PUBLIC EDUCATION RELIGION STUDIES

AMERICAN ACADEMY OF RELIGION
AIDS TO THE STUDY OF RELIGION SERIES

edited by
Gerald J. Larson

Number 7

PUBLIC EDUCATION RELIGION STUDIES:
AN OVERVIEW
by
Paul J. Will, ed.
Nicholas Piediscalzi, assoc. ed.
Barbara Ann DeMartino Swyhart, assoc. ed.

PAUL J. WILL, Ed.
NICHOLAS PIEDISCALZI, Assoc. Ed.
BARBARA ANN DeMARTINO SWYHART,
Assoc. Ed.

PUBLIC EDUCATION RELIGION STUDIES: AN OVERVIEW

SCHOLARS PRESS

Distributed by
Scholars Press
101 Salem Street
P.O. Box 2268
Chico, California 95927

PUBLIC EDUCATION RELIGION STUDIES: AN OVERVIEW

Paul J. Will, ed.

Nicholas Piediscalzi, assoc. ed.

Barbara Ann DeMartino Swyhart, assoc. ed.

Library of Congress Cataloging in Publication Data

Main entry under title:

Public education religion studies.

   (Aids for the study of religion ; no. 7)
   Bibliography: p.
   1. Religious education—United States—Addresses, essays,
lectures. I. Will, Paul J. II. Piediscalzi, Nicholas. III. Swyhart,
Barbara Ann DeMartino. IV. Series.
LC405.P82   377   80-12237
ISBN 0-89130-402-9 (pbk.)

Printed in the United States of America
1   2   3   4   5
Edwards Brothers, Inc.
Ann Arbor, Michigan 48106

This volume is dedicated to

Edwin Gaustad
Robert Michaelsen
Robert Spivey

Early Leaders in Public Education Religion Studies

TABLE OF CONTENTS

ACKNOWLEDGMENTS

The editors express appreciation to Professor Gerald
Larson, Editor of the Aids in the Study of Religion Series,
and the American Academy of Religion for their interest in
and support of this volume.

The editors also are grateful to the members of the
American Academy of Religion's Group on Religion Studies
in Public Education for their active involvement in the
development of this project and for providing funds for its
completion. Additional grants from Central Michigan
University's Faculty Research and Creative Endeavors Fund
and Wright State University College of Liberal Arts Research Fund facilitated production of the final manuscript.

Dolores Lawrence and Veda Horton patiently typed and
re-typed many of the draft chapters for this book. Annette
Davis is singled out for her typing of the final copy.
Their efforts are greatly appreciated.

Nicholas Piediscalzi prepared his contributions to the
volume and fulfilled his duties as associate editor while
on professional development leave from Wright State University, participating in a 1978-79 National Endowment for the
Humanities Faculty-in-Residence Seminar at the University
of California, Santa Barbara under the direction of Professor Walter H. Capps.

ix

PREFACE

This volume presents an overview of public education religion studies in elementary and secondary schools after more than a decade of unprecedented growth. During this period, the field has undergone significant maturation. Through the initiative of those who actively support religion studies in public education, numerous states are involved seriously in developing programs which meet the legal guidelines established by the United States Supreme Court and the highest academic standards. An increasing number of scholars are addressing themselves to the needs of public education religion studies and the authors of the chapters reflect this diversity of interest, with both religionists and educators from public and private institutions contributing.

This publication had its genesis in Dayton, Ohio during a 1976 meeting of the Steering Committee of the American Academy of Religion Group on Religion Studies in Public Education. While formulating a program format for the Group's work, the overall needs of this relatively new field were discussed. Barbara Ann DeMartino Swyhart suggested several possible publications, including a theoretical work, a practical guide and resource volume, and a collection of both previously published and unpublished manuscripts in the field. The editors took their guidance from this meeting. The present work seeks to incorporate these needs in a single volume, including both theoretical considerations for defining the goals and methods of public education religion studies and practical approaches and materials for implementing them. Some of the chapters are revised and updated versions of significant papers presented originally at AAR meetings or published previously in professional journals.

This contribution to the Aids in the Study of Religion Series complements studies of religion studies on the collegiate level. It represents not only insights into the state of the art but the refined deliberations produced by the AAR Group. This work should provide a useful resource for those who wish to familiarize themselves with public education religion studies and implement programs of their own.

SECTION I

THEORY

The chapters in this section are a representative sampling of theories and models developed by leaders in the field of public education religion studies. After an introductory chapter that outlines the professional efforts and programs which are related to these theories, a variety of positions are presented that have been argued before meetings of the AAR Group on Religion Studies in Public Education including those of Nicholas Piediscalzi, Guntram Bischoff, Henry Hoeks, and John Boyle. Significant emerging issues and theories are revealed clearly. A critical review of the scholarly work of the AAR Group itself further summarizes the progress made and issues discussed in the past four years as well as proposes questions and problems which require further attention.

During the past decade, several significant attempts have been made by educators in Great Britain to replace indoctrination in Christianity and the Bible with an academic and pluralistic study of religion in state-supported schools. Many of these theories and approaches, in addition to the problems they have encountered, are applicable to the American scene as the contribution by Ninian Smart, England's foremost theorist, illustrates.

Finally, William Collie's analysis of published religion studies curricular materials not only shows how theory relates to actual materials but provides a transition to the second section of the volume in which the question of the implementation of public education religion studies program is addressed.

CHAPTER ONE

A SURVEY OF PROFESSIONAL EFFORTS TO
ESTABLISH PUBLIC EDUCATION RELIGION STUDIES

Nicholas Piediscalzi

Numerous professional efforts to establish the
academic study of religion in public schools have occurred
since the early 1960's. They cover a wide range of activities including the sponsorhip of national conferences,
the publication of books and articles, the introduction of
courses, the production of curriculum materials, the
establishment of teacher education and certification
programs, and the founding of national and state organizations. Some of these endeavors were spurred by the 1963
U.S. Supreme Court decision (Schempp) which encouraged the
public schools to study religion academically at the very
time it prohibited them from requiring students to pray
and read devotional passages from the Bible.[1]

Others were stimulated by individual teachers and
students who became convinced that it is impossible to
conduct a complete study of world history, American history,
literature, art, music, and a host of other subjects without including a consideration of the religious factors at
work in these areas. Still others, while well-intended,
were inappropriately instigated by either individuals who
were desirous of finding a new form of religious life or
those who wanted either to re-institute a lost Protestant
hegemony over the schools or return Christian values to
the schools. These efforts have taken place in many
different parts of the country and, for the most part, have
been unrelated and uncoordinated. A summary and description of them follows. This survey is not an exhaustive

Nicholas Piediscalzi, Ph.D., is Chairman, Department of
Religion, and Codirector, Public Education Religion Studies
Center, Wright State University.

report but presents a representative selection of each of
the different activities which have taken place and thereby illustrates the general character of each of the many
and varied types now transpiring.

National Conferences

Since 1964 a series of national conferences have been
conducted by several different organizations.[2] Three of
them will be mentioned here. As a follow up to the 1964
report of its Commission on Religion and Public Schools,
which endorsed the academic study of religion in public
education, the American Association of School Administrators (AASA) invited thirty officials from the Jewish,
Catholic, and Protestant communities to discuss whether
the AASA should embark on an active program to develop
curriculum materials on world religions and religions in
history for use in the secondary schools.[3] Even though
the various officials did not reach agreement on philosophical issues, they achieved consensus on four matters.
First, all agreed that the AASA should

> take the lead with teachers of art, music, and
> literature--the humanities as they are found
> in secondary schools--to make a topic-by-topic
> analysis of the separate courses in order to
> seek out the appropriate ways to teach the
> reciprocal relationship between religion and
> other elements in human culture.[4]

Second, substantial agreement was reached "on the need
for material of the highest educational and technical
excellence on religion in history (rather than the history
of religion) and on understanding of the world's religions
and ideologies (rather than comparative religion.)"[5]

Third, the group agreed that since teachers play a
crucial role in the development of religion studies in
public education, it is imperative to provide sound pre-
and in-service teacher education programs in this area.

Fourth, the group agreed that materials developed for
classroom use "should represent the co-operative efforts of
scholars in religion, in history, in various subject fields,
and in education generally."[6]

A year later (May, 1966), a conference on "The Role
of Religion in Public Education" was held at Harvard
University under the sponsorhip of The National Conference
of Christians and Jews and the leadership of Theodore R.
Sizer who, at the time, served as Dean of Harvard's
Graduate School of Education. A variety of papers on
several different topics were presented. Some argued
forcefully for the inclusion of religion studies in the
public schools while others opposed it with equal vigor.
The conference did not seek to establish a consensus;
rather, its aim was to provide "different approaches and
perspectives and run a broad ideological spectrum." [7] In
his introduction to the collected papers from this
conference which he edited, Sizer commented:

> Few issues in American Society have been argued
> more irrelevantly and more misleadingly than
> that of the place of religion in public school-
> ing. Few issues have been argued for so long
> or so passionately. And few issues have come
> to so little resolution. [8]

Sizer also stated that anyone interested in covering
this area adequately should take into consideration four
opposing points of view which he placed in sharp contrast
to each other: (1) sectarian teaching; (2) information-
giving either about people's differing beliefs or about
religions through comparative religion studies; (3) a subject of study and discourse in its own right; and
(4) psychological adjustment. [9]

In June of 1973 the Public Education Religion Studies
Center (PERSC) conducted a symposium recognizing the tenth
anniversary of the Schempp decision and the founding of
PERSC in October of 1972. "Religion Studies in the
Curriculum: Retrospect and Prospect, 1963-1983" served as
the symposium's theme. After the late Justice Tom C.
Clark, author of the Schempp majority opinion, delivered
the keynote address, educators, academicians of religion,
and professional leaders heard and discussed papers on
three concurrent and interrelated developments in public
education religion studies during the period 1963-1973:

(1) clarification of legal issues; (2) publication of
curriculum materials; and (3) development of teacher
education and certification programs. The symposium also
considered the professional needs of these areas and other
related issues for the period 1973-1983.

The authors of the closing chapter in the volume of
selected symposium's papers wrote that there are several
areas which require the immediate and long range attention
of those involved in the development of this profession.
These include: further clarification of (a) the legal
distinction between the profession of a religion and the
study about religion, and (b) the meaning of the terms
"religion" and "objectivity," and the establishment of
standards and criteria for guiding and development and
evaluation of (a) high quality curriculum materials,
(b) pre- and in-service teacher education programs, and
(c) certification curricula in public education
religion studies. The recorders of these observations
conclude that it is not clear that public education
religion studies will:

> continue to expand and become a new element in
> public education. However, it is absolutely
> clear that the present moment demands that all
> concerned with public education religion
> studies devote their energies and attentions
> to improving the quality of existing programs
> and curricular materials, expanding and up-
> grading teacher education and certification
> programs, and establishing sound criteria for
> evaluating programs, materials, and teacher
> education programs.[10]

The national conferences described above and several
others have been occasions for professionals in this newly
emerging field and interested groups and citizens to share
opinions and information as well as to improve their own
work. However, they have neither dispelled the innumerable misunderstandings and tensions which exist in this
controversial area nor stimulated the expansion of
religion studies in public education. The latter has been
accomplished by the grass roots efforts of teachers and
students.

Books

A number of books on public education religion
studies have been published during the past fifteen years.
Three, already mentioned, are the results of commission
studies and conferences: the AASA report, the Harvard
Conference, and the PERSC symposium.[11]

James V. Panoch and David L. Barr co-authored
Religion Goes to School, a presentation of legal and
educational justifications for the inclusion of religion
studies in public education and several different examples
of the ways in which teachers may introduce such study in
the curriculum through either existing courses or new
ones.[12]

Robert Michaelsen published Piety in the Public
School: Trends and Issues in the Relationship Between
Religion and the Public School in the United States in
1970.[13] After conducting "a superlative study of the
relation of religion and education throughout the entire
span of American history," Michaelsen presents a justification for the inclusion of the academic study of religion
in the public schools.[14]

Four years later, David E. Engel edited an anthology
under the title Religion in Public Education.[15] This work
presents selections on historical, legal, theoretical, and
practical problems in addition to examples of curriculum
projects, courses, and teacher education projects.

Teaching About Religion in Public Schools was
published in 1977.[16] This volume contains chapters which
report and describe in detail curriculum projects, courses,
and units of study in religion studies. They were written
by classroom teachers, school-district curriculum specialists, curriculum project directors, university subject
matter and teacher educators, and scholars of religion.
According to the editors of this volume, these articles
"detail current practice and hold portent for future
religion studies development in elementary and secondary
schools."[17]

To date, the books published in this area provide
historical surveys of and justifications for public education religion studies in addition to examples of what can
and is being done in the classroom. However, no major
theoretical work on public education religion studies has
appeared.[18]

Courses[19]

Reports from many different sections of the United
States reveal that religion studies have been increasing
in public schools. In 1975 PERSC located over one
thousand schools in the United States where courses or
units about religion were offered. These offerings ranged
from "Religious Literature" and "The Bible as/in Literature" to "World Religions" and "Religious Issues in
American History." Thomas Love of California State
University, Northridge, reported that at least eighty
religion courses were introduced within a sixty-mile radius
of his campus during the period 1968-1972. He also noted
that many units of various courses, and many enrichment
programs, also are offered in religious studies. At least
fifteen new religion courses appeared in the Dayton, Ohio
area during this same period. Ninety-six Michigan high
schools responding to a survey conducted by Lambert J.
Ponstein, Hope College professor, reported that they
included religion studies in their curriculum. Fifty-nine
of these ninety-six stated that they had introduced these
new courses about religion since 1970. A 1974 follow-
up study by Professor Henry Hoeks of Calvin College in
Michigan discovered 19 additional high schools offering
religion studies courses, a substantial number of religion
courses in junior high schools, and many units in regular
courses at both levels. The number of students studying
religion in Pennsylvania schools increased from only 700
in 1967 to 12,000 in 1974.

Harold Hosel, formerly of Grinnell College, discovered
in a 1974 study that 58% of 327 Iowa schools responding to
his survey listed courses or units on religion studies. In

1977, a less representative study, conducted by Professor
Maria Della Bella of Coe College showed twenty percent of
sixty-five responding Iowa schools reported that they
offered a course, unit of a course, or a mini-course on
religion.

Similar developments were reported from New England:
in the Fall of 1974, new programs were instituted in
Oxford, Medford, and Needham, Massachusetts high schools,
as well as Stowe, Vermont. In January of 1979, Lynn Taylor,
Director of the Kansas Center for Public Education Religion
Studies, wrote that approximately 600 teachers who had
received training at the Kansas Center were engaged in
teaching about religion in the schools of Kansas. The
Bible as Literature and World Religions are, according to
recent surveys, proving to be popular elective options in
public high schools.[20]

The increase in religion studies is not without
problems. Hosel discovered in his survey of Iowa schools
that only 13% of the courses and units offered are taught
by teachers trained in the academic study of religion.
Hence there is need to upgrade the quality of teaching
about religion. Hosel also learned that the courses
offered and the curricula developed by teachers need to be
improved "through the adoption of explicit rationales, the
use of more realistically descriptive categories, the
employment of functional definitions, and the conscious
avoidance of normative methodologies, procedures, and
judgements."[21]

Hosel's findings are not limited to Iowa. They are
applicable to every other part of the United States where
religion studies are being introduced. Hence criteria need
to be developed by which competent teaching about religion
can be evaluated. Some individuals and organizations have
developed and published such criteria. Examples of these
may be found in the Resource Section of this volume.

Curriculum Materials

In general, four types of curriculum materials on religion studies have been produced since 1965: integrated curricula, textbooks, courses, and units. Each of these is described below.

The Educational Research Council of America (Cleveland, Ohio) designed and produced a K-9 social studies curriculum which includes the study of religious themes, issues, and problems wherever they arise naturally in the material under study. According to Raymond English, director of this program,

> the case for religion in public education rests
> on the assumption that knowledge . . . is of
> central importance, and that transmitting knowl-
> edge -- including knowledge of great ideas or
> great revelations--is the major function of
> education . . . For more than ten years, the
> Educational Research Council of America has
> been attempting to put the rationale into prac-
> tice in its Social Science Program.[22]

Religious Literature of the West, a textbook for a one semester course designed under the direction of a team of scholars at Pennsylvania State University pursuant to an act of the General Assembly of the Commonwealth of Pennsylvania, contains selections from the sacred litera-ture of Jews, Christians, and Muslims; introductory materials; and study questions.[23]

An ecumenical group of scholars prepared The Bible Reader, a special edition of the Bible for use as a text in public schools.[24] This volume contains key biblical passages in various translations with introductory arti-cles, essays, and notes from the Jewish, Catholic, and Protestant traditions.

The Bible as/in Literature and The Enduring Legacy are two texts designed for use in English classes on the Bible.[25] Both deal thematically with key biblical passages from creation through the fall to redemption, and they demonstrate how English and American literature derive content, symbols, and style from various parts of the Bible. The former excludes introductory materials

because the editors believe that it is not possible to
provide any which are appropriate for use in the public
schools. The latter includes such materials since the
author holds that it is not possible to study the Bible
in public education without resources from contemporary
biblical scholarship. Both of these texts reveal that a
study of the Bible either as literature or a literary
source for English and American literature does not do
justice to the Bible as scripture and that such study does
not provide adequate training in religious studies. There
is need for a text on the Bible itself which would be
suitable for use in public education religion studies
programs. Given the pluralistic nature of our nation and
the public schools, there also is a need to develop an
approach to and a text for introducing public school
students to the scriptures of the major living religions
of the world.

The Many Faces of Religion: An Inquiry Approach and
The Great Religions by Which Men Live are two texts
designed to introduce students to the major religions of
the world.[26] Both suffer some serious deficiencies. To
date, no adequate single text on the living religions of
the world has been published for use in public education.

The World Religions Curriculum Development Center
(Minneapolis, Minnesota), funded by a Title III-IV C grant
under the Elementary-Secondary Education Act, developed a
multi-media course about world religions which was published by Argus Communications.[27] According to the
project's directors, the course is designed for use in
high schools

> to enhance human dignity . . . and to maintain
> the imprecise, delicate, and very human quali-
> ties religions represent. It is a course which
> helps students learn about the religious diver-
> sity of the world and develop attitudes of
> understanding and respect for the beliefs and
> practices of others and the legitimacy of those
> beliefs and practices in a world of pluralism
> and mobility.[28]

The University of Nebraska Press published The God
and Man Narratives in 1968, a unit on religious literature
which is included in the seventh grade level English
Curriculum for Nebraska Schools. Four different narratives,
"Classical Myths," "Ancient Hebrew Religions Narratives,"
"American Indian Myths," and "Stories of the American
West," are studied. Emphasis is placed on developing an
understanding of what the narratives meant to those who
wrote them and to their intended audience and what they
have meant to subsequent generations.

The Florida State University Religion-Social Studies
Curriculum Project produced units on religion for inclusion
in junior and senior high school social science classes
and a set of units for inclusion in elementary school
curricula.[29] The former are three separate volumes,
Religious Issues in American Culture, Religious Issues in
Western Civilization, and Religious Issues in World
Culture, which are designed for use in social studies and
history courses. The units may be included individually
at the appropriate time in a given course, e.g. there is a
unit on the religious dimensions of the Revolutionary War
for inclusion when that period is studied, or the ten
units may be used together to form an integral part of a
course. The major aim of the units is to help students
learn how to distinguish and analyze religious issues and
problems as they arise in societies, cultures, and
histories. The elementary materials which consist of
separate multi-media units for grade levels 1 through 6
are designed to provide students with the basic concepts
necessary for learning about religions in a cross-cultural
and pluralistic setting. The Nebraska and the two Florida
State University units are only three examples of a host
of units which have been published in recent years.

These different types of curriculum materials illustrate various attempts which have been made to correct the
exclusion of academic religion studies from public
education. The integrated approach restructures an
entire curriculum so that the religious dimensions are

considered as they arise naturally in the area under
study. This is the ideal approach since it considers
religion as it appears in actuality. Hopefully, the
writers and publishers of all curriculum projects and
textbooks eventually will rewrite their materials in this
manner. Until that time arrives, it will be necessary to
provide curriculum units like the ones described above
which can be used as supplements to existing curriculum
materials. Moreover, the integrated approach will not
eliminate the need for individual courses in religion
studies at the upper levels of public education. In fact,
it may lead to the establishment of a greater variety of
advanced content courses, e.g., The Scriptures of the
World Religions, The Bible in Western Culture, American
Religions, etc. which will require the publication of new
types of textbooks in religion studies.

The recent appearance of curriculum materials and
textbooks points out two other deficiencies in this area:
sound criteria to guide the development and evaluation of
curriculum materials and the lack of teacher education in
religion studies both at the pre- and post-certification
levels. While the materials described above meet, with
the noted exceptions, academic standards set by the public
schools and the legal criteria suggested by the United
States Supreme Court, many other materials which are
published do not. Therefore, there is an urgent need to
provide criteria for evaluating religion studies curriculum materials and to train school administrators and
teachers to evaluate materials according to those
criteria before adopting them for classroom use.

Teacher Education and Certification Programs

The publication of new curriculum materials in religion studies also accentuates the fact that teacher
education programs have not included training in religion
studies. Hence the appearance of such materials is only a
partial solution to problems which arise when religion
studies are introduced into the curriculum. There remains

the need to educate teachers in the appropriate methods
and techniques for public education religion studies.
Efforts to educate teachers and future teachers require
the establishment of in-service training and the addition
of this new field to existing pre-service or certification
programs. Such programs are beginning to appear. During
the summer of 1978, according to an informal survey conducted by PERSC, about fifteen summer institutes and workshops were offered in different parts of the United States
on various aspects of integrating religion studies into the
public schools curricula. Also, at the instigation of
colleges and universities, four states, California, Michigan, Massachusetts, and Wisconsin, approved certification
programs in religion studies. Efforts are underway in a
number of other states to introduce similar programs. In
support of these endeavors, several institutions of higher
education inaugurated master degree programs in public
education religion studies. These efforts are described
in detail elsewhere in this volume.

National and State Organizations

Several national and state organizations were
established during the past fifteen years to stimulate and
assist the growth and development of public education
religion studies. James V. Panoch, founded the Religious
Instruction Association (RIA) in the early 1960's. RIA
gathered information on public education religion studies
from every area of the United States and served as a
clearing house for and disseminator of these materials.
No attempt was made to evaluate them. In addition, Panoch
and his associate, David L. Barr, served as consultants to
schools, religious groups, and community and professional
organizations. They presented papers at the annual meetings of almost every major professional group in the
United States, e.g., American Association of School
Administrators, National Council for Social Studies,
National Council of Teachers of English, and the American
Academy of Religion. In addition, they published articles

in the journals of these organizations and helped others
to do the same. Some of RIA's functions were assumed by
PERSC when Panoch became one of its co-founders and first
field co-ordinator.

Through the efforts of the Religious Education Association under the leadership of Boardman W. Kathan, the
National Council on Religion and Public Education (NCRPE)
was established in 1971. The purpose of NCRPE is to provide a "means for cooperation among organizations and institutions concerned with those ways of studying religion
which are educationally appropriate and constitutionally
acceptable to a secular program of public education."
NCRPE seeks to fulfill this purpose by striving to: (1)
create public and professional awareness and support for
the purpose of the Council; (2) serve as a clearing house
for information regarding resource persons, programs, projects, curriculum materials, teacher education opportunities,
and legal decisions; (3) provide a forum for continuing
dialogue on issues, programs and projects in religion and
public education; (4) collect, coordinate, and disseminate
materials and methods for the study of religion; and (5)
establish liaison with professional and lay organizations
and other appropriate groups.[30]

In 1972 the Public Education Religion Studies Center
(PERSC) was founded at Wright State University, Dayton,
Ohio with grants from Religious Heritage of America and
the Lily Endowment. PERSC's stated purpose is "to encourage and facilitate increased and improved teaching
about religion within constitutional bounds, mainly in
elementary and secondary public schools and where applicable in relevant areas of post-secondary education."
PERSC stresses the natural inclusion of study about
religion within regular curricular offerings and the
addition of specific courses or units. The improvement
of pre- and in-service training for teachers is another
concern. PERSC's activities include: (1) conducting and
recommending workshops, seminars, and conferences throughout the nation; (2) serving as a resource center on

available curriculum materials; (3) providing a research
center for scholars studying religion studies in public
education; (4) making its staff and/or other nationally
recognized experts available for consultation with
governmental, educational, and community groups or with
individuals; (5) publishing a quarterly newsletter; (6)
encouraging and initiating responsible review and evaluation of existing curriculum materials and programs and
the development of necessary new materials; and (7) making
available through Wright State University a master's degree
program in education (M.E.D. or M.A.T.) which can be designed to meet the candidate's individual needs for
training in religion studies and education.[31]

From its inception PERSC has been assisted and
advised by a Professional Advisory Council which consists
of thirty scholars, educators, and professional leaders
from throughout the United States. At its first two
meetings the Council drew up criteria for evaluating
curriculum materials, teacher education programs, and
teacher competency. Members of the Council have written
evaluations of curriculum materials and teacher education
programs for the PERSC Newsletter. These criteria also
have been used as models for guidelines developed by
several state organizations and for the design of curriculum materials and teacher education and certification
programs.

PERSC conducted a two-year (1976-78) teacher education project which was funded by the National Endowment
for the Humanities. After holding several projects--
mainly consultations--in conjunction with the American
Academy of Religion, PERSC became an affiliate member of
the Academy in 1977.

Public education religion studies became an official
concern of the American Academy of Religion (AAR) in 1973
when the officers of the AAR convened a consultation on
the topic at the 1974 annual meeting. Those who attended
the consultation heard a panel describe recent developments and problems in this newly emerging area and ways in

which the AAR could serve its needs. The consultation
members voted unanimously to request the AAR Program
Committee to establish a Group on Public Schools-Religion
Studies (subsequently the title was changed to Religion
Studies in Public Education Group). The Program Committee
acted positively on the request and appointed a steering
committee to lead the Group. The Group chose the follow-
ing areas to study and discuss during its first five years
of operation: "The Problem of Norm in Public Education
Religion Studies: Enlightenment, Emancipation or Sociali-
zation?" (1975); "Distinguishing Moral Education, Values
Clarification, and Religion Studies" (1976); "Public
Education Religion Studies as a Discipline" (1977);
"Paradigms for Public Education Religion Studies Curriculum" (1978); and "Professional Programs for Religion
Studies in Public Education" (1979).[32]

The Group singled out these areas as those most
requiring study at the time and the ones which point to
those elements which constitute public education religion
studies as a distinct academic discipline. Furthermore,
the Group concluded that it is imperative to delineate and
describe succinctly the unique characteristics of this
academic discipline in addition to establishing its
theoretical foundations.

This Group provides the only organized and ongoing
professional forum for the systematic study of theoretical
and practical problems and issues in public education
religion studies. The publication of this volume is the
culmination of five years of intensive work by the Group's
membership both individually and collectively.

Several state organizations developed during the same
period in Connecticut, Iowa, Kansas, Michigan, Minnesota,
Missouri, North Carolina, Ohio, and Wisconsin for the
purpose of encouraging the development of religion
studies, teacher education programs, and teacher certification programs in public education religion studies.
Several of the organizations are composed solely of
representatives from universities and colleges with

teacher education programs. Others include organizations,
e.g., councils of churches, in addition to public school
teachers. Several of these organizations have sponsored
statewide awareness conferences with funds from the
humanities councils in their states.

Conclusions

The preceding selected sampling of numerous and
varied professional activities on behalf of public education religion studies are intended to delineate the
present status and characteristics of the newly emerging
profession in almost every part of the United States.
From this survey, the following conclusions are offered
as theses for study, discussion, and testing against
reality.

There is a small but vigorous number of individuals
and groups dedicated to the establishment of sound and
responsible academic religion studies in public education.
Those involved in these efforts come from the ranks of
highly dedicated students, teachers, university and college
professors; leaders of professional, educational, and religious organizations; and lay people.

On the whole, the majority of public school teachers
and administrators, members of colleges and departments of
education, and state board of education officials are
notably absent from these efforts. Their lack of involvement may be explained by a variety of possible reactions
to the new call for the introduction of religion studies
in public education. Most of them still misunderstand the
Schempp decision and believe that the Court proscribed
religion studies in public education; some fear that the
introduction of such studies will produce unnecessary and
destructive controversy. Others maintain that the public
schools already are overburdened with new programs and
cannot handle or afford any more, and still others see no
genuine educational need for introducing religion studies
to the curriculum. Until these negative attitudes can be

changed extensively, public education religion studies will
remain on the periphery of the curriculum.

This is unfortunate since students on the whole appear
to be receptive to and benefit from the introduction of
religion studies and since some publishers have invested a
great deal of talent and money in the development of some
excellent curriculum materials. However, since there are
so few adequately trained teachers and since there always
is the possibility of rekindling semi-dormant religious
controversies which polarize communities into unresolvable
conflicts, it may be best for those involved in this field
to maintain a low profile. They need to work slowly but
consistently at efforts to train future teachers in pre-
professional training programs and practicing teachers
through in-service training programs and to continue conducting awareness and consciousness raising programs for
administrators, state education officials, and the public
at large. In the long run, those presently involved in
this small, quiet, and almost unrecognized movement may be
able to establish a more secure and lasting foundation for
public education religion studies than a nationally mounted
campaign or projects with highly visible profiles can.

Along with these efforts it also is suggested that
those AAR members now engaged in this area devote a great
deal of their time to cultivate and sustain working relations with faculty members from the field of education.
Without their co-operation and support, much of what is
taking place may come to naught.

When he addressed the Ohio Committee on Public Education Religion Studies in the Spring of 1978, Guntram
Bischoff argued convincingly that those religionists and
educators dedicated to the growth and improvement of
public education religion studies should devote more of
their time and efforts to meeting regularly with teachers
and to assisting them in forming their own professional
groups in their districts and states. Bischoff maintains
that the future growth and development of public education
religion studies is dependent to a large part upon the work

of the classroom teacher and that scholars of religion and
education must view themselves as "servants" of this group
in order to help this newly emerging profession survive
and flourish. Bischoff's suggestions should be taken
seriously since they address some of the most important
needs in this area.

Since the major curriculum areas of American public
education will not change dramatically in the immediate
future and since only a few individuals have sought to
develop models of religion studies for inclusion in humanities programs, it is suggested that leaders in the field
begin to direct their efforts to this area. Relegating
religion studies, by default, to the areas of the English
Bible and social studies makes it almost impossible for
religion studies to emerge in its proper place within the
curriculum. Public education religion studies must find,
just as religion studies in higher education does, its
rightful place in the humanities. The methods and
approaches most appropriate for the study of religion are
found not in the narrow confines of English literature and
the social studies but, rather, in the humanities. Certainly, these disciplines have contributions to make to
religion studies but their contributions can be made best
when they are integrated into an interdisciplinary humanities approach to the study and interpretation of religion.

NOTES

[1] See 374 U.S. 300: "The holding of the Court today
plainly does not foreclose teaching about the Holy Scriptures or about the differences between religious sects in
classes in literature or history. Indeed, whether or not
the Bible is involved, it would be impossible to teach
meaningfully many subjects in the social sciences or the
humanities without some mention of religion. To what
extent, and at what points in the curriculum religious
materials should be cited, are matters which the courts
ought to entrust very largely to the experienced officials
who superintend our Nation's public schools."

[2] For more detailed descriptions of some of these conferences see: Arthur Gilbert, "Reactions and Resources," in Theodore R. Sizer, ed., Religion and Public Education (Boston: Houghton Mifflin, 1967), 37-83; and John W. O'Brien, "Religion in Public Education: Toward the Implementation of an Idea," 1974 paper reproduced and distributed by the Public Education Religion Studies Center, Wright State University, Dayton, Ohio 45435.

[3] Religion in the Public Schools: A Report by the Commission on Religion in the Public Schools (Washington, D.C.: American Association of School Administrators, 1964). This report was published by Harper and Row (Harper Chapel Book, B 13) in 1965.

[4] Gilbert, "Reactions and Resources," 51.

[5] Ibid., 52.

[6] Ibid.

[7] Sizer, Religion and Public Education, XIX.

[8] Ibid., XV.

[9] Ibid., XV-XIX

[10] Peter Bracher, et al., eds., Religion Studies in the Curriculum: Retrospect and Prospect, 1963-1983 (Dayton, Ohio: Public Education Religion Studies Center, 1974), 96.

[11] In addition, the papers delivered at the founding meeting of the National Council on Religion and Public Education were edited by Richard U. Smith and published in a special issue of Religious Education, Part II (July-August, 1972), under the title Religion and Public School Curriculum (Proceedings of the National Council on Religion and Public Education).

[12] New York: Harper and Row, 1968.

[13] New York: Macmillan.

[14] Philip Gleason, "Blurring the Line of Separation: Education, Civil Religion, and Teaching About Religion," Journal of Church and State 19/3 (1977), 529, n. 31.

[15] New York: Paulist Press, 1974.

[16] Nicholas Piediscalzi and William E. Collie, eds., (Niles, Illinois: Argus Communications).

[17] Ibid., 2.

[18]In addition to separate volumes, articles on public
education religion studies, too numerous to list here, have
been published in professional journals during the past
fifteen years. A partial listing of these articles may be
found in a bibliography compiled by Ronald B. Flowers and
published in Journal of Church and State 14 (Autumn 1972).
This issue also contains the proceedings of a consultation
on public education religion studies conducted in Texas in
1971 by a coalition of religious and educational groups.

[19]This section and the following ones on Curriculum
Materials and Teacher Education and Certification Programs
are abridged and revised versions of paragraphs which first
appeared in Nicholas Piediscalzi, "Public Education Religion Studies Since the Schempp Decision (1963)," in Marvin
J. Taylor, ed., Foundations of Christian Education in an
Era of Change (Nashville, Tennessee: Abingdon, 1976).
c 1976 by Abingdon Press and used here with permission
granted by Abingdon Press.

[20]George Hillocks, Alternatives in English: A Critical
Appraisal of Elective Programs (Urbana, Illinois: National
Council of Teachers of English, 1972), 25.

[21]"Religion and the Public Schools: An Analysis of
Current Curricula in Iowa Secondary Schools" (unpublished
Master's thesis, Graduate College, University of Iowa,
1974), 120.

[22]"Reflections on Ten Years' Experience with Teaching
about Religion in Public Schools," PERSC Newsletter 1/3
(Spring, 1974): 5. The K-9 social science curriculum has
been published by Allyn and Bacon (Boston).

[23]John Whitney and Susan Howe (Minneapolis, Minnesota:
Augsburg Press, 1971).

[24]Milwaukee, Wisconsin: Bruce, 1969.

[25]James S. Ackerman and Thayer S. Warshaw (Glenview,
Illinois: Scott, Foresman, 1976). Ackerman and Warshaw
have served as general editors for six teacher-oriented
resource volumes for courses on the Bible in/as literature
published by Abingdon Press. Douglas Brown (New York:
Schribner, 1975).

[26]Steward Dicks, et al., (Boston: Ginn, 1973) and
Floyd H. Ross and Tynette Hills (Greenwich, Connecticut:
Fawcett, 1973).

[27]Religion in Human Culture (1978).

[28]Lee H. Smith and Wesley J. Bodin, "Religion in
Human Culture," Nicholas Piediscalzi and William E. Collie,
174-175.

[29]Robert A. Spivey, et al., Issues in Religion, 3 vols. (Menlo Park, California: Addison-Wesley, 1972-74) and Robert A. Spivey, et al., Learning about Religion/Social Studies (Niles, Illinois: Argus Communications, 1977).

[30]The National Council on Religion and Public Education. By-Laws, 1973.

[31]Public Education Religion Studies Center, descriptive brochure.

[32]The papers from the first year were published in Anne Carr and Nicholas Piediscalzi, eds., The Academic Study of Religion: 1975 Proceedings and Public Schools Religion-Studies: 1975 Proceedings (Missoula, Montana: Scholars Press, 1975), and the papers from the second year were published in Nicholas Piediscalzi and Barbara Ann Swyhart, eds., Distinguishing Moral Education, Values Clarification and Religion-Studies (Missoula, Montana: Scholars Press, 1976).

CHAPTER TWO

A SUGGESTED PURPOSE AND GOALS FOR
PUBLIC EDUCATION RELIGION STUDIES IN LIGHT OF LEGAL,
THEORETICAL, AND PRACTICAL PROBLEMS

Nicholas Piediscalzi

This chapter suggests a purpose and set of goals for
public education religion studies in the United States.
Both are derived from the author's understanding of the
problems which arise out of the unique history of the
public school system in relation to established religions
as well as recent Supreme Court decisions pertaining to
the practice and study of religion in public education.
These areas will be considered in the first section of
this chapter which serves as a prolegomena to the second
where a purpose and several goals are delineated.

Public Schools

The public schools in the United States have developed
in large part according to a model conceived in the
eighteenth century by Thomas Jefferson. Because the
churches were in conflict over the essentials of basic
theology, especially concerning the beliefs necessary for
salvation, and because of his own philosophical presuppositions and concerns for national political unity, Jefferson, according to Robert Michaelsen, called upon the public
schools to serve as "America's established church." The
faith of this church, which is democratic in nature,
combines aspects from both the Jewish and Christian
traditions and dimensions from other world views which are
not consonant with orthodox Christianity--"elements from

---

*Nicholas Piediscalzi, Ph.D., is Chairman, Department of
Religion, and Codirector, Public Education Religion Studies
Center, Wright State University. This chapter is a revi-
sion of a paper given at the annual meeting of the American
Academy of Religion in San Francisco, December, 1977.*

eighteenth century rationalistic deism; elements which . . .
[our founding] fathers regarded as being common to all
religions, the best in all religions, and the only aspect
of any religion necessary to civic orders and well being."[1]

Jefferson's model made it possible and at times
necessary for the public schools to conduct civil religious
rituals. Their goal was to foster national unity and well-
being by inculcating young people in a national democratic
faith and morality. In practice, these rituals did not
always achieve their intended end. In fact, they often
produced just the opposite. This failure occured because,
when the Constitution was ratified, the First Amendment was
applicable only to the Federal Government. States were
allowed to establish religions. Thus the theology and
morality of majority groups in each state or region determined educational policies and practices. For example,
the Calvinists of New England established a school system
to serve their theological interests.

This being the case, the history of public education
in the 18th, 19th, and 20th centuries is rife with religious controversies. At first, the conflict was among
diverse Protestant denominations and sects. Horace Mann's
solution--reading from the King James Version of the Bible
without note or comment--was viable only as long as Protestants maintained control over their communities and
remained in agreement. However, Mann's pan-Protestant
approach proved ineffective as soon as large numbers of
non-Protestant immigrants entered the population. Conflicts arose because Jewish, Eastern Orthodox, and Roman
Catholic parents objected to the schools forcing their
children to read from the King James Version of the Bible,
recite Protestant prayers, and receive indoctrination in
Protestant theology and morality. On occasion, the conflicts erupted into violent clashes. A parish priest in
New England was tarred and feathered for exhorting his
parishoners not to send their children to the public
schools where the King James Version of the Bible was read.
The Rifle War was fought in the streets of Cincinnati over

what version of the Bible would be read in the public
schools. Immigrant groups founded parochial schools
during this period as a means of preserving their ethnic
and religious heritages and identities. Like the public
schools, they inculcated youth in one faith and did not
study religion from a pluralistic perspective.

Toward the end of the 19th century the conflict sub-
sided when many schools discontinued Bible reading and the
recitation of prayers. However, the conflict was re-
kindled after World War I when schools re-instituted Bible
readings and prayers and inaugurated "released-time"
religious instruction programs. After World War II, the
conflict intensified when parochial schools renewed their
efforts to obtain state and federal assistance. At the
same time, a call went out for the re-introduction of
spiritual values into the schools. (This also was the
period when Congress added the phrase, "one nation under
God" to the pledge of allegiance and authorized the
Treasury Department to imprint "In God We Trust" on our
coins and bills.)

The conflict in the 19th century not only took place
among various religious groups but also between a growing
number of secularized intellectuals and many different
religious communities. The latter conflict produced,
according to Guntram G. Bischoff, "an almost simplistic,
two-dimensional development of thematic attitudes toward
religion. The traditional, seminary cultivated theology
of church and synagogue found itself in a kind of permanent
and progressive confrontation with the great debunkers who,
more often than not, spoke from the rostrum of colleges and
universities."[2] This bifurcation prevented the vast
majority of Americans from becoming acquainted with the
rise and development of Religionswissenschaft in European
universities during this period and thereby deprived both
groups of learning about the emerging European differen-
tiation between indoctrination in religion and the study
of religion.

The public schools which, according to Jefferson, were
to inculcate the young in a democratic faith which would
transcend religious conflicts and thereby foster national
unity never fulfilled his dream. In fact, many of the
religious conflicts continue today in modified form despite
(or is it in spite of?) Supreme Court decisions which have
asked the schools to become genuinely pluralistic. Now
groups of Protestants, Catholics, and others are protesting
that the schools are dominated by "secular humanism" and
that their faiths and traditions do not receive equal and
fair treatment.

Some within these groups hold that our nation's crises
are caused by those who have foisted a godless religion
upon the schools.[3] Actually, the conflict is not between
devious secular humanists and "true believers" but, rather,
between those who believe that the schools should be
genuinely pluralistic and those who do not. Those who
oppose pluralism come from different sub-groups such as
those who maintain a strong belief in God, family ties,
and a traditional morality, e.g., the Appalachian families
involved in the textbook disputes.[4] Others object to the
introduction of the inquiry method and moral and values
education programs into the schools because they believe
that these innovations are directly responsible for
students not learning how to read, write, and calculate;
producing a lack of respect for authority and a breaking
down of discipline; and promoting a relativistic attitude
towards all values.[5]

The Jeffersonian model for public education, the
conflicts among various religious groups, and arguments
between the religious groups and secularists have left the
public schools and the public at large with a legacy of
ignorance about the nature of the academic study of religion and a truncated view of religion. Most Americans
continue to equate the study of religion with indoctrination in a specific religion and/or morality. Also, they
view religion as a set of rational beliefs derived from
texts and creeds to which individuals must give assent.

They do not consider myth, rituals, symbols, and communal
life to be expressions and "texts" of religious life. Moreover, even though they hold that being religious entails
holding the beliefs of a given tradition, they also view
religion, paradoxically, as a private matter. Religion is
what one holds by himself or herself. Hence it is neither
available nor open to study. This tendency ignores the
social, cultural, and historical dimensions of religious
life. Finally, the highly moralistic character of America's religious roots and the demand placed upon the
schools to be inculcators of a specific morality tend to
lead people to identify erroneously inculcation in morality
with the study of religion. These are one set of factors
which must be considered when the purpose and goals of
public education religion studies are developed.

Supreme Court Decisions

The United States Supreme Court between 1948 and 1963
heard a series of cases pertaining to the practice and
study of religion in the public schools. In McCollum
(1948), the Court ruled unconstitutional "released-time"
programs (religious instruction on school grounds by
clergy). Four years later, "dismissed-time" programs
(dismissing students from school to attend religious instruction classes in their own religious institutions) were
judged constitutional by the Court (Zorach). In 1963
(Engel) and 1963 (Schempp), the Court ruled unconstitutional
required recitation of prayers and devotional readings from
the Bible.

Each of these cases contain dicta which state that on
both educational and legal grounds religion, which is a
significant dimension of human history, should be neither
ignored by the schools nor omitted from the curriculum on
allegedly constitutional grounds.

Justice Robert H. Jackson wrote in McCollum (1948),

> For good or for ill, nearly everything in our
> culture worth transmitting, which gives mean-
> ing to life, is saturated with religious
> influences, derived from Paganism, Judaism,
> Christianity . . . and other faiths accepted by
> a large part of the world's people. One can
> hardly respect a system of education that
> would leave the student wholly ignorant of
> the currents of religious thought that has
> moved the world society for a part in which
> he is being prepared.[6]

In 1963, the late Justice Tom Clark reaffirmed this
opinion: "It might well be said that one's education is
not complete without a study of comparative religion or
the history of religion and its relationship to the advancement of civilization."[7]

Justice Arthur Goldberg added the legal justification
for including religion studies in public education in his
1963 concurring opinion to Schempp:

> Neither the State nor this Court can or should
> ignore the significance of the fact that a
> vast portion of our people believe in and
> worship God and that many of our legal, poli-
> tical and personal values derive historically
> from religious teachings. Government must
> inevitably take cognizance of the existence
> of religion and, indeed, under certain circum-
> stances the First Amendment may require that
> it do so. And it seems clear to me from the
> opinions in the present and past cases that
> the Court would recognize the propriety of
> providing military chaplains and of the teach-
> ing about religion, as distinguished from the
> teaching of religion, in the public schools.[8]

In addition to providing an educational and legal
rationale for public education religion studies, the
Supreme Court in these cases also expounded what it
believed to be a constitutionally sound approach to religion studies in public education. According to the
Justice's writing in Schempp, religions should be taught
objectively within a secular program of education according
to the canons of comparative religion and historical and
literary scholarship. Expositions of these terms follow.

Justice Brennan held in Schempp that a secular program
of education is one which is "free of parochial, divisive,

or separatist influences of any sort . . . ."[9] In the 1947
Everson decision, Justice Jackson called for a "strict and
lofty neutrality" which is free from all religious assumptions and teachings. (Schempp substituted "wholesome
neutrality" for this phrase in 1963.) From these opinions,
it may be inferred that a secular program of education is
one that is not controlled by any religious assumptions
and/or group. Furthermore, all forms of religious indoctrination are eschewed. It is in this context that Justice
Goldberg's distinction between teaching of and teaching
about must be understood. The Justices equated sectarian
approaches to religion with the teaching of religion and
secular approaches as teaching about religion. While this
distinction may be helpful to jurists, it is not entirely
satisfactory for those who seek to study religion academically. It fails to consider, for example, whether this
very commitment to secular education constitutes an
"ultimate" world view.

To be objective, according to the Court, is to be
neutral, open, free, and scholarly. This does not reduce
teaching to bland recitation of dates, facts, and statistics. There is room for responsible "passionate" and
"committed" scholarly teaching in public education religion
studies. However, proselytizing and evangelism are to be
avoided.

Michaelsen concludes from a careful study of several
Court decisions, both state and federal, that the Justices
determine the objectivity and neutrality of a given religion course or program by deciding whether it is taught by
professionally competent teachers who utilize the "tools
and methods appropriate to achieving the fullest possible
understanding of the subject" and espouse open and free
inquiry in schools which guarantee and protect academic
freedom.[10]

While the Justices did not spell out what they meant
by comparative, it is safe to conclude from their remarks
on objectivity and neutrality that normative comparisons
are prohibited and that only descriptive comparisons as

found in the phenomenology and history of religion are
allowed. Teaching that is free from religious assumptions
and controls cannot include normative value judgments.

The Justices emphasized two points when they employed
the word historical. First, they stressed that religions
grow and develop within specific societies and cultures.
Second, they suggested that religions influence the course
of history by acting in and through cultures and societal
institutions. Hence an historical approach to religions
is an investigation into the ways in which these transac-
tions take place.

"Literary qualities" is one of the phrases used in
Schempp to describe how the Bible may be studied in public
education. From this usage, it is possible to infer that
both the Bible and the scriptures of other religions are
to be studied according to the canons of literary scholarship and criticism. Justice Clark also added that the
Bible should be studied for its historic qualities. Again,
it may be inferred that both the Bible and the scriptures
of other religions are to be studied in the historical
manner described above. In addition, according to James
Ackerman and Thayer Warshaw, while the literary and historical study of the Bible, and by inference other scriptures, must be free, open, and critical in the same way
other literature is studied, such study also "must maintain
respect for the various religious backgrounds represented
in . . . [the] classroom so that no pupil is led to conclude
that his religious training is inappropriate or academically indefensible when pitted against the approach of his
authority figure teacher."[11] Finally, when the Scriptures
of religions are taught as literature, mention also should
be made that they are the scriptures of given communities
who do not regard them merely as literature but as one of
the sources and canons of their faiths, i.e., sacred
literature.

The Court has utilized recently both broad and narrow
definitions of religion in different but related cases. In
1961 (Torcaso), the Court distinguished between religions

which base themselves on theistic beliefs and those that
are founded on other types of belief. According to the
Court, Buddhism, Taoism, Ethical Culture, and Secular
Humanism are illustrations of the latter. Following this
precedent in 1970 (Welsh), the Court held, when exempting
an individual from military service on the grounds of
personal conscience, that personal beliefs derived solely
from readings in history and sociology may constitute a
person's religion.[12] However, in 1972 (Yoder), when the
Court exempted persons from compulsory school attendance,
a narrow definition of religion which had been used in
other previous cases was invoked, i.e., a recognized sect.
Hence, in an apparent effort to meet specific needs in
different concrete situations, the Court abandoned consistency and invoked different definitions of religion.[13]

One question remains: Are these descriptions and
definitions to be followed to the letter? Michaelsen
shows that the Justices did not intend their dicta to
become iron-clad, immutable laws.[14] This is true for two
reasons. First, even though they are intended to be taken
seriously, dicta are not binding laws; they are only
opinions of the Justices. Second, the Justices themselves
suggested that their dicta on public education religion
studies should be viewed as flexible guidelines. Michaelsen establishes the latter point by noting that the
Justices did not use a noun but, rather, an adverb,
"objectively," to suggest how religion should be taught
and that:

> Justice Jackson observed in McCollum that "since
> neighborhoods differ in racial, religious and
> cultural composition . . . it must be expected that
> they will adopt different customs which will give
> emphasis to different values and will enduce dif-
> ferent experiments . . . . We must leave some
> flexibility," he urged his colleagues, "to meet
> local conditions, some chance to progress by
> trial and error."[15]

Justice Brennan's concurring opinion in Schempp supports further this interpretation: "To what extent, and
at what points in the curriculum religious materials

should be cited, are matters which the courts ought to
trust very largely to the experienced officials who superintend our Nation's public schools."[16]

In conclusion, the Justices of the Supreme Court provided
flexible legal parameters and definitions for the public
schools to use in teaching about religion. It is the
responsibility of the schools to be well versed in these
and to fulfill their intent as religion studies programs
based on the canons of responsible scholarship are introduced.

The Purpose of and Goals for
Public Education Religion Studies

The preceding summary of Jefferson's model for public
education, the religious conflicts in the schools as a
reflection of the religious conflicts in the wider community, and Supreme Court decisions pertaining to religion
studies in public education provide the foundation for the
following proposed statement of the purpose and goals of
public education religion studies. They are offered as a
possible means for fulfilling the spirit of the Court's
decisions, for providing educational objectives for
religion studies in the public schools, and for meeting
accepted scholarly theories and approaches to the study of
religion. They also are suggested as a means for correct-
ing the truncated way in which most Americans view religion.

The purpose of religion studies in public education is
to help students attain by means of methods commensurate
with their stages of intellectual, emotional, religious,
and social development, a broad and balanced understanding
of the nature and function of religions in their personal,
social, and historical lives and the lives of others.

Religion as used here refers to both the narrow and
broad definitions offered by the Supreme Court, i.e., the
major traditional monist, monotheistic, and deist religions and the atheistic, ethical, and secular ideological
systems which perform religious or quasi-religious functions in many societies, e.g., Theravada Buddhism, Taoism,

Ethical Culture, Secularism, Scientism, and Marxism.
These definitions presuppose that all human beings require
a world view by which to order the meaning and conduct of
their lives and that these world views constitute one of
the major elements in the religious dimension of life. At
the same time, it is assumed that religions are the symbol
systems of specific cultures and sub-cultures and, therefore, every individual religious commitment possesses a
social element. The personal and social dimension of
religions always are related inextricably and, therefore,
should not be considered as independent entities. Primary
emphasis is placed in this definition on concrete historical, social, and personal lives because living communities
and individuals always precede abstract study of them.
Hence any definition of religion must maintain concrete
referents.

Broad and balanced understanding includes developing
a complementary relation between an analytical study of
religious phenomena according to the canons of empirical
investigation and an empathetic grasp of the experienced
world view of the religious group and individuals under
study. The holding of these two approaches in a harmonious
polar relation will enable students to gain an understanding of how religions develop and change in history and the
ultimate meanings they hold for their adherents.

Since the public schools generally include students
from the ages of five through eighteen and since there are
major developmental differences between the first and
twelfth grade students, religion studies must select
methods for developing balanced understanding which are
appropriate to the age level of the students. Therefore,
it is not adequate to suggest, as Bischoff does, that the
most appropriate method for studying about religion in
secondary public education is that of existential hermeneutics.[17] It may be an appropriate method to introduce at
the eleventh or twelfth grade but hardly at lower levels.

Henry Hoeks is correct both psychologically and pedagogically when he states that "religion studies in the elementary and secondary schools ought to develop that modicum
or more of knowledge as a basis for advanced (usually
college or university) inquiry . . . ."[18] (Usually, should
be underscored here, because the students who begin the
process of forming their own identities in the eleventh or
twelfth grades are capable of raising and handling, in
elementary ways, existential hermeneutical questions.)

In light of these considerations, the following seven
goals are suggested as a means whereby the above suggested
purpose of public education religion studies may be
attained. In each instance, the objective is to develop a
broad and balanced understanding of

    (1) the many and diverse ways in which the religious
        dimension of human life is manifested;

    (2) how religions influence societies and in turn are
        influenced by them;

    (3) the meaning and significance of making a religious
        commitment through either acculturation, nurture,
        or conversion or a combination of these, and
        living by the commitment;

    (4) the history of religions in America and the in-
        teraction of religions and culture in America in
        addition to the conflicts between religions in
        America;

    (5) the relation of religions to moralities, and the
        difference between the two;

    (6) the numerous and different ways in which religions
        may be studied, including their strengths and
        weaknesses, and the dimensions of religions which
        seem to elude analytic investigation; and

    (7) the difference between studying about religions
        in a pluralistic context and practicing religion
        within a specific community, and the significance
        of each for the other.

Ideally, these seven goals should be fulfilled in
programs whose basic design, content, and approach progress
from the simple to the complex and from the concrete to
the abstract. This progression, moreover, should be based

on learning and teaching theories informed by sound
psychological studies of human development. Much of what
is published today does not do this and as a result, is
pedagogically ineffective.[19]

Goals 1 and 2 seek to take full account of the
plurality and variety of religions in the world and of
their historical and social dimensions. While pursuing
these goals students should be introduced to both narrow
and broad definitions of religion so that they will learn
how to gather information about and come to some understanding of formal and informal, communal and personal, and
inherited and experienced manifestations of religions. At
the same time, students should be made aware of the different and diverse "texts" of religions which communicate
the meanings and values of religious communities--rituals,
myths, ceremonies, festivals, symbols, stories, music, art,
literature, communal structures, and social action.
Finally, students should be introduced to the dialectic
relation between religions and cultures.

Goal 3 is intended to help students gain an insight
into the different ways in which individuals become members
of religious communities and the emotions, actions, and
thoughts that accompany these approaches in addition to the
rituals attached to each. Students should be assisted in
developing an understanding of the meaning and significance
of making a commitment and fulfilling it in each of these
different ways.

Goal 4 is included to introduce students to their own
American heritage and provide them with information and
insights to understand the present religious situation in
which they live. This introduction should help them
become aware of the way in which civic religion and
morality were welded together to form an established democratic faith in the United States and how this faith,
because it was pan-Protestant in emphasis and intent,
produced conflicts in the wider society and the public
schools. Also, it should enable students to recognize the
religious significance of the new pluralism which is being

introduced into American society and education. Lastly,
this goal should help students develop an acquaintance
with and understanding of the religious and moral significance of the religious and moral conflicts produced by the
almost unrecognized change in America's value orientation
from commitment to the cultivation of individuality and
self-mastery to mass conformity and mass consumerism.
According to Harry S. Broudy,

> Not only are foods and cars and credit avail-
> able for purchase, but also opinions and
> tastes and value norms. And just as enormous
> sophistication has been invested in the mass-
> produced material goods of our society, so
> have enormous amounts of knowledge and thought
> been invested in the mass-distributed ideas,
> ideologies, and images.
>
> In a strange way this is a return to Eden,
> where Adam and Eve did not have to toil for
> anything; where knowledge, especially of good
> and evil, was superfluous. They forfeited
> that bliss by yielding to a forbidden curios-
> ity. Today the technologically mature society
> in its bumbling way offers to decrease the
> toil of mind, body, and spirit while supplying
> an ever greater degree of health, pleasure and
> stimulation. The price is abandonment of the
> desire to be one's own man, to be one's own
> conscience, and of the hunger to develop one's
> intellectual and moral powers.[20]

This shift in personal and societal values is related
to the religious life of the American people and needs to
become recognized as such. It is a departure from some of
the major tenets of the commonly held democratic faith and
morality which still are included in the symbol system of
America's civil religion but no longer receive support
from the socio-economic structures.

Goal 5 is included to develop an understanding of how
moralities are derived from world views, and why moralities
do not necessarily constitute religions. Also, it is
intended to assist students in discovering the sources of
particular moralities, e.g., a theistic or humanistic
world view.

This goal should help American students discover the
relationship among moralities, religions, and politics in
American culture and to be able to come to a clearer understanding of how this relationship shapes their society
and impinges on their personal lives.

Goal 6 is included to introduce students to the
various ways in which religion may be studied, and the
limitations of each approach. Since religions are highly
complex phenomena and because religions are historical,
social, and personal in character, no single method of
study is adequate in and by itself. A broad understanding
of religions requires the utilization of a combination of
several different methods which complement each other.
It requires a synthesis of insights from the natural and
social sciences and the humanities, and the establishment
of a delicate balance between the analytic and intuitive
approaches to reality.

Goal 7 seeks to assist students in overcoming their
society's propensity to identify erroneously the practice
of religion with the academic study of religions. This
tendency, as pointed out earlier, is the result in part of
the public schools inculcating students in Jefferson's
"democratic faith," a particular Protestant theology or a
pan-Protestant set of beliefs and morality. Therefore,
this goal should demonstrate how it is possible to study
religions academically without advocating one.

It should help students learn that, no matter how
firmly one may hold a faith, entirely new dimensions of
one's own faith and the faiths of others may be gained
from an academic study of religions. At the same time,
this goal should introduce them to the way in which the
academic study of religion is based upon presuppositions
which must be examined critically since they, too, are
derived from particular world views. Finally, this goal
should lead students to discover that genuine pluralism
does not necessarily imply relativism. On the contrary,
it requires a strong commitment to one's own stance in
order to grant recognition and validity to the position
of another. In the words of Joseph Watras,

A quest for values cannot be satisfied by half-
truths. Over sociologizing is equally mislead-
ing for it can be used to sidestep or denigrate
deeply felt concerns . . . . The school system
that takes a chance and affirms genuine pluralism with . . . [all] sides interacting, maintaining the possibility of one finally dominating,
[and] searching for the truth all within limits
will revolutionize education.[21]

Pluralism, in this view, also assumes that students,
as they move toward psychological and emotional maturity,
will be open to modifying their own views and commitments
in light of their study of other religious positions and
their dialogues with their teachers and fellow students.

Eventually, this type of pluralism must either replace or modify dramatically Jefferson's democratic religio-
political model and the pan-Protestant approach as the
unifying points of the public schools. As we have seen,
both have been unable to cope with the problems and
dynamics of an ever growing pluralistic and secular society.
Both have substituted the practice of religion for the
academic study of religions. The introduction, development,
and refinement of public education religion studies as outlined in this chapter may make a modest and long lasting
contribution to the resolution of these problems.[22]

NOTES

[1]"The Public Schools and 'America's Two Religions,'"
Journal of Church and State, 8/3 (Autumn, 1966), 383.

[2]"A Call for the Study of Religion as an Academic
Discipline," in Religious Education, Part II (July-August,
1972), 101.

[3]See: James E. Wood, Jr., "Secular Humanism and the
Public Schools: Myth or Reality?", PERSC Newsletter 5/2
(Winter, 1978), 1-4.

[4]See: Joseph Watras, "The Textbook Dispute in West
Virginia: A New Form of Oppression," Educational Leadership, 33/1 (October, 1975), 21ff.

[5]See: Guy B. Hammond, et al., "Secular Humanism: Social Studies Teachers and the Concern over Morality," The Social Studies, 69/4 (July-August, 1978), 145.

[6]333 U.S. 203 (1948).

[7]374 U.S. 319 (1963).

[8]374 U.S. 260 (1963).

[9]374 U.S. 257 (1963).

[10]"Constitutions, Courts and the Study of Religion," Journal of the American Academy of Religion, 45/3 (1977).

[11]James S. Ackerman, "Teaching the Bible as Literature in Secondary Schools: A Report on the 1970 Indiana University Summer Institute," (mimeographed), a paper presented at the 1970 Annual Meeting of the American Academy of Religion in New York, 7.

[12]Thayer Warshaw, "Religion Studies, Moral Education, and Values Clarification in American Public Schools: Definitions," (mimeographed), a paper distributed to the Religion Studies in Public Education Group of the American Academy of Religion, December, 1976, 2.

[13]Ibid.: "Too narrow a construction in Welsh would have tended to destroy our selective service system by restricting the privilege of exemption to members of religious sects, which would be unconstitutional advancement of religion over irreligion. Too broad a construction in Yoder would have tended to destroy our public school system by granting exemptions to anyone whose values were opposed to the philosophy of the local schools. Theoretical consistency gave way to practical considerations."

[14]"Constitutions, Courts and the Study of Religion," 296.

[15]Piety in the Public School: Trends and Issues in the Relationship between Religion and the Public Schools in the United States (London: Macmillan, 1970), 205.

[16]374 U.S. 257 (1963).

[17]"The Pedagogy of Religiology," Ann Carr and Nicholas Piediscalzi, eds., The Academic Study of Religion: 1975 Proceedings and Public Schools Religion-Studies: 1975 Proceedings (Missoula, Montana: Scholars Press, 1975), 132-134.

[18]"A Multi-Disciplinary Approach to Religion Studies in the Schools," (mimeographed), a paper presented to the Religion Studies in Public Education Group at the 1977 Annual Meeting of the American Academy of Religion in San Francisco, 3.

[19]For examples of how this may be done, see: Harold
M. Stahmer, "Religion and Moral Values in the Public
Schools," Religious Education, 61/1 (January-February,
1966), 24-26; W. Owen Cole, ed., World Faiths in Education
(London: George Allen and Unwin, 1978), 18-22 and 53-56;
Joan G. Dye, "Learning About Religions through the Elemen-
tary Social Studies Program," Nicholas Piediscalzi and
William E. Collie, eds., Teaching About Religion in Public
Schools (Niles, Illinois: Argus Communications, 1977),
107-118; and Joan G. Dye, Robert A. Spivey and Rodney
Allen, Learning About Religion/Social Studies (Niles,
Illinois: Argus Communications, 1976).

[20]General Education: The Search for a Rationale
(Bloomington, Indiana: The Phi Delta Kappa Educational
Foundation, 1976), 28.

[21]"The Textbook Dispute in West Virginia," 21-23.

[22]The author expresses appreciation to Professors
Catherine L. Albanese, David L. Barr, William Collie,
Robert Michaelsen and Paul J. Will for their criticism
of and suggestions for improving the original paper presented to the AAR.

CHAPTER THREE

PUBLIC EDUCATION RELIGION STUDIES AS A BRIDGE
DISCIPLINE: TOWARD A PEDAGOGY OF RELIGIOLOGY

Guntram G. Bischoff

Public education religion studies, as distinct from
theology or the credal extrapolation of religious groups,
is still a rather recent phenomenon on the American educational scene. Public school religion studies in a
constitutionally acceptable form are not yet two decades
old and can hardly be called well-established. Public
education religion studies at institutions of higher
learning have only a slightly longer tradition, and while
it is true that the discipline of religion studies as such
has made major advances, one cannot say the same with
reference to its pedagogical dimension, particularly its
didactics.[1] It is, therefore, not surprising that so far
few efforts have been made to stake out the entire field
of public education religion studies as an identifiable
area of academic inquiry, i.e., as an academic discipline
in its own right.

It is the purpose of the following reflections to
contribute to such efforts not only (1) by arguing the
merit of a systematic academic inquiry into the teaching
of the academic study of religion as a comprehensive cross-
discipline, but (2) to roughly sketch what might be an
appropriate though obviously incomplete outline of this
discipline, and (3) at the same time to suggest some
answers to problems which inevitably arise in the course
of treating this discipline. In an attempt to escape
imprecise or awkward terms and lengthy circumlocutions, we
call the discipline the pedagogy of religiology. In order
to meet the stated objectives within the available space,

*Guntram G. Bischoff, Th.D., is Professor of Religion,
Western Michigan University.*

it will be necessary to reduce, somewhat arbitrarily, the
complexities of the subject area to some manageable pro-
portions. This is accomplished by addressing the rather
limited thematic question of why and how should public
(secondary) school students study religion?

General Theory of Education:
The Nature and Function of Education

Any pedagogy of religiology should proceed and
devolve from a general theory of education because it is
not possible to construct such a pedagogy in abstracto.
Like all special pedagogies, the pedagogy of religiology
deals with a specific aspect of education only and is,
therefore, in theory at least interrelated with all other
special pedagogies. Both individually and in their
totality, special pedagogies necessarily imply prior
assumptions and choices, and it would seem desirable that
such implied elements be rendered explicit in form of a
general theory of education.

The first question to be considered is that of the
anthropologically based need for education. Education in
whatever form is necessary, it might be argued, for at
least two reasons. First, the young human being must
learn to cope with his or her physical environment.
Second, since humans are essentially social beings and
such coping with the environment can take place only
within the social context, the integration into the group
must be learned.

A first requirement then is to study the historical
development of educational theory and practice in particular
societies. With regard to American public education, and
in view of the present focus on religion, two principal
and intimately related factors stand out vividly. The
first is the experience of pluralism, the other that of
secularity. Both have come to function as normative
principles precipitated into law and guarded by legal
institutions. During the 19th century, the First Amendment gradually came to be understood not only as

recognizing de facto pluralism--religious and otherwise--
but as establishing it de jure. Secularization and its
attendant result, secularity, are merely the obverse side
of this affirmative acceptance of pluralism.

Today's public school is thus the institutional as
well as the symbolic expression of these fundamental
norms. It is in principle both pluralistic and secular,
and it should be noted that "secular" here does not mean
"non-sectarian," as is sometimes suggested, but it means
quite literally "a-religious," without religion. If it
took a good century to arrive at this interpretive conclusion, this is not surprising; for historical consciousness
invariably limps behind the events that shape it. Indeed,
the very question of why and how school students should
study religion implies that such study may not be taken
for granted as are, for instance, the study of literature
or history.

It would seem that current theory generally lists
three primary goals of education: (1) the development and
training of skills needed to cope with the demands of a
highly advanced industrial society, (2) socialization into
the norms of such society, and (3) the development of the
individual student's personal potential. It would seem to
be unreasonable to take exception to any of these goals as
it is impossible to conceive of a society functioning without its members having attained to a certain measure of
skills, some form of socialization (though certainly not
just any form), and a degree of self-actualization. One
does miss in such enumeration of divergent goals, however,
a focus in which the intimate interrelatedness of all
goals becomes apparent, a central purpose that would
indicate the integral nature and function of the educational process. The formulation of such a purpose must
reckon, of course, with the historical experience of
pluralism and secularity. With this caveat in mind, it
may be suggested that it is the over-all purpose of
education to help and enable persons, according to their
capacity and ability, to autonomously order their

environment and themselves into a meaningful world to
which they acknowledge themselves to be responsibly
related.[2]

No such autonomous construction of a meaningful world
is possible without the understanding of what is "given,"
i.e., the world as it presents itself. Nor is such
autonomous construction possible without the understanding
of the self willing and doing the constructing. Hence
world-understanding and self-understanding are fundamental
goals of education in that they inform, to a large extent,
a person's motivation and action.[3]

Speaking of the "world" to be constructed means, of
course, the act of conceptualizing both the world of
nature and the world of culture, since both are data,
"given" to personal consciousness. The term "self-
understanding," however, requires elaboration. It is
meant to denote the process of rendering conscious a
person's attitudes, convictions, beliefs, doubts, motives
for action and decisions, values, etc. All of these are
mediated through the self-understanding of other human
beings, individuals or groups, and its expression in a
variety of ways, such as literary, artistic, philosophical,
ethical, and religious documents. By exposing oneself to
the self-understanding of others, by grasping, reflecting
upon, and evaluating such self-understanding of others, a
person is enabled to more fully appreciate and understand
himself or herself, to "place" oneself in the "world,"
and hence to meaningfully and responsively relate oneself
to the natural and cultural worlds in which one finds oneself.

Such relating may, of course, be either positive or
negative. One may accept or reject either the self-
understanding of others or the world in which one finds
oneself, or both. One even may accept or reject oneself
as one is at that moment in time. Hence the process of
self-understanding inevitably involves decision-making.
Obviously, the educational process cannot and should not
make such decisions for the student lest the goal of

autonomy be vitiated by keeping the student heteronomously captive. On the contrary, it should enable the student to make such decisions by and for himself or herself as an act of genuine responsibility. This it can do only by confronting students with the self-understanding of others in such a way as to render their various claims to meaning-giving truth and value as genuine possibilities for themselves and for their adoption of them and identification with them.

School theory must deal with the particular problem posed by the distinction between public and private schools. In which sense is public school education different from that of private schools? Should it be that way? It was suggested earlier that the public school is as much symbol as it is institution. Is it, one might ask, the best possible educational institutionalization of the social norms of pluralism and secularity? What is to be its integrant if it is not to be some sort of vague patriotism or the "civil religion?"

Finally, a general theory of education must deal with the student, both individually and as a group. Who are today's students? What motivates them? What are their goals and ambitions? What unites them and what divides them? These and similar questions while of course not unrelated to problems of developmental psychology, primarily focus on the problem of the socio-psychological identity of today's students for whom unconscious social forces and influences are at least as important as is their own conscious self-image. Is it correct, for instance, to say that large numbers of young people are victims of anomie? And if so, what are its causes? Should the recent trends toward individualization and "permissiveness" be interpreted as part of the emancipation from tradition, and if so, to which extent have these trends affected religion? What is the contemporary student's cultural image of religion? Must we understand this whole development as a sort of accelerated secularization? Whatever the answer to this particular though

representative problem, it should be clear that a general
theory of education cannot be formulated without a careful
analysis on several levels of the identity of the contemporary student.

The Reason and Purpose of Education in Religiology

Next, it is necessary to address the question of the
reason and purpose of public school religion studies: why
should public school students study religion? The purpose
of education in religiology cannot be different from the
larger purpose of education in general but is and should
be integral to it, that is, it is to guide the student to
an adequate world-understanding and self-understanding.
Religion studies will at best be considered a special frill
unless one can convincingly demonstrate that such studies
are an integral part of good education for all.

Three arguments are most often cited in support of
religion studies. The "genetic argument" reasons that
religion has always been a powerful cultural force, and
that in order to understand one's own or any other culture,
one must know the role religion played or plays in it.
The "socialization argument" holds that since religion is
an ineradicable factor in the make-up of our national
identity, successful socialization implies familiarity
with religion and religious values. The "character or
behavioral argument" claims that the study of other and
less known religions develops tolerance and other desirable
character or behavioral features.

While there is a measure of validity in all three of
these arguments, none of them is really convincing. The
view of religion implied in them is questionable since it
is exclusively instrumental or functional. Religion
appears only as epiphenomenon, as a variable of human
culture or behavior. Moreover, secularization and secularity are taken either too seriously or not seriously
enough. They are taken too seriously insofar as the reduction of religion to its social and psychological
functions is itself a secularistic notion. They are not

taken seriously enough in that the powerful counterreli-
gious forces of secularization, including the force of
modern ideologies, are naively ignored. One tends to
forget the fact that about half of the United States'
population does not identify with institutional forms of
religion. Finally, the assumption that religion studies
will foster tolerance appears doubtful. The opposite may
well be the case, but the behavioral argument is at any
rate much too simplistic since it does not recognize the
dialectic of tolerance. Systems proclaiming tolerance may
indeed do so with considerable intolerance.

The desirability of, and need for religion studies
may be persuasively argued, however, if one derives them
from the educational goals of world-understanding and
self-understanding. It appears unquestionable that
individuals and societies of all ages have understood
themselves in religious terms, i.e., in terms of the
structures of ultimate reality, norm, and meaning. This
self-understanding of others is objectivated in all areas
of their culture but perhaps most obviously and accessibly
in their literature, art, philosophy, ethics, and religion.
As such it becomes the object of the educational goal of
world-understanding which students study as data, i.e., as
part of the historical environment, the world in which
they find themselves. This objective world-understanding
is necessarily and dialectically related to the students'
own subjective or "existential" self-understanding. In
this way, the self-understanding of others, past and
present, becomes not only "knowledge," but a challenge, a
claim, a question to the students' own self-understanding
in form of a continuous dialogue.

The Content of Education in Religiology

The preceding considerations lead inevitably to the
problem of the content of religion studies: why and how
should public school students study *religion*? Past
experience suggests that attempts to argue the desirability
and purpose of religion studies often become entangled in

the effort to define religion. The problem seems both
endemic and intractable; for not only does every so-called
definition of religion reflect a particular approach and
methodology, but it may well be that religion can be defined only when regarded as an epiphenomenon. In its
authentic self-claim, however, the intended object of
religion is the totality of reality in its infinitude and
absoluteness, rendering religion undefinable. What is
definable and in need of definition are limited objects of
the study of religion which means that definitions of
religion are at best heuristic.

To begin with, the study of religion in the public
school must orient itself, like the study of any other
subject, to its academic referent discipline. This is
necessary for at least two reasons. First, the study of
religion is probably most concentrated, intensive, and
advanced within the community of its expert scholars.
Second, it is imperative that the study of religious
phenomena on any level not be bastardized for whatever
purpose and reason but that its integrity and authenticity
be jealously guarded. This is true, of course, for any
field of knowledge. It would hardly do to insist, for
whatever reason, that the sun revolves around the earth.
The referent discipline for the study of religion in the
public school is the academic study of religion, or
religiology.

Religiology is not a simple discipline. It is rather
a complex discipline, or a bundle of disciplines, such as
the history, sociology, psychology, philosophy, and pedagogy of religion. The term religiology indicates that all
of these sub-disciplines share the same general object,
however much they may differ with regard to their particular objects and methods. The problem of definition
mentioned above must be seen against this background.

The notion of the complex identity of the discipline
of religiology has a number of corollaries which may be
formulated by way of postulates. (1) Religiology should
not be regarded as confined to any one exclusive approach

and method.   (2) Religiology is not possible if the
phenomenon of religion is reduced to an epiphenomenon.
(3) Religiology, though related to theology, should be
distinguished clearly from it.

    Particularly the last point requires further comment.
Religiology is inevitably related to theology because the
experience of, and the quest for the "unconditioned conditioning" of all reality is inseparable from both the
self-understanding of the religious person and the
intentionality of the phenomenon of religion as such.   If
this element were eliminated or ignored, nothing would be
left but an epiphenomenon. On the other hand, religiology
is different from theology in that religiology stops short
of the decision to symbolically identify the "unconditioned
conditioning" or to choose among "contents" of the formal
identification of "reality as a whole". Religiology
declares itself incapable and incompetent of such decision.
It recognizes the quest and the form but suspends judgment
as to the validity and the content of the claim of any
given tradition or person. Theology does the opposite inasmuch as a Christian, Islamic, or Jewish theology without
a positively identifiable Christian, Islamic, or Jewish
"credal" affirmation is quite inconceivable. Religiology,
therefore, regards theology itself as a religious form.
While religiology is thus essentially in harmony with the
experience and consciousness of pluralism and secularity
(though by no means necessarily with secularism), theology
is not. This should not surprise us in view of the fact
that religiology is historically the child of secular
consciousness.

    It should now be clear why a strict religiological
definition of religion is neither possible nor desirable.
It is not possible because this would entail either the
reversion to theology or the denial of religion. It is
not desirable because it would have to be necessarily
exclusivistic. One should instead proceed with limited,
heuristic definitions such as the following example:
Religion is the expression of a visionary perception of

reality in its ultimate wholeness. The term "visionary perception" in this context is to indicate that it is the very signature of the human condition that humans experience and know its finitude through their necessarily partial perception of reality.

Due to its nature as a bridge discipline, the pedagogy of religiology shares the general objects of its parent disciplines. To the extent to which it may be seen as a subdiscipline of religiology, it shares the general object of that discipline, i.e., the general and particular phenomena of religion. With the educational sciences, on the other hand, it shares the general object of the conditions, nature, and function of the particular forms of communication which we call education. This dualism of general objects is important because it substantially affects the specific object, purpose, and content of the pedagogy of religiology, and it does so not only qualitatively, but also quantitatively.

While in principle its content is no different from that of religiology, it is sharply distinguished in practice; for the specific purpose of the pedagogy of religiology is not the study of religion as such, but the communication and appropriation, the teaching and learning of religion as studied by religiology. Hence the specific object of this discipline is the communication and appropriation of the study of religion under various conditions which determines its content and methods. First among these conditions is, of course, the age of the student. It is obvious that the teaching of kindergartners is not the same as that of college students or adults notwithstanding the fact that the general contents to be communicated and appropriated are identical in principle.

The Didactics of Religiology

The preceding considerations lead to a final major section of the pedagogy of religiology which addresses itself to questions of approach and method concerning the study of religion: why and *how* should public school

students study religion? This area of the discipline, the
didactics of religiology, divides into a theoretical and a
practical part. Limitation of space dictate confinement
to the first of these, with a mere allusion to the second.
The didactics of religiology may be regarded in many ways
as the crux of the entire discipline; for not only is it
closest to the practice of teaching and learning, but in
it the bridge character of the discipline is put to the
test.

A number of difficult problems demand attention, and
since all of these problems are interrelated, it is important to find the proverbial Archimedian point. It may be
argued that this point is the problem of the proper
approach to, and the methodology of public school religion studies. Before proceeding, it may be useful to
recall two postulates stated earlier. Like the teaching
of any subject, public school religion studies must be
guided by the students' need, capability, and ability.
Moreover, public school religion studies must preserve and
respect both the authenticity of the phenomenon of religion studied and the purpose and goals of education in
general.

First of all, it should be axiomatic that no approach
can be educationally successful which does not address and
involve students in their personal center. After all,
students are persons and not containers to be crammed and
stuffed with facts and information, quite apart from the
question whether or not the assumption of such uninter-
preted mere-facts and information is tenable. Students
are engaged--or should be so engaged--in a vital search
for identity, truth, and values. They neither want nor
need just facts; they want and need facts related to
themselves. They are not, and need not be, ashamed of
their subjectivity. They are existentially engaged in
attempting to arrive at a full, coherent, and satisfying
self-understanding, and any approach to the study of
religion ignoring this personal dimension of learning is
not likely to succeed.

A second, equally important requirement is that any
proper approach to the study of religion should be
critical. The demand for criticalness derives from the
purpose of education itself. If this purpose is the
student's autonomous construction of a meaningful world,
and if this is possible only through the medium of an
adequate world-understanding and self-understanding, it
follows that criticalness is the sine qua non of successful education. The achievement of autonomy, the emancipation from parental tutelage and other forms of heteronomous
authority, and the attainment of a mature self, all require
decisions among alternatives which cannot be made without
criticalness.[4]

Religion studies must be critical so that the student
may discern genuine and authentic possibilities of world-
understanding and self-understanding of others, past and
present, with which to confront his own world-understanding
and self-understanding as a matter of genuine choice. In
this way the critical study of religion can contribute to
the enabling process of developing personal autonomy. Of
course, the teacher must not make the choice for the
student. This would be quite counterproductive and pre-
vent rather than aid the student's growth into autonomy.
Neither should teachers avoid their task by pedestrian and
boring descriptiveness or by picking out juicy tidbits of
the sensational and exotic that cannot be taken seriously
by the student.

Two marginal qualifications are in order at this
point. Criticalness must at all times imply self-critique.
This is as important for the teacher as it is for the
student since mere instrumental criticism which is unwill-
ing to risk its own presuppositions does not lead to
emancipation but only to a new, however subtle form of
dependency. Furthermore, it should be stressed that
criticalness as the condition of free choice is in harmony
with the experience of both pluralism and secularity. Not
to be critical can only mean either to deny pluralism or
to make it into an absolutist idol, beyond critique, and

ruling in untouchable heteronomy. As such it would be an instance of secularism, not secularity. It is for this reason that one should plead for and welcome the inclusion of modern religion-critique in any study of religion. The often-heard call for an uncritical study of religion that emphasizes only the so-called positive aspects of religion is not only untrue, excluding much of modern self-understanding, but it is also dishonest and an affront to the intellectual and moral integrity of the students denying them the very autonomy toward which it is to guide them.

One of the most difficult problems associated with the methodology of the study of religion, particularly public school religion studies, is that of "objectivity." It would appear that prevailing opinion insists that the only proper, correct, and viable approach to the study of religion is the descriptive one, whereby "descriptive" is taken to be synonymous with "objective." Proponents of this view usually invoke the language of the U.S. Supreme Court's Schempp decision which seems to relate objectivity to the teaching "about religion," opposing both to the practice of religion. However, while the question of constitutionality is certainly a pressing one, the real problem is not that of the use of certain words and phrases, but their interpretation and particularly the assumptions underlying this interpretation. As far as the advocates of mere-description are concerned, the assumption seems to be that a rationalistic view or theory of science and knowledge is alone capable of yielding objectivity; but such an assumption is highly dubious both in epistemology and in education.

One may on the contrary argue that the merely descriptive approach to the study of religion is worthless both educationally and academically. It is worthless educationally because it does not engage the students in their deepest concerns or interests, regardless of whether or not they can as yet articulate such concerns or interests. It is academically worthless because it ignores the very heart of the phenomenon of religion and

because it is essentially uncritical, refusing to admit
that non-interpretation constitutes an interpretation of
sorts.

The problem of a proper approach is not insoluble,
however. Its solution requires an approach which is
objective without being objectivistic, critical without
being reductionist, rational without being rationalistic,
and secular without being secularistic. Its solution
requires an approach which respects the students' search
for ultimate meaning without being theological or religious
itself, which supports the students' discovery of the
significance of religion for themselves without yet being
indoctrinating or authoritative. It requires an approach
which allows the phenomenon of religion its own transpar-
ency and depth without either at once explaining it away
or remaining the captive of prior commitments. It requires
an approach which interprets while it describes, and which
is not afraid to accept its own limitations. In short,
the solution of the problem requires an approach which is
in systematic dialogue with the phenomenon and which may
be called the hermeneutical or dialogical approach.

A few salient points must suffice to indicate aspects
of this approach. Hermeneutics in the broad sense is the
science of interpretation and understanding through the
medium of language. Language, of course, is not confined
to the spoken or written word. We rightly refer to the
"language" of gestures and ritual, the "message" carried
by actions, and ancient artifacts or institutions "speaking" to us. Yet it is a simple fact that the vast bulk of
historical data, past and present, is available to us only
through written texts of one kind or another.

The heart of the hermeneutical or dialogical approach
and method is that it allows the "reader" (or "listener")
to enter into a critical dialogue with the "text." No
religious text can speak fully and freely if the questions
directed to it violate its own intentionality and if it is
not allowed to first disclose the world-understanding and
self-understanding of its author. On the part of the

reader this requires first of all a readiness to listen
and to critically re-examine his questioning of the text.
But beyond this it requires that the reader be willing and
prepared to risk his own world-understanding and self-
understanding in the ensuing dialogue with the text and
its author.

With regard to the educational situation, this
approach requires that the teacher should serve as
experienced guide, leading the student to become a good
listener, reader, and partner in the dialogue with the
text. The educational objective here is the genuine dialogical confrontation with the religious claim of text and
author in which the student's inchoate world-understanding
and self-understanding are risked and re-formed. Under no
circumstance should the student be shielded from this claim
of the text out of a mistaken fear of breeching the canons
of a false objectivity. On the contrary, students can
develop an authentic world-understanding and self-understanding only if over and beyond mastering the hard data
of facts they risk their own "pre-judices" in confrontation
with the objective claim of the text.

The hermeneutical-dialogical method thus turns upside-
down, as it were, the mistaken notion of objectivity. The
reading of a text through a preconceived framework of explanation is precisely not objective. True objectivity,
on the contrary, demands that one allows the text to speak
its own message without forcing prior conditions on it.

Advocacy of the hermeneutical-dialogical approach does
not imply its exclusive validity. One may consider it,
however, the most adequate approach and method as far as
public school religion studies are concerned and urge its
use in addition to the widely accepted methods taking their
cue from a strictly empirical methodology. Moreover, it
has like all approaches, definite limits. Inasmuch as the
transempirical and non-rational elements of reality are
co-constitutive to the very phenomenon of religion itself,
they should not be suppressed. What should be suppressed
is the dysfunctional desire to relieve the students of the

necessity of making their own decisions. In this sense,
public school religion studies--unlike theology--can be
more than propaedeutical. They should lead the students
to the threshold of the mysterium but may not cross it
with them.

Some other subjects and problems a didactic theory
should include can be listed only briefly. The problem of
values and norms in relation to religion studies should
receive explicit attention and treatment. The problem is
entirely unavoidable. Reality-perception is never divorced
from value-perception, neither in thought nor in action,
and the problem of norm is endemic to religion. The gods
do not just create the world but in doing so they also
determine its norms and set sacred law. The experience of
transcending is intrinsically normative. Secondly, the
problem of the place of religion-critique, together with
the wider problem of secularization should be carefully
examined. Thirdly, the place of religion studies within
the total curriculum needs detailed attention if the
process of education is to lead to an integral rather than
a fragmented experience. Fourthly, there is the obvious,
but difficult problem of the selection of data. Public
school religion studies obviously cannot and should not
cover the entire field of religiology. Selectivity is
necessary, but what are to be its criteria? In practical
terms, what should be the content of a religion course:
the grand sweep of world religions, or a smorgasbord of
religious items from Primitive to Zen, or a clearly defined
religious phenomenon such as mysticism? Finally, one needs
to ask what the role of the students' own tradition is to
be in the teaching of religiology. What, in terms of education, is the relationship between their own and foreign
traditions? To which extent and how is hermeneutical
mastery of "foreign" religious traditions possible?

The examination of didactic practice should consider
such problems as the local school situation; student motivation and goals; and curricular questions such as whether
to treat religion within existing courses and structure or

to offer separate courses, minicourses, or units. Reflection on didactic practice also will have to consider
teaching aids and materials, especially their critical
evaluation and use under particular conditions and circum-
stances. Further, testing procedures, goals and objectives
of standard accountability systems, etc., need to be investigated. Finally, there is to be covered the large area
of teaching strategies and techniques.

The Pedagogy of Religiology and Teacher Education

The pedagogy of religiology, it has been argued, is a
discipline in its own right--or should be at any rate. As
such it is neither identical with religiology nor with the
educational disciplines, nor is it simply a compound of
the two. It is not just an "applied" discipline in the
sense that it merely applies the principles of religiology,
its content and methods, to particular practical situations
under the guidance of educational theory. The pedagogy of
religiology--like any special pedagogy--rather owes its
existence to the fact that in the process of teaching and
learning particular contents, something happens to both
ends of the relational scale. Various contents affect the
teaching-learning process variously, even as various
teaching-learning situations affect the same particular
content variously. Furthermore, the religiological data
themselves may change, as it were, in the process of
mediation and appropriation. The teaching and learning of
a particular content establishes a particular hermeneutical
frame of reference and process, and these often change with
the content taught or learned.

This dynamic of the hermeneutical frame of reference
is bound to have consequences with regard to the preparation of competent teachers. The present institutional
separation between academic departments and departments of
teacher education--often pitifully and precariously linked
by a meagre "methods course"--breaks the hermeneutical
frame, leaves the young student-teacher to his or her own
devices in pulling the two heterogeneous ends of

subject-discipline and the educational disciplines together
and thus misses the very heart of the educational process,
i.e., the simultaneous study of content and appropriation.
Only if this simultaneity is preserved, can prospective
teachers have the opportunity of learning to critically
reflect the process of appropriation in themselves while
studying.

To accomplish this, one would have to have, of course,
highly competent didactitians who are also specialists in
the discipline or disciplines involved. Obviously, one
cannot hope to prepare competent teachers in religiology
if one leaves reflection on educational and didactic
theory and practice to a single course or to the whims of
a semester of practice teaching. Such reflection should,
on the contrary, be a sustained effort and integral part
of teacher education programs in religion studies.

One can only hope that the near future will see a
greater awareness, on the part of the academic community
as well as the teaching profession, of the importance of
the pedagogy of religiology as a necessary bridge
discipline.

NOTES

[1] The discipline is variously referred to as Religion,
Religious Studies, Religion Studies, History of Religion,
Comparative Religion, Religiology, etc. It should be
noted, that although its character as discipline is still
arduously debated, this character is assumed in the
following.

[2] Autonomy in this sense assumes what traditionally
has been referred to as free agency and the capacity for
critical understanding.

[3] The term "understanding" is meant inclusively; for
unlike mere knowledge, understanding includes the affective as well as the actional spheres besides the purely
cognitive.

[4] The term "criticalness" as used here is not to be
understood to mean detraction and debunking but rather in
its primary meaning as referring to the ability and the
will to discern alternatives.

CHAPTER FOUR

A MULTI-DISCIPLINARY APPROACH TO
RELIGION STUDIES IN THE SCHOOLS

Henry J. Hoeks

Some theorists view public education religion studies
as an autonomous or singular discipline. One of them
labels the field "religiology" to dramatize this point.[1]
I adopt a different position in this chapter by presenting
a case for a multi-disciplinary approach to religion
studies in the schools.[2] The term "schools" is used here
in the broad sense in order to include private as well as
public lower education since I believe this multi-disciplinary approach is applicable in both.

The theoretical foundations of my argument reflect to
no small degree both my tutelage under Philip H. Phenix,
Professor of Philosophy and Education at Columbia Univer-
sity-Teachers College, and my allegiance to the educational
philosophy of Calvin College which makes an inter-discipli-
nary approach to liberal arts education the heart of the
academic preparation for future teachers.

Definitions

When one speaks of "religion studies as a discipline"
particularly in the context of the schools, what does one
understand by "discipline" and "religion studies?" By
"discipline" I mean the scientific or theoretical study
of some aspect of reality according to previously
developed and commonly accepted canons or patterns of
procedures. A scientific, theoretical study enables one
to distinguish between knowledge and mere opinion. It
involves the use of conceptual frameworks and certain

*Henry J. Hoeks, Ed.D., is Professor of Religion and Educa-
tion, Calvin College. This chapter is a revision of a paper
presented at the annual meeting of the American Academy of
Religion in San Francisco, December, 1977.*

methods, techniques, and procedures which have been
developed in the scholarly community for the purpose of
understanding particular aspects of experience more consistently and profoundly than occurs in common sense
analysis. Hence, the disciplines are media or paths for
arriving at particular understandings by means of particular questions properly put to different aspects or
phenomena of reality.

> Thus the special office of the academic
> communities is to create schemes for
> critically analyzing interpretations
> originating in non-academic communities;
> those, for example, associated with eco-
> nomic, social, military, political, or
> religious interests. That is to say, a
> major function of the academic disciplines
> is to interpret interpretations, to gain
> perspectives on perspectives arising from
> the variety of shared concerns of particu-
> lar groups.[3]

In what sense and in what way is or ought religion studies
in the schools to be a "discipline" in the manner just
articulated? What scheme or conceptual framework and
methodology for analysis should be used to gain perspective on and interpret religious phenomena? Rather than
propose a unique conceptual framework and methodology, this
chapter proposes the use of several disciplines, commonly
accepted and prevalently practiced in the schools, as one
way of understanding and interpreting religions and religious phenomena.

By "religion studies" I have in mind "the basic
distinction between the study of specific religions and
the history of religions," as Kitagawa put it.[4] This
distinction has a bearing upon methodology and pedagogy in
that the history of religions approach, as Kitagawa subsequently defined it, involves an abstract and holistic
"scholarly inquiry into the nature and structure of the
religious experience of the human race."[5] The history of
religions approach presumes, it seems to me, a foundation

of general knowledge of many world religions. It is my
contention that religion studies in the elementary and
secondary schools may be offered as a unit or course in
which the beliefs and practices of past or present religious tradition and/or the literature (sacred writings,
creeds, and mythologies) of particular religions are
studied. The overall aim of such studies, also considering
developmental psychology, would be to develop an awareness
and understanding of specific religions as a basis for
advanced (usually college or university) inquiry which
makes use of the history of religions approach. For this
reason, religion studies should begin with consideration
of the particular and more concrete religious traditions
in order to explore later, perhaps even in one's final year
in high school, the universal and more abstract phenomena
and forms of religious experience. Moreover, a second
crucial aim for religion studies in the schools would be to
help students perceive of religious traditions as comprehensive world-and-life orientations comprised of many
facets which have shaped civilization, past and present.
This leads us to a consideration of what we mean by
"religion."

     When one attempts to define what he or she means by
"religion" as an object of study, the task becomes touchy
to say the least. For the purposes of this chapter, I
conceive of a "religion" as a total perspective on life of
an intentional faith community, located in a particular
place and time, which is embodied and manifested in
ideology, codes of conduct, cultic practices, and social
communal structures.[6] This conception of religion intends
to include extinct religions, extant "primitive" or pre-
literate religions, and traditional complex world religions,
as well as "quasi-religions," which is one way of naming
ideologies which function or act like religions.

     Implied in the foregoing "definition" is the recogni-
tion that religions are comprised of multi-faceted and
multi-dimensional phenomena. The world-and-life view of
any religion in its historical particularity includes not

only literary sources such as sacred texts, recorded
mythologies, beliefs, and creeds but also a constellation
of religious expressions through music and dance, art and
architecture, biography and history, rites and rituals,
sociological relationships and institutions, and individual
and group psychology. Moreover, any religion has its
"official" and "popular" expressions, its professed and
operative ways of life.

     Now if the preceding is conceded, at least for the
time being, what are some pedagogical possibilities for
the school?   One possibility, now proposed, is that
academic religion studies be viewed in prism-like perspective. This perspective assumes that each of several
religions may be seen as comprised of a continuum of
several "colors" or components. Each component, each
aspect of religious reality--given a disciplinary view of
education--may best be examined through the "spectacles"
of the discipline which have been developed by the community of scholars for study of that aspect of reality.
Hence, I propose a multi-disciplinary approach to religion
studies, in which not one discipline but several disciplines provide the means by which the complexity of
religions may be studied, analyzed, and interpreted. This
approach is not to be interpreted as merely taking students
on excursions through literature, the arts, and social
sciences as they relate to religion. Rather, the approach
is to engage students in the use of the various disci-
plines--employing appropriate conceptual frameworks and
their respective methodologies--in order to imaginatively
understand the components of religions and how those
components express peoples' ultimate concerns and perceptions of ultimate transformation or salvation.

     Why propose a multi-disciplinary approach? Which
disciplines could be used? How might this approach be
handled in school curriculum and teaching? To these
questions we now turn.

Rationale

Concerning the reasons for a multi-disciplinary approach, this chapter has implied somewhat of a rationale already, but more explicit primary and secondary reasons can be given. The first has to do with the multi-faceted nature of religion. To examine a religious tradition from only one perspective such as in historical or literary perspective alone, or to study only the ideological, mythic, or social component, is not to do justice to that tradition; it invites reductionism and a myopic or one-sided view of a religion. Because religion is multi-faceted and impinges upon almost every aspect of human experience and reality, it seems to me that the appropriate way to examine, however briefly, the several dimensions of religions is by means of the respective disciplines which address and question those aspects in generally accepted scholarly ways. Care must be taken to consider several components in the interests of gaining an understanding of each component in relation to the whole of the tradition. Hence, the multi-disciplinary approach seems uniquely suitable for achieving the following goals developed by the Florida State University Religion-Social Studies Curriculum Project and espoused by the Public Education Religion Studies Center (PERSC):

> An understanding of . . . the place (or role
> of religion, 1. . . . in its cultural con-
> text, 2. . . . Its relation to economic,
> social, political, education, and domestic
> institutions, 3. . . . Its relation to man's
> humanistic endeavors: art, music, language,
> literature, etc. . . . [and] the methods of
> study of religion . . . [especially] the variety
> of ways of inquiry. . . .[7]

Another primary reason for a multi-disciplinary approach is that it is a way to deal seriously with the fact that adherents of a religion view their commitment comprehensively and holistically. For the faithful, religion is all of life. The essence of a religious

tradition is the passionate subjectivities and ultimate
commitments of a faith community as it orders its total
way of life. A variety of disciplines provides a set of
scholarly frameworks and methodologies necessary for
entering imaginatively and empathically into these comprehensive subjectivities by probing the feeling as well as
the cognitive elements of a particular way of life as it
is manifested in creed, cult, code, and cultural institutions.

Disciplines appropriate to religion studies also
provide appropriate questions for appreciative, yet
critical and interpretive, inquiry into the meaning of
faith to the faithful of any religious tradition while at
the same time not requiring a compromise of the inquirer's
own commitment. I echo Professor Phenix's conclusion:
"The most productive way of setting up a curriculum of
religious studies is to apply these disciplines, which
have their own covenants of objectivity, so as to make
explicit and vivid the subjectivities that constitute the
meaning of faith in the various religions of mankind.[8]

A third reason for this approach is found in the
pedagogical insight that repetitive use of several different disciplines can help the student develop enduring
skills for creative, constructive, and critical (discerning) reflection upon any religion or quasi-religion, old
and new. Our multi-faithed society is changing and so are
its religious values, commitments, and mores. Some old
traditions are decaying and new forms and phenomena are
thriving or emerging. If persons are to be adequately
prepared for reflective and responsible living in an
increasingly global and fast-changing society, they should
be equipped with a conceptual "tool box" with which to
assess long-standing traditions as well as the changing
winds of values and religious phenomena. A multi-
disciplinary approach can provide a variety of conceptual
"tools" for understanding and exercising discerning
judgement concerning religious phenomena. Such an approach
can also develop an increased capacity to appreciate, and

appropriate meaning from, the diversity of religious
artistic and institutional expressions of religious
communities which are unfamiliar to the student. Thus the
development of skills in "perceptive application of the
processes of inquiry to religious concepts (and) careful
description of religious phenomena ..." may be enhanced by
familiarity with the use of a variety of disciplines
appropriate to religion studies.[9]

Another argument for the utilization of several
disciplines in religion studies is derived from the basic
knowledge provided by the disciplines themselves. Familiarity with a variety of conceptual frameworks and academic
methodologies can contribute invaluably to the general
education of students by providing them with a variety of
ways of knowing which foster growth in structured and
scientific understanding of the whole of man's culture,
over against learning by rote or from mere opinions, fad-
dish concerns, and purely pragmatic approaches to
education.

The Disciplines

Let us now consider which disciplines could be used
in a multi-disciplinary approach to religions. For
example, each religion is rooted in some spatial environment and the religion both influences and is influenced by
the physical characteristics of its people and setting.
The discipline of *geography* may aid in delineating why a
particular religious tradition was and is found in a
particular environment. Geography of religions also
furthers understanding regarding the nature of possible
interrelationships between the physical environment and
the religious beliefs and manifestations of a particular
time and place.[10] So we speak about particular religions
of the Ancient Near East, such as Egyptian religion, of
Hinduism in India, or of North American Roman Catholicism.

Among the great writings of human civilization are
the sacred scriptures, mythologies, creeds, and codes of
conduct (not to speak of secondary documents) of the

religions of mankind. A *literary* approach to writings
such as the Bhagavad Gita, the Hebrew and Christian Bible,
the Qur'an, et al, and designed to acquaint students with
the genius of writings which have helped shape religious
traditions. Critical understanding of their content and
form is gained by means of the tools of literary criticism.
The methods of textual and higher criticism help unpack
content, form, style, and concepts of composition. Moreover, empathic appreciation for the literature of a
religion by means of imaginative identification with the
religious community which produced it and lives by it
would help one to answer questions such as: How has and
does the literature function among, and what does it mean
for, its "leaders"? its educated adherents? its "common
folk"?

In most religious traditions there are powerful
aesthetic and sensory expressions of the thought and
feelings of the faithful. An approach to religion
studies through *music* (and dance) seeks to acquaint persons with the variety and modes of religious musical
expressions. The music of a religious tradition is a
vehicle for imaginative reflection upon and empathic
understanding of the deepest emotions, ideas, and religious commitments--the "soul"--of a people's hopes and
fears, questions and affirmations. The Negro spiritual,
the Protestant hymn, the Jewish Kol Nidre are well-known
musical examples.

Similarly, the expressions of faith depicted in the
visual arts can enable persons to more fully "feel" and
appreciate the faith of a particular community. While the
Gothic cathedral cannot be fully understood apart from
some knowledge of the faith of the people who built it, an
imaginative study of the architecture (or a sculpture or
painting) can help inquirers to comprehend more fully the
particular ideas, beliefs, and commitments among people
in a given place and time and culture. Think of the
insights one can attain into Egyptian religion through
reflective examination of the funerary art of the Treasures

of Tutankhamun exhibit. And since the religious artist
frequently seeks to express the inexpressible through the
media of the visual arts, one provocative visual used in
religion studies may be worth a thousand descriptive
words.

All religions and "quasi-religions" are a way of life
either concomitant with a total culture or a "sacred" part
of a larger "secular" culture. For example, prehistoric
and "primitive" religions characteristically are coexten-
sive with their culture; but Eastern Orthodoxy in the
United States is a small part of secular American culture.
The discipline of *anthropology* provides a way of examining
how patterns are acquired and transmitted in a culture.
Religious beliefs and behaviors are internal to these
patterns to a greater or lesser extent depending upon the
nature and historical particularity of each religion.
Rituals and rites of passage observed in archaic societies
are imbued with religious significance. Basic to the
cultural anthropological approach is description and
understanding of the reciprocal relationships between the
religious beliefs of a people and their particular physical
environment, and how those people deal with the perennial
questions of human existence throughout their life-cycle.

Religions in modern societies are manifested in group
activities and social institutions which in turn interact
with other social structures, such as marriage and the
family, government, business, and education. The inter-
actions and reciprocal relationships which are primarily
religious or belief-related are the concern of *sociology*
of religion, and to some extent, political science, economics, and the psychology of religion, though the latter
concentrates more on the effect of religious beliefs on
the nature and behavior of individuals. In many ways,
these social science disciplines touch on issues which are
of the highest existential concern to students. One can
ask how beliefs influence practices, and cultural practices reshape beliefs, concerning the roles of men and
women, marriage and family life? What various views of

the State are held by religions and "quasi-religions?"
How do religious codes of conduct vary according to religious tradition and social standing? Of what significance
is the "institutional church" in contemporary society?
What is the role of religion studies in public education?
Hence, the analytical tools of the social sciences ought
to find a prominent place in religion studies if the latter
is to help students clarify their autonomous thinking on,
and ordering of, their own world-and-life view.

The discipline of philosophy is omitted from the list
of disciplines, partly because it is normally not a subject
which is taught in the schools or for which teachers have
been adequately prepared and certified and partly because
the discipline raises the truth question and explores the
validity of religious perspectives, a most difficult if not
a well-nigh illegal undertaking in the public school. However, a philosophic spirit and outlook permeates proper use
of all the above-named disciplines in that alternative ways
of belief and practice are recognized and critically considered (without assuming or affirming that all alternatives
are equally true, valid, or desirable). Of course, no one
way may be absolutized and promulgated in public school
religion studies.

It may be noted by some readers that the "discipline"
of religion per se is also omitted from the disciplines
suggested in this multi-disciplinary approach. The reasons
for this omission are as follows. First, scholars and
educators have not been able to reach agreement on whether
there is an identifiable discipline of religion studies
for lower education. This chapter argues that "religion
studies" must be viewed as a multi-disciplinary synoptic
venture in which several commonly known and prevalently
practiced disciplines are viewed and used together as
vehicles, auxiliaries, and servants in the task of uncovering and unpacking the comprehensive, multi-faceted
phenomenon we call "religion." Thus public education
religion studies, need not be a separate autonomous
discipline alongside other disciplines but may be composed

of several disciplines which together view explicit aspects
of religious reality and hence seek to be comprehensively
integrative and holistic. In this view, religion studies
is analogous to light which is comprised of a spectrum of
colors, no one color being dominant or exclusively peculiar
to light.

Second, the purpose and aim of religion studies in the
schools is primarily religious literacy concerning specific
religious traditions. This literacy becomes the basis for
more advanced inquiry. However, this aim ought not be
perceived merely as introduction and preparation for more
formal religion studies at which time questions of ultimacy
would then be addressed. Issues of ultimate meanings will
and should arise in viewing an unparalleled piece of
religious art or monumental architecture, in listening to
a particularly poignant musical composition, in reading
the intensity of belief and commitment in a literary work,
or whatever. "The pursuit of ultimacy may occur through
many different symbols, beliefs, rites, codes and institutions."[11] When and where this occurs, the teacher and
students must address these issues in sensitive, honest,
fair, and impartial ways appropriate to the developmental
level of the children and to the nature of the school,
whether the latter be public or sectarian.

Pedagogical Implications

Having considered several disciplines which seem to
be feasible for religion studies, we may now consider the
"how," i.e., the curricular and teaching implications of a
multi-disciplinary approach. The schematic diagram which
follows is designed to provoke several questions such as:
Which disciplines are applicable to which religions? In
what order should the disciplines be used? Which is more
feasible, proceeding vertically applying one discipline,
then another, to several religions or proceeding horizontally applying several--if not all--disciplines to a single
religious tradition, then to another tradition? What questions from the disciplines would one ask of the religions
in order to perceive them aright?

A SCHEMATIC OF A MULTI-DISCIPLINARY
APPROACH TO RELIGION STUDIES IN THE SCHOOLS

Geography	Literature	History	Music (and Dance)	Visual Arts	Anthropology	Social Studies
Prehistoric and "primitive" religions							
Buddhism							
Hinduism							
Ancient Near Eastern religions							
Judaism							
Christianity							
Islam							
"Quasi-religions"--e.g. Atheism, Nationalism, Civil Religion.							

It should be noted that not all the disciplines shown
on the schematic diagram are applicable equally to the
study of all the religions cited. This is the case because
not every category is found in every religion. Consider
the following examples. Literature is non-existent in
pre-historic and "primitive" religions, whereas music and
dance are. Therefore, they are crucial for obtaining an
accurate understanding of this way of life. The importance
of historical events and the views of time differ between
Eastern and Western religions even though each religion
has a history. The visual arts, other than the architecture and furnishings of the temples and synagogues, have
had a limited place in Judaism. Higher criticism of the
Qur'an or the Bible may be in violation respectively of
the Muslim or conservative Christian conviction concerning
its authorship and authority. A multi-disciplinary

approach, therefore, does not entail necessarily the use of all the disciplines when studying a particular religious tradition. Here is where the religion studies teacher's expertise, decision-making, and guidance come into play.

The order in which the disciplines are to be applied to any religion is quite arbitrary, pedagogically speaking. One could begin with the more sensate and concrete materials of a historical religion, such as its music or visual arts, in order to introduce basic themes or to evoke student hypotheses or affective responses. Next, one could proceed to study the sacred literature or the history of the religion, whichever is more appropriate, and then geography, anthropology, and/or sociology of religion. Or one could begin with the central historical events of a religion, then consider its geography, literature, and manifestations in music, visual arts, and sociological institutions. Or small groups of students could be inquiring concurrently into the same religion via different disciplines. The order in which one uses the disciplines seems to be more dependent upon pedagogical objectives and strategies than the dictates of logic. So too is the selection of the number of religions, which religions, and in what order they are studied within the limitations of a semester or year.

Regarding whether a "vertical" or "horizontal" strategy is best, my answer--based upon somewhat limited experience as a student and as a teacher of the multi-disciplinary approach to religion studies--is that the most coherent tactic is to proceed horizontally within one religion, moving from one discipline to another. The vertical strategy tends to emphasize the use of the disciplines whereas the horizontal strategy placed the religions in primary focus. The latter is more consistent with the primary reasons previously stated in favor of a multi-disciplinary approach.

But, you ask, how many school teachers today have obtained the kind of synoptic and comprehensive liberal arts education that would enable them to use competently

all these disciplines? Probably not many of them nor
perhaps many of us. One solution is team-teaching, in
which two or more teachers from different disciplines combine their expertise. There are also some aids available
for the individual teacher's continuing education. An
excellent theoretical discussion of the academic disciplines is found in Philip H. Phenix's Realms of Meaning, a
book presenting a philosophy of the curriculum for general
education.[12] Furthermore, the handbook which the author
has published applies Phenix's disciplinary emphasis more
extensively to religion studies.[13] The many questions
posed in this handbook for each of nine disciplines
selected for their appropriateness to religion studies in
the schools were designed to be of practical assistance
to the teacher who wishes to use the multi-disciplinary
approach. Moreover, several specific pedagogical strategies are suggested, with particular emphasis given to the
use of the inquiry approach to teaching. So the classroom
teacher is not bereft of resources for the use of a multi-
disciplinary approach.

Summary

I have argued for an approach that is narrower than
the natural inclusion of religion studies in either fine
arts, language arts, or social studies and broader than a
uni-disciplinary approach to religion and its phenomena.
In effect I have also argued for a separate course approach
to religion studies in the schools which is multi-disciplinary, synoptic, and integrative in nature. My contention has been that religions are total perspectives on
life which are manifested in and through many different
phenomena. When a religion is studied in a multi-disciplinary way there is less tendancy toward reductionism
than when one makes use of only one discipline. An
examination of the many-faceted manifestations of a religion can best take place by means of the methodological
"spectacles" provided by an array of disciplines, each of
which has been developed to analyze a particular facet or

phenomenon. Moreover, the inner significance of a geogra-
phically and historically particular tradition may be more
closely approximated and empathically appreciated through
a disciplined study of its visual arts, music, and literature, its historical events and meanings, and its patterned
way of life and social institutions. Finally, where there
is emphasis upon the use of a variety of conceptual frameworks and disciplinary techniques as tools for enlarging
and deepening one's understanding of religions, there is
promise of the development of skills for creative, constructive, and critical personal reflection upon, and
evaluation of, both traditional and avant garde religious
perspectives which one may confront or experience in our
pluralistic society.

NOTES

[1]See Guntram G. Bischoff's provocative paper on "The
Pedagogy of Religiology," The Academic Study of Religion:
Public School Religion Studies - 1975, ed. by Anne Carr
and Nicholas Piediscalzi (Missoula, Montana: Scholars
Press, 1975) 127-135, and chapter three in this volume.

[2]This case was also put forth in "Issues and Guide-
lines for the Academic Study of Religions in Michigan
Public Secondary Schools," (unpublished Ed.D. dissertation,
Teachers College-Columbia University, 1975) and in Studying
the Sacred in the Schools (Grand Rapids, Michigan: Calvin
College, 1976).

[3]Philip H. Phenix, "Religion in American Public
Schools," Religion and the Public Order (1965), ed. by
Donald A. Gianella (Chicago: The University of Chicago
Press, 1966) 94.

[4]Joseph M. Kitagawa, "The Making of a Historian of
Religions," Journal of the American Academy of Religion,
XXXVI/3 (Sept. 1968) 199.

[5]Ibid.

[6]As we all know, definitions of religion abound.
This formulation is a tentative, eclectic one to which
many recent authors of textbooks and articles have un-
knowingly contributed.

[7]Peter Bracher, et al., PERSC Guidebook: Public Education Religion Studies: Questions and Answers (Dayton,
Ohio: Public Education Religions Studies Center, 1974) 4.

[8]Philip H. Phenix, "Religion in Public Education,"
Religion and Public Education, ed. by David E. Engel (New
York: Paulist Press, 1974) 68.

[9]Bracher, Guidebook, 4.

[10]See, for example, David E. Sopher, Geography of
Religion (Englewood Cliffs: Prentice Hall, 1967) and Hans
J. Klimkeit, "Spatial Orientation in Mythical Thinking as
Exemplified in Ancient Egypt: Considerations toward a
Geography of Religions," History of Religions, 14 (May,
1975) 266-281.

[11]Philip H. Phenix, Realms of Meaning (New York:
McGraw Hill, 1964) 251.

[12]Ibid., and see also the articles by Phenix,
previously cited in this paper, in which he briefly
applies his disciplinary thinking to religion studies.

[13]Studying the Sacred in the Schools.

CHAPTER FIVE

PARADIGMS FOR PUBLIC EDUCATION RELIGION
STUDIES CURRICULA: SOME SUGGESTIONS AND CRITIQUE

John P. Boyle

This chapter examines in detail and critically three
issues that emerged from the Religion Studies in Public
Education Group's deliberation at the 1977 annual meeting
of the American Academy of Religion in San Francisco.
They are: (1) What are appropriate aims, goals, and
objectives for religion studies in the American public
school? More particularly: what is the place of non-
cognitive objectives in public school religion studies?
(2) Granted the usefulness of studying religion through
the social sciences, the arts, and philosophy, what is the
role of methods specific to the study of religion that have
been developed in the last century or more? More particularly: is there a content to religion studies that could
not be appropriately dealt with using other methods?
(3) What are the implications for public school religion
studies curricula of the constitutional and political
realities in the United States?

In theory it is possible to construct paradigms for
religion studies curricula on the basis of principles and
procedures drawn from methods for the academic study of
religion developed at the highest levels of modern scholarship. Using such an approach, one could, perhaps, construct
a curriculum paradigm from each of several scholarly
approaches. I have chosen not to follow such a procedure
for several reasons. The first is that there is a considerable variety of academic approaches to the study of

John P. Boyle, Ph.D., is Director, School of Religion, and
Associate Professor of Religion, University of Iowa. This
chapter is a revision of a paper presented at the annual
meeting of the American Academy of Religion in New Orleans,
November 1978.

religion. But what makes matters worse is that the various
approaches rarely appear in unalloyed form, recognized and
agreed to by nearly everyone. The methods employed by
scholars tend to be varied and often mixed, while one
scholar, Wilfred Cantwell Smith, has expressed his suspi-
cions of the modern emphasis on method and prefers instead
to insist only on the general canons of scholarship for
religion studies, insisting that specific methodologies
are unnecessary.[1]

Given this multiplicity of approaches to the academic
study of religion, it seemed better to me to examine curriculum paradigms drawn from the actual practice of
religion studies in the public schools of the United
States. Once these paradigms have been established,
questions can be addressed to them. In particular one can
then ask whether the curricula approach the study of religion descriptively, historically, and comparatively as do
methods of study broadly accepted among contemporary
scholars.

It should be noted early in this study that the
development of the academic study of religion, especially
the struggle to separate the academic study of religions
from theology, led to a heavy emphasis in academic study
on objectives which are cognitive. It should occasion no
surprise, therefore, that when the word "understanding" is
commonly used to describe an objective of the study of a
religion, a scholar like Robert D. Baird presents as a
"functional" definition of understanding religion "any
valid knowledge about religion communicable in proposi-
tional form."[2] Baird acknowledges a traditional emphasis
in religion studies on a need for empathy as well, but he
prefers to refer that dimension to a "psychology of
understanding," while reserving the purely cognitive
dimension for the "logic of understanding."

I propose, then, to describe several paradigms for
public school religion studies curricula and address
questions to each of them: (1) What method or methods for
the study of religions underlies the paradigm? (2) Are

the aims, goals and objectives, and methods proposed for
the paradigm consistent with a method of study that is
descriptive, historical, and comparative? (3) Does the
paradigm yield an "understanding" of religion? (4) Is the
paradigm pedagogically sound? (5) Is the proposed paradigm
legally appropriate to the American public school setting?

In selecting paradigms for this study I have thought
it best to draw from what is known of the actual practice
in American public schools without pretending to be
exhaustive, while taking advantage of the paradigm as a
theoretical construct to emphasize differences in
approaches to the study of religion. I only will present
approaches whose intentions are to function within constitutional limits.

<h2 style="text-align:center">Natural Inclusion</h2>

By "natural inclusion" I mean that approach to
religion studies which gives attention to religion insofar
as it is or can be made a part of existing curriculum
offerings. Thus, attention to various manifestations of
religion is made a part of existing public school programs
in literature, the fine arts, geography, history, and the
other social sciences.[3]

There are rather obvious reasons for suggesting
"natural inclusion" as an approach to study about religion.
One is the practical consideration that the curriculum of
the public schools is already long established and difficult to change. It is much easier to deal with, say, the
history of a religion or the impact of a religion on
historical events than to create a new religion studies
course, much less a new program or department. The fact
that teachers whose primary teaching field is another area
can also teach about religion makes this approach attrac-
tive to many public school administrators.

A variation on the pattern of natural inclusion is a
"multi-disciplinary approach" to the study of religion in
the schools, like that suggested by Professor Henry Hoeks.
This approach not only has the advantage of using already

existing programs, it points to another reason for the
"natural inclusion" approach: the study of religion by a
variety of disciplines is already well established at the
college and university level. Courses in the history,
psychology, sociology, philosophy, etc., of religion are
a part of academic life. Moreover, each of these disciplines is already defined and has a methodology or methodologies accepted within the discipline and regarded as
empirical and objective. The natural inclusion approach
then would study about religion in the disciplines already
established when questions about religion fit naturally
into the subject matter of those disciplines.

The definition of religion which underlies this
approach is clearly a functional one. Using the methods
of the various disciplines, especially the social sciences,
religion is studied through what it does. For at least
some students of religion, like Malinowski, "one has
understood a religious rite when he has determined its
psychological or social function."[4]

It is not necessary to demonstrate here that functionalism is a widely accepted approach to the data of anthropology, sociology, and psychology as well as literature and
the arts. Nor is there need to argue that in the hands of
competent scholars and teachers the method is used consistently and critically. Moreover, the method lends itself
to a study of religions which is descriptive, historical,
and comparative and, therefore, appropriate to the secular
educational program of the American public school.[5]

A more perplexing question, however, is whether such
a method yields an understanding of religion. To be sure,
the method yields a great deal of information about
religion; but the issue is whether, having studied the
social and psychological impact of religion, one has
studied religion exhaustively, or for that matter whether
one has really studied "religion" at all or has merely
studied its effects. The charge is made that the
functional method of studying religion is a form of
"reductionism," i.e., that religion is reduced to its

social and/or psychological effects without remainder.
Critics who make such a charge argue that in a functional
method what is proper to religion never appears; it is
swallowed up in attention to the functions of religion.
Thus one can study religious literature and religious
organization, describe religious practices of every sort
and states of consciousness, or effects typical of religious people and their experiences--but never get at
religion itself. Similar comments have been made by
Guntram Bischoff and Paul Will.

Hoeks argues, convincingly I think, that the interdisciplinary approach is pedagogically appropriate to the
public schools both at the elementary and secondary levels.
Its concreteness in dealing with religion is one of the
strongest pedagogical arguments for such an approach.
Moreover, its objectivity is not in question and therefore
its legal appropriateness seems assured. It is small
wonder that descriptions of courses which deal with religion in literature, the social studies, or the humanities
are not difficult to find.

However, if the "natural inclusion" approach to the
study of religion is to escape the charge that it reduces
religion to social and psychological functions and
ultimately distorts the reality it purports to study and
teach, then ways must be found to keep the study of
religions open to the dimension of ultimacy, the sacred,
or the transcendent which many students of religion argue
sets religions and religious phenomena apart. That will
require the use of other paradigms, especially the
phenomenology of religions. It should also be asked what
aims, goals, and objectives are compatible with a functional definition of religion and the method of natural
inclusion.

It seems to me that to adopt a functional definition
of religion and methods which are descriptive, historical,
and comparative does not ipso facto include or exclude,
for example, non-cognitive goals such as the moral improvement of the student through knowledge of religion(s) or the

qualification of the student's understanding as "appreciative." To be sure, a method which is descriptive, historical, and comparative usually assumes cognitive goals and
objectives, but it might be used to promote others as well.
The logical distinction between cognitive and non-cognitive
objectives should not obscure the fact that the learning
process will certainly carry with it affective and behavioral learning as well as the conceptual as noted by
Professor Kniker.[6] The role of the teacher is important,
it seems to me, in understanding, defining, and promoting
appropriate teaching objectives which are not assured
solely by the choice of appropriate elements of
Religionswissenschaft or other disciplines in the public
school setting. The teacher is at least as important as
procedures and materials.

In summary, then, natural inclusion implies a definition of religion which is functional; it employs methods
derived from the social sciences, literature, philosophy,
and the arts; it is to that extent descriptive, historical,
and comparative. Functionalism is open to the criticism
that what is proper to religion does not appear with this
method, and it therefore requires complementing with
other methods. Natural inclusion is both pedagogically
sound and legally appropriate to the American public
school.

Surveys of the Religions

The presuppositions of survey of religions courses
and their aims, goals, and objectives or their chosen
methods are not immediately obvious. Alan Gore's
evaluation of materials resulted in diverse judgments
about a number of these courses and their materials,
judgments which were often negative because normative
elements incompatible with a descriptive and comparative
method had been introduced.[7]

Survey courses in the public school may often be
approaches to religion studies in search of a rationale, a
paradigm adopted in imitation of the college or university

without an adequate understanding on the part of the
instructor of appropriate aims, goals, and objectives or
even of the reason for the adoption of the survey approach
itself--one which obviously allows for considerable
diversity.[8]   It might be observed, however, that surveys
do seem to imply description and permit comparisons. But,
as Gore discovered, what is possible is not always
realized: normative rather than descriptive elements can
be introduced by those who do not understand the methods
of religion studies.

     The confusion of purposes which can surround a survey
make it virtually impossible to know whether an understanding of religion will result or be desired. Even if the
materials used are suitable to the elementary or secondary
school level, even if the intentions of the teacher who
undertakes such a survey are beyond reproach, it is
apparent that imitating at the secondary school level an
approach to the study of religions from the college and
university level which suffers from unclarity and even
confusion of purposes and methods will introduce problems
which can call the religion studies program in the public
school into serious question on both legal and educational
grounds. Good intentions are no substitute for competence.
An acceptable paradigm for public school religion studies
must therefore be one in which the aims, goals, and
objectives are clearly understood and suitable methods
are chosen in the light of those objectives.

Religion Studies

     In contrast to the rudderless survey model is the
religion studies paradigm in which the aims, goals,
objectives, and methods of a course or unit have been
carefully thought out by competent teachers. Such teachers
are not only well-versed in the study of religions, but
they have been trained in historical, descriptive, and
comparative methods of study and are aware of the need to
avoid importing normative elements into a descriptive
study. In short, they are methodologically self-conscious.

The competent teacher is also a master of judicious
selection of the materials for study, choosing those
appropriate to the chosen objectives as well as to a
balanced and integral presentation given the level of
instruction. But dedication to descriptive methods does
not require a kind of pretentious inclusiveness that
offers a superficial and undirected survey in place of
the study of materials carefully selected to meet objectives while respecting the integrity of the religious
phenomena under study. Nicholas Piediscalzi has helpfully
underscored the complexity of religion in its cultural
setting in choosing Geertz' definition of "religion," so
the range of materials is vast.[9]

I need hardly say that the kind of religion studies
paradigm I am describing somewhat abstractly is both
methodologically and pedagogically sound and legally
appropriate. However varied the courses, methods, and
objectives, they are informed by the imperative of
Religionswissenschaft to employ a descriptive, historical,
and comparative approach, to maintain scrupulous respect
for the integrity of the religions or religious phenomena
under study, and openness to the consideration of the wide
range of phenomena which may upon examination be appropriately described as religious, if Geertz' view is
accepted.

Methods typically employed in the history of religions
or comparative religions have been criticized for being
insufficiently sensitive to an understanding of the vast
range of religious phenomena. Therefore the religion
studies paradigm, for all its strengths, needs to be com-
plemented by the phenomenology of religion.

Phenomenology of Religion

Although courses explicitly labeled "phenomenology of
religion" are not as common at the secondary level as they
are at the college and university level, nonetheless units
and courses at the secondary level do explicitly deal with
the phenomenology of religion. I use the term "phenomenology

of religion" here somewhat loosely to designate those
approaches to the study of religion which emphasize a
careful description of religious manifestations of all
sorts with the aim of allowing the nature or essence of
religion to appear. Phenomenology has been the subject
of intense discussion, criticism, and debate in the field
of the academic study of religion, and it would take us
far from our present concerns to pursue that discussion.

Yet, it does seem fair to say that when a phenomenological method is employed, the emphasis will be on
careful description of a wide variety of religious
manifestations, i.e., of symbols, myths, rituals, systems
of belief, ethical codes, and cultic practices with the
intention of helping the student to arrive at an understanding of what "religion" and the "religious" is.
However, the public school classroom is not the place to
resolve the questions of whether such an understanding in
fact can be achieved or whether the "gods," the "sacred,"
or the "transcendent" have a metaphysical reality.

Critics have dismissed the phenomenology of religion
as subjective and uncritical, but the secondary school
teacher and curriculum planner might be pardoned for
choosing not to ignore the work of such scholars as van
der Leeuw, Wach, Otto, Eliade, and Smart. Whether or not
the study of the phenomenology of religion yields an
understanding of religion is much disputed. But I suggest
that the sort of short segment devoted to the phenomenology
of religion that Joseph Forcinelli incorporated in his
course at Claremont will succeed in helping the students
"become aware of what a serious adherent feels, when he or
she worships."[10] Moreover it does so comparatively by
examining religious phenomena from several different
religions.

This method emphasizes the need for careful definition
of the purposes for which a phenomenological approach to
religion is used in the schools. Among these purposes,
might be that of helping students to appreciate the
breadth of phenomena in our own and other cultures which

can be described as "religious," at least in the broad
sense. Therefore, I would argue that a phenomenological
approach in a segment or unit of a course could indeed be
useful and appropriate. In my judgment the method does
not lend itself to extended use (e.g., whole courses) at
the elementary or secondary level. It would be very
difficult there to do justice to the methodological
problems and the broad control of several religions the
method demands.

The objectives of the use of the phenomenology of
religion, e.g., the experience of the variety of things
considered "religious" in various cultures or at various
times, or acquiring a sense of the qualities proper to
"religious" phenomena are appropriate to the objective
study of religion. The study of religious manifestations
with the phenomenological method does not involve activities which are legally inappropriate in the public school.
The problems with the paradigm are not legal but
methodological. I therefore judge its usefulness limited
but nonetheless important.

Relational Humanities

When I use the term "Relational Humanities" I have in
mind the "personalist" approach suggested by Wilfred
Cantwell Smith.[11]   Briefly, Smith deplores the emphasis in
contemporary Religionswissenschaft on method and pleads
for a return to what he sees as the traditional willingness
of humanistic studies to employ whatever method or methods
are necessary and useful for the study of religion or any
other object of scholarly interest. Smith pleads that the
objective of the study of "religions" (a term he criticizes
severely) is an understanding of religious persons, of the
"faiths" of such persons, and not just an analytic understanding of "religion," i.e., the various symbols, myths,
rites, or texts. The academic study of religion is distinguished by its subject matter, not by a unique method
of study; for in Smith's view the scholar should employ
whatever method or methods seem useful.

A course of study about religon for the public school
which laid emphasis on understanding the faiths of "religious" persons rather than on "religions" as such, would
have much to commend it in a pluralistic society. Such a
humanities course would also, following Smith's suggestion,
be able to utilize a wide variety of evidence to approach
its study. Indeed the question must be asked whether what
Smith proposes is really a method or simply an objective
for the study of religion. To the extent that there can
be talk of a "method," it would have much in common with
the interdisciplinary approach described above--though
Smith himself is no more satisfied with "interdisciplinary"
approaches than with others, since again their emphasis is
on the study of things and not persons.

I have already suggested that an empathetic understanding of the faiths of a variety of persons is one
admirable objective for the study of religions in the
public schools. Smith does not propose a method and indeed repudiates concern for the fine points of a unique
methodology for the study of religions. He does insist,
however, an academic inquiry generally requires disciplined
study which is rational, critical, analytical, systematic,
deliberate, comparative, public, cumulative, inductive, and
in some sense empirical.[12] It seems fair to say that it
is thus objective. Understanding is precisely its goal,
although it is "personal understanding," i.e., understanding of persons and their faiths and not of "religion" as
such.

Is the method pedagogically sound? I would argue that
if it were possible to gain an extensive and personal
acquaintance with adherents of a variety of faiths, then
it surely would be. But generally that is precisely the
problem. The study of religions in American schools is
frequently a literary study. Most American communities
have great difficulty providing suitable opportunities for
students to become acquainted with persons whose personal
faith falls outside the traditions of Christianity and
Judaism, despite the feasibility of field trips in some

places. Moreover religion studies in the public schools
rarely has time at its disposal that Smith's approach
demands.

Personal contact is sometimes attempted by inviting
to the classroom persons of various faiths. This approach,
given the limits of time and selection which I have
mentioned, may produce legal problems unless there is
assurance that the study will be objective and under the
control of the teacher. This is not to say that field
trips and classroom visits are not a useful adjunct to
other appropriate teaching strategies, however.

"Relational humanities" of the sort advocated by
Smith will, therefore, rarely be an option for the
American school. But the objective Smith defends is
surely an important one toward which efforts to study the
religious faiths of people through their literary, symbolic, or other expressions ought to strive.

Historical-Critical Hermeneutics

Guntram G. Bischoff has argued the case for an
approach to religions, and especially to religious texts,
that is historical, critical, and interpretive.[13] While
such an approach might be largely literary, there is ample
scholarly precedent for the interpretation of symbols,
myths, and rituals as well. The critical approach implies
not only a critique of the object of study but also a
critique of the subject and the subject's world, including
the sociological context of the subject's knowledge. Such
an approach has as its goal the self-understanding of the
rationally autonomous subject and a correlative world-
understanding.

In addition to critical awareness, this approach is
explicitly aware of the historicity of human existence.
The hermeneutical enterprise is the outgrowth of the
modern consciousness of human individual and societal
historicity. An examination of the scholarly arguments
which have accompanied the emergence of hermeneutics in
modern scholarship is beyond the scope of this paper.

There is no question of its significance--nor of its
complexity. Some of the loftiest of modern "high"
scholarship thus suggests a method which is consistently
critical and historically self-conscious.

Can such a method yield an understanding of religion?
Professor Bischoff has argued persuasively that such a
method is one that permits religion to be itself, that
allows religious texts to be interpreted precisely as
religious, thus avoiding the reductionism which lurks in
a functionalist approach. The student interprets the
text historically and critically in the light of his/her
own developing and thus historical self-understanding and
world-understanding. Since it is religious texts that are
to be interpreted, no religious question is excluded from
the hermeneutical process, and Professor Bischoff has
argued vigorously that none should be if the Englightenment goal of rational autonomy is to be attained. For
him the rationally autonomous and the secular are the
same.

Is such a method pedagogically sound? It need
hardly be said that a great deal of careful teaching needs
to be done if a method developed at the highest levels of
modern university scholarship is to be used appropriately
at the secondary school level. The method presupposes
that questions raised by religious texts for the student
relate to human concerns which are a part of every life,
and perhaps, especially those of the student whose understanding of self and world is still emerging. Given
student willingness to engage in careful thinking, the
method at least opens the possibility of asking authentically religious questions of texts (or of being questioned
by them) and doing so with critical and historical methods.
Perhaps not many secondary school students can engage in
such sophisticated thought (although their numbers ought
not to be underestimated) but at least the possibility
would be open to them.

Is such a procedure legally appropriate in the public
school? Here I confess to some reservations which are both

legal and political. Professor Bischoff insists on the
purely rational, and therefore, secular character of the
hermeneutical approach he proposes. By equating the
secular with the rationally autonomous, he seeks to avoid
the obvious constitutional problem. I doubt that he
succeeds, since it seems to me that the difference between
what is constitutionally permissible in the schools and
what is not effectively vanishes. Moreover, I question
whether local communities and their school boards are
prepared to have students pursuing their self-understanding in matters religious under the auspices of the public
schools. I doubt that the problem can be evaded by
insisting that any question taken up under the rubric of
pursuing rational autonomy is ipso facto secular.

Perhaps the consistent application of the Englightenment ideal of the rationally autonomous individual as the
goal of education should extend to religion as to any
other field. Certainly the Englightenment writers thought
so, and the philosophy of religion is the product of that
era. But the gnawing question is whether the relationship
of religion studies to the state and its schools in the
United States has been defined by the consistent application of a philosophy of either government or education or
instead has been defined by constitutional and legal
arrangements which are the product not of theory alone
but of practical political judgments made in the course of
American constitutional history. I believe the history of
the First Amendment suggests the latter.

There is an important issue here relating to the
relationship of theory to political and educational praxis.
There is also a question of the role of coherence to which
Robert Michaelsen alluded.[14] Sidney Mead may well be
right in arguing that many orthodox believers are
schizophrenic in their simultaneous allegiance to their
religious orthodoxies and to the principles of American
religious pluralism.[15] The issue for religion studies in
the public schools, however, is whether it is the role of
the public schools to encourage the resolution of the

tension Mead describes in the name of theoretical coherence, or to say, as Michaelsen does, that patriotism, if
it is coherently explained, would demand the same thing.
I can only record here my unease with this position,
since it places the state through its public schools in an
adversary role vis-à-vis the religious beliefs of some of
its citizens. I understand the constitutional protection
of such beliefs to be virtually absolute. The free exercise of religion is not absolute, but how each citizen
reconciles religious pluralism with religious orthodoxy I
take to be a matter of belief beyond the competence of
the state, and therefore, of the public schools.

The issue here is important, since it touches not
only the suggestions made by Professors Bischoff and
Michaelsen but some of Professor Kniker's as well. In
each case a valid position is being pressed to its logical
conclusion. I argue that theoretical consistency here
collides with constitutional and legal restraints and
American political reality which are not the product of
theory consistently applied but of pragmatic judgments
made in response to quite concrete realities of American
life. I would also argue, without agreeing wholly with
Ivan Illich's thesis in Deschooling Society, that if
religion studies is to be viable in the American public
school, it must impose upon itself restraint that avoids
the impression that the school, especially the state's
school, is the only vehicle of education. To suggest as
Kniker does that "constructive action" such as examining
"various value systems with the avowed purpose of
developing one for himself/herself," or initiating "efforts
to cope with injustices that are resoluble," are desirable
objectives of religion studies seems to me to step over
the line which separates religious beliefs and practices
rooted in those beliefs from the sphere of state activities.[16] Non-cognitive goals and objectives, especially
"constructive action," constitute an especially sensitive
area.

I do not think that it is a sufficient defense to
counter-argue that rational autonomy or religious individualism is not so much something the state promotes in
matters religious as it is a freedom for each person that
the state protects and with which it ought not to interfere
in its schools. It will require a good deal more sophisticated analysis than we have produced thus far to
differentiate the sphere of the "religious" in which the
state must not sponsor or promote practices (and decisions)
from the sphere in which religious texts precisely as such
produce a rational exigency for self-and-world understanding with which the state should not interfere. It is this
reduction of the difference between the religious (the
heteronomous?) and the secular (the autonomous?) to the
vanishing point that gives rise to my unease. A purely
verbal difference is not enough. It is just possible that
one person's "theoretical incoherence" is another person's
"balanced tension" that permits practical pluralism in a
very diverse society.

Perhaps a skillful and sensitive teacher could use
the hermeneutical paradigm. It may well be argued that
interpretation is inevitable in any case. I am prepared
to concede that. But, surely, it is important that some
clearly recognizable line stand between what is constitutionally permissible and politically acceptable and what
is not if religion studies on this model is to be legally
and politically viable.

Conclusion

This chapter has addressed itself to three questions.
The first regards appropriate aims, goals, and objectives
for public school religion studies, with particular
attention to the place of non-cognitive objectives. The
second question had to do with the role of methods
developed specifically for the study of religion and the
need to use them if religion as such is to be studied in
the schools. The third question concerned the implications
for public school religion studies of constitutional and

political realities in the U.S. These questions have been
addressed in the course of describing and criticizing
several paradigms for public school religion studies.

The search for appropriate objectives results in the
conclusion that while cognitive objectives are those which
Religionswissenschaft has tended to emphasize, religion
studies as a humanistic discipline has seen the need for
an empathetic and appreciative study of religion as well
as an objective, descriptive study. We have, however,
been led to question the appropriateness of some non-
cognitive objectives on both legal and political grounds.

The role of Religionswissenschaft is complex.
Therefore, the omission of a "history of religions"
paradigm from this summary of paradigms may appear to be
a serious error. However, what public school religion
studies has to learn from the highly developed methods of
university researchers is not a single paradigm but
guidelines and the incentive to employ a variety of
methods and to study a variety of religious phenomena
including texts, symbols, rituals, and myths. This should
be done while retaining a sense of what Piediscalzi aptly
has called the mysteriousness of religion.[17]

While insisting that objective methods of religion
studies are legally and constitutionally appropriate, I
have argued for restraint in the formulation of objectives
that are not cognitive if religion studies is to be viable
in American public schools.

NOTES

[1]Robert D. Baird, ed., Methodological Issues in
Religious Studies: Wilfred Cantwell Smith, Jacob Neusner,
Hans Penner (Chico, California: New Horizons Press, 1975)
1-25.

[2]Robert D. Baird, Category Formation and the History
of Religions (The Hague: Mouton, 1971) 59.

[3]Peter S. Bracher, et. al., PERSC Guidebook: Public
Education Religion Studies: Questions and Answers
(Dayton, Ohio: Public Education Religion Studies Center,
1974), and Charles R. Kniker, "Approaches to Religion-
Studies in Public Schools" (paper presented at the annual
meeting of the American Academy of Religion, San Francisco,
California, December 1977).

[4]Baird, Category Formation, 60.

[5]Nicholas Piediscalzi, "Towards Defining the Purpose
and Goals for Public Education Religion Studies in the
U.S.A." (paper presented at the annual meeting of the
American Academy of Religion, San Francisco, California,
December 1977).

[6]Kniker, "Approaches," 5.

[7]Alan Gore, "The Teaching of World Religion in the
Public High Schools of the United States: A Critical
Evaluation of the Curricular Materials in Current Use"
(unpublished Ph.D. dissertation, University of Iowa, 1971)
273-287.

[8]Gore, "Critical Evaluation," 115.

[9]Piediscalzi, "Defining Purpose and Goals," 6-8.

[10]Nicholas Piediscalzi and William Collie, eds.,
Teaching About Religion in Public Schools (Niles, Illinois:
Argus Communications, 1977) 14.

[11]Baird, Methodological Issues, 1-25, and Wilfred
Cantwell Smith, The Meaning and End of Religion (New York:
New American Library, 1962).

[12]Baird, Methodological Issues, 3.

[13]Guntram G. Bischoff, "The Pedagogy of Religiology,"
Public Schools Religion-Studies: 1975, Anne Carr and
Nicholas Piediscalzi, eds., (Missoula, Montana: Scholars
Press, 1975).

[14]Robert S. Michaelsen, "Some Preliminary Comments on
N. Piediscalzi's 'Toward Defining the Purpose and Goals
for Public Education Religion Studies in the U.S.A.'"
(paper presented at the annual meeting of the American
Academy of Religion, San Francisco, California, December
1977).

[15]Sidney E. Mead, The Old Religion in the Brave New
World: Reflections on the Relation Between Christendom
and the Republic (Berkeley, California: University of
California Press, 1977).

[16]Kniker, "Approaches," 15.

[17]Piediscalzi, "Defining Purpose and Goals," 10-11.

CHAPTER SIX

A CRITICAL REVIEW OF AAR PAPERS (1970-1978) ON PUBLIC EDUCATION RELIGION STUDIES

Nicholas Piediscalzi

Since 1970, twenty-five papers on public education religion studies have been presented to members of the American Academy of Religion. Of these, nineteen are full length papers, five are responses to papers, and one is a preface to a volume of working papers discussed at the 1976 AAR annual meeting. Twelve of these papers present general theories of public education religion studies; five deal with theoretical and normative issues and practical problems involved in teacher education programs in public education religion studies; two report on and critically evaluate curriculum projects; five are responses to papers; and the preface traces briefly the histories of the interrelation of religion studies, moral education and values clarification in public education, and the Religion Studies in Public Education Group.[1] This chapter presents a summary of some of the significant areas of convergence and divergence in these papers, a criticism of some of their theories and approaches in addition to suggesting some of the more important problems and issues which still need to be analyzed and addressed by members of the Academy and leaders in the field of public education religion studies.

Nicholas Piediscalzi, Ph.D., is Chairman, Department of Religion and Codirector, Public Education Religion Studies Center, Wright State University. This chapter is a revision of a presentation given at the annual meeting of the American Academy of Religion in New Orleans, November, 1978.

Areas of Convergence and Divergence

1. The Legality of Public Education Religion
Studies--Virtually every paper mentions or presupposes
that the legality of public education religion studies was
settled definitively by the 1963 Schempp decision of the
United States Court. (Schempp and one or two quotations
from the majority opinion are invoked almost ad nauseam.)
The papers present four criteria which are derived from
Schempp: religion studies in public education should be
academic, pluralistic, objective, and critical. All also
agree that religion studies programs which fulfill these
four criteria share four characteristics in common: freedom from ecclesiastical and/or theological control; a
plurality of sources, presentations, and interpretations;
"intra-subjectivity" as defined by Philip Phenix; and
instruction in criticism. To this list Guntram G. Bischoff
adds a fifth, instruction in self-criticism which is "a
sustained process of confrontation where the student risks
his inchoate self-understanding."[2]

Although the terms "secular" and "pluralistic" are
employed frequently, they very seldom are defined carefully. Bischoff is the only author who attempts to
define "secular" systematically and to apply this definition with consistency. "Secular," according to him, means
freedom from religious presuppositions and freedom from
church control and orientation.[3]

2. The Purpose and Goals of Public Education--Several
papers maintain that it is necessary to consider the nature
and purpose of public education before attempting to define
the goals of public education religion studies. They hold
that the latter must be derived in part from and related
integrally to the former. Most of those taking this position agree with Bischoff's description of public education
and its purposes and goals. According to him, public
schools reflect the pluralism of our society and culture.
This being the case, they should uphold what is common to
all segments of society as opposed to that which is

partial and private. This includes actively cultivating
and maintaining ideological neutrality. Bischoff then
states that the purpose and goals of public education are
to train students in the basic skills for survival in
society and introduce them to (1) the process of forming
meanings for life, (2) the different ways in which people
define their self-meanings and moral responsibilities. In
Bischoff's own words, the primary educational objective of
public education is to provide "the enabling process which
helps develop the young person's world-understanding and
self-understanding."[4]

In 1978 John Boyle stated that the decentralized and
diffuse nature of the public school system makes it most
difficult to define public education. Therefore, he
recommended that only a very general description should be
used, viz., public schools are those institutions of
learning "which are operated under the authority of
federal government or of the states or their political sub-
divisions and paid for with tax monies."[5]

3. Definition of Religion--With two exceptions, the
papers define religion as either an ultimate commitment or
as a world view which provides ultimate meaning for human
existence and an implicit or explicit code for moral conduct. This definition makes it possible to include under
the academic study of religion both traditional religions
and secular or quasi-religions.

Henry Hoeks defines religion as the ultimate world
view of "an intentional faith community."[6] The addition
of this qualifying phrase makes the definition too narrow,
possibly too Protestant. There are religions which neither
view themselves nor conduct their affairs as self-con-
sciously willing communities. Hoeks' definition does not
account for these.

Thayer Warshaw rejects the broad definition for two
reasons. First, it covers such a wide range of different
phenomena it practically eliminates the distinction between
what is religious and what is not. Second, teachers who
employ a broad definition of religion may find themselves

in an impossible legal dilemma. According to the Courts,
public school teachers are expected to foster specific
American moral values without inculcating a religious
faith. However, once a broad definition of religion is
established in public education, it would encompass, in
all probability, the moral values the teachers are man-
dated to foster, thereby making the teachers inculcators
of a religion--a function prohibited by law. For these
reasons, Warshaw defines religion as "a belief in the
divine, a consequent code of moral values, membership in
a sect, and cultic practices."[7]

The justification which Warshaw uses to reject a
broad definition of religion is the very reason why it
should be used. If the goal of religion studies is, as
most agree, to introduce students to the ways in which
human beings are religious and act out their commitments,
then it is necessary to study these religious commitments
and actions wherever they appear--even if this means presenting the teacher with an almost "pathological" situation. To do otherwise would be to misrepresent the
numerous and different ways in which religious commitments
and traditions emerge and evolve.

Likewise, if the Court presents the teacher with a
dilemma, the way in which to deal with the problem educationally is not to deny or avoid the dilemma but to explore
with the students why and how this dilemma arose and why it
continues to persist. Also, this particular dilemma raises
for teachers and students alike two questions: (1) What is
the relation of religion to morality in the U.S.A.?
(2) Can a pluralistic society survive without unifying
"religious" or moral principles? The latter question is
significant because Supreme Court decisions seem to answer
it in the negative while holding to a fairly strict separation of Church and State in public education.

Some of the papers recommend the use of functional
definitions of religion while others do not. The latter
hold that functional definitions fail to point out the
unique essence or character of religion; they only

describe how religion operates. This may be true for some
early functionalists but not the more recent sophisticated
ones such as Clifford Geertz. Moreover, Robert Hall, Rodney Allen, and several others in our Group have demonstrated that functional definitions can provide descriptions
of religion which point to or uncover the essence of
religion in human experience. Therefore, it is counter-
productive to dismiss summarily a functional approach to
the study of religion.

    4. Rationale for Public Education Religion Studies--
All papers agree that there is only one justifiable
rationale for public education religion studies--an
educational one. If one of the major purposes of education
is to help students understand all facets of reality, then
religion must be studied since it is an integral part of
human history, society, and culture. There is no way to
avoid this reality and remain true to the purpose and
goals of education. In the words of Robert Michaelsen,

> Religion is a fact . . . . To be sure one can
> debate . . . whether religion is sui generis or
> merely the function of something else more
> fundamental . . . . But to deny the fact of
> religion by ignoring it is to engage in a kind
> of irresponsibility which does not befit the
> proud heritage of the community of learning.
> The question then, is not whether to study
> religion but how to study it.[8]

    5. Goals for Public Education Religion Studies--The
papers present a variety of goals for public education
religions studies, most of which, if not all, are compatible
with each other. All support the general goal that religion studies should develop a critical understanding of
the universal phenomenon of human religiousness through a
critical examination of its many and varied manifestations.
Some do not go beyond this general goal while others add
to it. The additions come primarily from those who have
been or are involved in secondary education or teacher
education programs. For example, Charles Knicker of the
School of Education at Iowa State University lists four
major goals: the development of religious literacy,

passionate inquiry, open and accurate communication, and
constructive action.[9]

Others add as a goal the task of developing or understanding the process of making moral and ethical decisions
with special reference to the role of religious beliefs
and practices in this process. While accepting these
goals, Lee Smith, Wes Bodin, Thayer Warshaw, James Ackerman, and Joseph Forcinelli add two others--developing
(a) attitudes of respect for the religious ideas and
practices of others as derived from our commitment to the
value of human dignity and the value of the right to individual choice, and (b) the ability to live effectively
in society by treating people as personal ends in themselves rather than impersonal means or categories and by
using their knowledge and talents to help solve religious
problems in society and in the world. Others also include
the attainment of a respect for pluralism and an understanding of the interaction of religion and history,
religion and culture, and religion and institutions. A
few others add a final goal--developing the ability to
distinguish between religion and morality and the interaction between the two.

6. Methods--John Boyle's 1978 paper presents an
excellent summary of the various methods proposed by AAR
members for studying about religion in public education:
natural inclusion, multi-disciplinary, surveys, phenomenology, relational, and historical-critical. Boyle's
description of the historical-critical method does not
take into consideration the difference between those who
follow Guntram Bischoff's claim that the historical-
critical method "is concerned exclusively with uncovering
the past and trying to understand it on its own terms,
without ideological or dogmatic impediments of a commitment to a particular faith," and those who contend that
this approach must be combined with "making students aware
of contemporary religious interpretations, traditions and
predispositions other than their own, so they will become
more conscious of their own presupposition and biases and,

perhaps, more sensitive to cultural pluralism of American society."[10] The difference between these two approaches may be traced in part to a difference between those who approach public education religion studies primarily from the theoretical perspectives of higher education and those who include experience from public education.

7. Teacher Education--There is general agreement on eight points concerning the development and conduct of teacher education programs in public education religion studies. Teacher education programs in this field should: (1) be joint ventures of religionists and educators; (2) utilize the same standards that are used for accrediting teachers in other disciplines; (3) expose students to diverse traditions and methods; (4) provide instruction in the evaluation of printed and non-printed curriculum; (5) introduce students to theories pertaining to the psychological development of children, and teach them how to apply this knowledge to teaching about religion; (6) include supervised practice teaching in religion studies; (7) train teachers to become aware of their own biases and how to correct the errors which they might impose on their teaching; and (8) provide adequate courses on religions in America and the history of the relationship between American religions and public education.

While there is consensus on these points, most existing programs do not fulfill all of these requirements. The specialties of given departments and programs tend to determine which ones will be emphasized. Paul Will's evaluation of the way in which teacher education programs in Michigan fulfill the guidelines provided by the State Board of Education illustrates this point. He shows how the research biases of departments shape the program on each campus and how the state guidelines which are quite specific are bent to meet the emphasis of departmental priorities. Will also demonstrates that even though scholars call for the inclusion of the study of non-Western religions they are usually ignored or given secondary emphasis.[11] In evaluating actual programs

according to these eight criteria I also discover that the
study of American religions is omitted or given insufficient attention even though there is general agreement that
it should be a major element in teacher education programs.

Areas Requiring Further Attention

Reflection on these areas of convergence and divergence leads me to suggest areas which require further study
and deliberation by those actively involved in the development of public education religion studies.

First, it would be of value to study and discuss the
meaning of the term "secular education" and its implications for public education religion studies. To state that
secular means freedom from ecclesiastical and theological
control is not enough, especially since the history of
American public education is replete with controversies
which may be traced to attempts to make the public schools
inculcators of a civic faith and morality or to use Robert
Michaelsen's apt phrase, "America's established church."
Perhaps it would be fruitful to re-introduce Harvey Cox's
distinction between secular and secularism (The Secular
City) and proceed from there. An oversimplified approach
to the concept of "secular education" does not help us
understand or overcome the problems and conflicts caused
by the way in which the public schools have been expected
to serve as an "established church" of a secular order
which may be as constricting as a theological order.

Second, attempts should be made to clarify what is
meant by "pluralism" and "pluralistic approach" and the
implications of these concepts for public education in
general and religion studies in specific. The shift to
pluralism is relatively new in public education; it has
produced innumerable shock waves in the public sector
which, for the most part, have been ignored by educators
responsible for the shift. At the same time, they do not
realize that they produced a conflict between different
ultimate belief systems which cannot be resolved rationally
or by appeals for the establishment of neutrality and

tolerance. I agree with Joseph Watras who stated, after
analyzing the underlying issues and problems in the West
Virginia textbook controversy, that the protestors were a
people who felt painfully trapped in a technological and
pluralistic society which ignored or denied their loyalty
to family ties, their faith in the God of the Christian
tradition, and their sense of moral certainty. "It is a
form of culturecide," states Watras, to ask these people
to surrender or compromise these strong beliefs in order
for their children to achieve greater success than their
parents in school and society. "The protestors showed us
that pluralism cannot be served if traditional values are
trivialized."[12]

Moreover, schools usually become repressive, according
to Watras when they seek to evade conflict by refusing to
make a value decision in the name of neutrality. Genuine
pluralism, according to him, encourages dialogue and interaction between both sides, "maintaining the possibility of
one finally dominating . . . [while each searches] for the
truth . . .within limits . . . . Just as the Appalachian
people have to lose their paranoia, we have to lose our
fear of strongly held values."[13] From this perspective,
and in this context it would be of value to consider the
nature of pluralism in public education religion studies.

Third, time could be well spent by examining in
detail the history of the public schools with special
emphasis on the way in which they have been expected to
serve as "America's established church" and the conflicts
this expectation produced. Most American Academy of
Religion discussions about the purpose and goals of public
education and public education religion studies lack concreteness because they fail to take this expectation and
these conflicts into account. This comes out clearly in
John Boyle's paper when he opts for a very simple definition of public schools after reviewing some offered by
members of the AAR Group which are highly theoretical.
Boyle is correct in stating that our theories about public
education should be based on historical study rather than

idealistic and abstract philosophical views. However, it
is not adequate to conclude, as he does, that it is better
to define public education in "a concrete rather political
way."[14] The history of public education must be viewed in
its entirety. The role of public education as defined by
those in the Protestant "Establishment" and those in the
immigrant groups must be assessed. Recent attempts at
neutral pluralism must be analyzed. Only after all of
this work is done, should attempts be made to define the
purpose and goals of public education and the purpose and
goals of public education religion studies. When these
tasks are completed, then attention should be turned to
developing and implementing new models for courses on
America's religions for teacher education programs and the
public schools.

Fourth, there remains a need to find more effective
ways to include greater emphasis upon non-Western religious traditions both in teacher education programs,
curriculum materials, and courses. As pointed out
earlier, most of the work in these areas is Western
oriented and excludes consideration of non-Western traditions. This presents a truncated view of the multiplicity
and diversity of religious traditions in history both past
and present.

Fifth, it would do us well to return to a major
question raised by Paul Will in his 1975 paper: Should we
design teacher education programs according to existing
structures in the public schools or should we pattern our
work according to what we believe ideal religion studies
should be? It is my opinion that we should begin with the
existing structures, seeking to operate as effectively as
we can within them while maintaining a long-range goal of
achieving significant changes in the departmental and curricular structures so that religion studies will not be
viewed solely as an adjunct to other fields. This order
is suggested since it would approach the question of change
from within the existing structures and not appear so
threatening as would a direct approach from without.

Sixth, with the exception of a few professional educators and two or three others, most of those in the
American Academy of Religion who are involved in public
education religions studies have not had any working
experience in or ongoing contact with the public school
classroom and teacher education programs. Often when I
visit a public school classroom, a teachers conference,
or a consultation with professors of education, I discover
that much of what most religionists recommend for inclusion
in public education religion studies programs is irrele-
vant. Those who commit this error need to immerse themselves in actual public school situations and teacher
education programs before they pronounce ex cathedra what
religion studies should be within public education. In
addition, it behooves them to establish more effective
working relationships with their colleagues in education
and public school teachers. I realize that these are
difficult tasks but they must be done, if their work is to
produce significant results. Fortunately, there are three
good models to follow: the Florida State University
Religion-Social Studies Curriculum interdisciplinary staff,
the Michigan Day Seminars, and Wright State University's
team-developed and team-taught curriculum.

Furthermore, religionists who seek to establish
working relationships with educators and classroom
teachers must sacrifice the luxury of their liberal arts
snobbery which holds educators and teachers to be lower
than the lowest of illiterate technicians. They also need
to cultivate a healthy sense of humility and to offer
themselves to their colleagues and teachers as resource
experts on religion rather than masters of public education. Their actions should reflect the following attitude:
As religionists we have knowledge and insights to offer
which can be of help. However, we also realize how little
we know about the public school system. We have a great
deal to learn from you as we offer our assistance. (I
commend for your reading that section in James Ackerman's
1970 paper where he confesses how surprised he was to

discover during the first year of the Indiana Institute on
Teaching the Bible in Secondary Schools that public school
teachers have creative ideas. This revelation forced him
to reject his rigid model of biblical studies and to take
seriously models suggested by the teachers.)[15]

Developing a sense of humility and an attentiveness to
the concerns and ideas of educators would enable religionists
to move more rapidly towards what Guntram Bischoff calls the
formation of a "Bridge Discipline" in which a dialectical
working relationship among religionists, educators, and
teachers can lead to significant innovations in public education. Please note that what is called for is a dialectical relationship. Up to this point I have stressed the sins of the
religionists and their need to undergo metonoia. Their colleagues in education and teachers also have committed and
continue to commit multitudinous professional sins which require attention. However, religionists need to put their own
house in order before they can expect to help educators and
teachers repent of their professional sins and contribute to
the formation of a "Bridge Discipline."

Seventh, many religionists ignore the insights
available from psychological studies of human development.
They theorize about public school religion studies models
without recognizing the significant psychological,
emotional, and intellectual differences between first and
second graders and juniors and seniors in high school, not
to mention the differences between high school freshman
and high school seniors. For example, I believe it is
incorrect to state, as Bischoff does, that the primary
method for secondary public education religion studies is
the historical-hermeneutical one. Freshmen and sophomores
and many juniors are not ready psychologically, emotionally,
and intellectually to test their incohate identities
against world views different from theirs. According to
Erik H. Erikson, the process of human identity formation
as described by Bischoff takes place in the post-high
school years. In light of this, I have tended recently to
support Henry Hoeks' assertion that the goal of public

education religion studies should be to provide students
with "that modicum (or more) of knowledge as a basis for
advanced (usually college or university) inquiry which can
use the history of religion approach."[16]

Valuable assistance in this area may be obtained by
devoting more attention to the way in which insights from
the psychology of human development are utilized by those
who are developing religion studies programs and curricula
in Great Britain and the authors of the Florida State
University Religion-Social Studies curriculum for the
elementary grades.

Eighth, I would like to call for a reconsideration of
the validity and efficacy of the way in which the question
of the "transcendent" is bracketed in the "scientific"
study of religion. To make my point more clear I shall
refer extensively to one of Guntram Bischoff's essays and
do so not to single him out as the main offender. All are
culpable in this area. I choose his thought because he is
the one who has stated the position so precisely and
systematically. Bischoff states that the science of
religion requires its practitioners to examine religion and
religious experience solely as a human phenomenon. Transcendent gods who usually are included in the content of
these phenomena must be viewed only as a dimension of
human experience since they are not available for empirical
investigation. "Hence transcendence must appear as
immanence, as the understanding of the gods must appear as
self-understanding."[17]

Bischoff further contends that teachers who, out of
either fear or a mistaken understanding of objectivity,
shield students from a specific theological or other
religious claim, short-circuit the educational process.[18]
This is the case because one of the major purposes of
secondary public education, helping the student achieve
self-understanding and autonomy, can be attained only if
the student is confronted authentically with "the various
historical and contemporary claims to meaning-given truth
and value" as genuine possibilities for the establishment

of his or her own self-image. Bischoff concludes, "In this
sense, the study of religion is, strictly speaking, propaedeutical to the student's own theologizing."[19]

It is time to raise anew several important questions
posed in the past: Are not the central cores of many religious experiences and religious lives violated by interpreting them solely as human phenomena? Are not communal
and individual descriptions of transcendent gods misrepre-
sented when they are studied only as immanent and
expressions of self-understanding? If the student is to
be confronted authentically "by the various historical and
contemporary claims to meaning-giving truth and value," is
s/he not denied such an authentic confrontation by a method
which claims categorically that "the transcendent gods . . .
are empirically available only as part of . . .[human]
experience, not as existing outside of and independent
from this experience."?[20] How can a student have an
authentic confrontation with the truth-claim of a person's
commitment to a personal god, if s/he knows that the method
employed by his or her teacher views such a commitment only
as self-interpretation? Furthermore, if we are to be true
to our devotion to the "scientific" method, are we willing
to view two of our basic normative claims--that the goal
of education is the formation of the autonomous self, that
transcendent reality does not exist outside of and independent of human experiences--and the "scientific" method
itself solely as immanent and as self-interpretations?
And are we willing to evaluate them as critically as we do
other normative claims to truth and other methods?

Please do not misunderstand my point. I am denying
neither the possibility of nor need for the objective and
critical study of religions. I am trying to point out that
there is a major difference between an objective study of
religions which treats all ultimate commitments equally
and one which brackets the truth claims of some because
they do not fit our empirical models without admitting or
dealing critically with the fact that such bracketing is
the result of a faith-commitment unverifiable by the

empirical method. Furthermore, I do not seek to re-
introduce an approach which would try to prove the
ultimacy and superiority of one world view over all
others. This would be counter-productive. However, I do
believe that it is time to re-examine the validity of our
dedication to bracketing the question of the "transcendent" and to ask whether we are not denying a most
important dimension of religious experience and life by
presenting the "transcendent" to our students as only
immanence and self-interpretation. (I believe Justice
Robert H. Jackson sought to raise this point in Everson
vs. Board of Education when he stated, "The assumption
[of public education] is that after the individual has
been instructed in worldly wisdom, he will be better
fitted to choose his religion. Whether such a disjunction
is possible, and if possible whether it is wise, are questions I need not try to answer.")

Ninth, although several claim that the study of the
Bible as/in Literature does not constitute religion
studies, they do not suggest what constitutes a proper
academic study of the Bible in public education. This is
another area which needs serious attention. Moreover, it
should be expanded to include consideration of the best
way to study in public education the sacred scriptures of
all religions.

Tenth, the attempts to distinguish moral education,
values clarification, and religion studies have produced
inconclusive results. Since several approaches to moral
education and values clarification erroneously present
themselves as free of ultimate truth claims and since many
parents and civic leaders confuse moral education and
values clarification with religion studies, it is necessary for educators, religionists, and ethicists to develop
some clear definitions of each field and suggest guidelines
for studying each in public education.

The foregoing survey and critique reveal that members
of the American Academy of Religion have reached accord in
several crucial areas. Their disagreements are not

serious. In fact, they provide an excellent opportunity
for further research, exploration, and discussion which
could produce significant contributions to the advancement
of public education religion studies.

NOTES

[1]See Nicholas Piediscalzi, "An Annotated Compilation
of AAR Papers on Public Education Religion Studies, 1970-
1978." (Duplicated and distributed to the members of the
American Academy of Religion Group on Religion Studies in
Public Education, 1978).

[2]"The Pedagogy of Religiology," in Anne Carr and
Nicholas Piediscalzi, eds., The Academic Study of Religion:
1975 Proceedings and Public Schools Religion-Studies:
1975 Proceedings, [Missoula, Montana: American Academy of
Religion, 1975], 134. (A revised version of this paper is
published in this volume.)

[3]Ibid., 128-29.

[4]Ibid., 129.

[5]"Paradigms for Public Education Religion Studies
Curricula: Some Suggestions and Critique," (1978), 3.
(A revised version of this paper is published in this
volume.)

[6]"A Multi-disciplinary Approach to Religion-Studies
in the Schools," (1976), 3-4. (A revised version of this
paper is published in this volume.)

[7]"Religion Studies, Moral Education, and Values
Clarification in American Public Schools: Definitions,"
(1976), 1. (Duplicated and distributed to members of the
American Academy of Religion Group on Religion Studies in
Public Education, 1976.)

[8]John R. Hinnells, ed., Comparative Religion in Education (London: Oriel Press, 1970), 11.

[9]"Approaches to Religion-Studies in Public Schools,"
(1977), 6ff. (Duplicated and distributed to members of
the American Academy of Religion Group on Religion Studies
in Public Education.)

[10]Bischoff, "The Pedagogy of Religion," (1975), 134,
and James S. Ackerman, "Teaching the Bible as Literature
in Secondary Schools: A Report on the 1970 Indiana
University Institute," 7. (Duplicated, 1970.)

[11]"Blueprints for the Future? Michigan's Certification Programs in the Academic Study of Religions," in Carr
and Piediscalzi, eds., The Academic Study of Religion:
1975, 93ff. (A revised version of this paper is published
in this volume.)

[12]"The Textbook Dispute in West Virginia: A New Form
of Oppression," Educational Leadership, 33/1 (October 1975),
22-23.

[13]Ibid., 23., cf. Edward Hulmes, "The Problem of
Commitment," in W. Owen Cole, ed., World Faiths in Education (London: George Allen and Unwin, 1978), 26-37.

[14]Boyle, 3.

[15]Ackerman, 4.

[16]Hoeks, 3.

[17]Bischoff, 130.

[18]Ibid., 134.

[19]Ibid., 133.

[20]Ibid., 134.

CHAPTER SEVEN

A CURRICULAR PARADIGM FOR RELIGIOUS EDUCATION

Ninian Smart

The question of the content of education in the field
of religion is not just a theoretical or logical one.   It
is also, and importantly, a political one.   I do not mean
this in a narrow sense but rather in the sense that whether
we adopt a pluralistic and descriptive approach to the
study and exploration of religion has profound effects on
our attitude to freedom.   I shall illustrate this in regard
to the development of religious education in the state
school system of England during the decade between 1968
and the present--which also as it happens covers the
period during which I have acted as director for the
Schools Council Projects on Religious Education at Lancaster University, which have had a wide effect on thinking
about religious education in the United Kingdom.[1]

It should be noted that religious education, which is
virtually a required subject in the schools in Britain,
was thought of, by the 1944 Education Act, for instance,
as Christian education; and it has in many areas been
largely based on the Christian Bible.   The curricular
revolution of the decade in question has in part to do
with freeing the subject from this confessional basis.   The
arguments for doing this are various and are of some
interest here as they help to throw light upon both the
logical and the political aspects of determining the content of a religion curriculum.   They are as follows:

*Ninian Smart, Ph.D., teaches at the University of Lancaster,
England and the University of California, Santa Barbara.
This chapter was first presented at the annual meeting of
the American Academy of Religion in New Orleans, November,
1978.*

First, the study of religion is in principle concerned
with the pluralism of traditions and in general with the
religious and existential dimensions of human behavior and
belief: that is, it is not rationally confined to the
study of just one tradition.

Second, though a society may be concerned with the
transmission of its values through the education process,
it is doubtful whether Britain can be sensibly defined as
a Christian country: indeed as a Western-style democracy
it espouses in theory religious and ideological toleration
within very broad limits, and this implies a higher-order
set of values.

Third, a religiate or religiously-literate person
ought to know something of the major patterns of religious
and ideological belief and practice in the world.

Fourth, studies such as those of Goldman already
showed how poorly the older instructional pattern of
religious education was functioning.[2]   Educationally and
psychologically the Biblical orientation of much of the
religion curriculum was deleterious. Paul may have had
the style of an angel, but he was not writing to children
in Birmingham.

Fifth, and connectedly, insofar as a religion curriculum
helps to illuminate choices in life for people, it must
speak to the existential condition of those individuals,
and here we are often far from the traditional values of
(say) Biblical religion. Rural metaphors in industrial
cities, polite dogmatism in a consumer society, educated
interpretations of faith in an intellectually crude environment:--these and other disadvantages can hobble the
teaching of religion in many of Britain's schools.

Behind such arguments, one can point to two motifs:
one is that there is a plural logic in the study of
religion itself. Since there is still some confusion as
to the nature of the study of religion even at the level
of higher education, I shall say something in brief compass
on this score. Incidentally, I consider that a subject
should in principle be the same throughout the levels of

education, even if methods of teaching and content may
vary: does mathematics actually turn into a different
subject just because it becomes more rarefied? (As for the
pure-applied distinction--again, does statistics for
instance change as we grow older?) The other motif behind
the above arguments is that the curriculum should be related to the social condition of those involved in it.

What, then, is the study of religion? One can look
at it in one way as like political science and economics.
In the case of these subjects we abstract from total human
behavior and look at man as acting politically or as an
economic being. Likewise we can look at that aspect of
human behavior and feeling, etc., which may be considered
firstly as aspectual. This is not to imply of course that
religion is everywhere much the same--nevertheless it often
deals with common themes and has common patterns: themes
such as death and suffering, patterns such as rites of
passage. In other words, the aspectual treatment of
religion tends towards comparisons. But these themselves
need to recognize the differences of traditions and therefore of the settings of that which exhibits similarity.
Thus the aspectual treatment of religion leads to a
recognition of pluralism.

That in studying religion we should explore religions
is not just common sense: it reflects too the nature of
our planetary culture. In Bradford, England, Islam
flourishes among Pakistanis; in California, patterns of
Buddhism and Taoism; in Paris, Vedanta--and so it is no
longer feasible to think that the question of religion can
be confined to a consideration of Western forms of theism.
And in a consumer society dedicated to individualism and
plurality of choice it is not at all surprising that the
multiple face of religious commitment should be unavoidable.

But not just religious commitment in the traditional
sense. For it is an obvious feature of the past and of
the planetary present that religions have been in interplay
with what on the surface at least are non-religious
ideologies--Victorian atheism, scientific humanism, Marxism,

Cambodian anarchosyndicalism, etc. It is artificial to
seal religious studies off from the study of ideology,
insofar as the latter presents alternative views on life
and death and alternative value-schemes. This is why we
may dub the study of religion "non-finite." It does not
have a closely marked boundary. It deals with worldviews,
not just religious worldviews; it deals with existence, not
just other-worldly aspirations.

We also consider the mode under which religion and
religions as described above are to be presented. Is it
just a matter of history and description, of the facts
concerning religions? Or are they to be presented con-
structively as teaching certain truths about the human
condition? Is the teacher a kind of preacher in the last
resort? Elsewhere I have explored the distinction between
describing a religious standpoint and expressing it. [3]

Pluralistic Approach

There is a logical and a political reason why it is
wrong to suppose that there is an identifiable set of
religious truths to be expressed by the teacher in the
course of exploring religion with students. The logical
reason is that the very pluralism of religions and
ideologies breeds an uncertainty about the criteria of
truth: religions are, however authoritatively presented,
essentially debatable. Or to put it another way: they
belong to the realm of faith rather than knowledge. Thus
to select certain truths out as being of the essence of
religion or of true religion is itself a religious act--a
choice within the field of faith. It belongs to the level
of the earthquake rather than that of seismology: it is
like the flight of a heron rather than ornithology. Moreover, at one level the justification for the teaching of
religion is that the religiate person is one who sensi-
tively knows about religions and ideologies and their
formative effect upon human history and individual lives:
religiateness is at the descriptive level. (But in a
moment we shall see that this terminology itself has to be
transcended.)

Second, the danger of teaching from a particular
religious standpoint is that it precludes appraisal of
other standpoints. It does not, politically, cohere with
the demands of a plural society. Pluralism itself is
desirable from a number of angles. First, it involves
toleration and the fair treatment of differing commitments,
except insofar as they are not incompatible with the demands of a plural society. Second, it is a component in
the open society, which itself is the best social precon-
dition of the pursuit of scientific and other truth, since
criticism is the root of science, as Karl Popper has
argued. Third, pluralism enhances the dignity of the
individual by encouraging responsible choice.

It might be objected that the pluralistic approach to
religious education could issue in a superficial description of so many varieties of religion and ideology: 57
varieties of faith, so to say. It would easily be woodenly
descriptive, and it could give the impression that there is
so to say a supermarket from the shelves of which you reach
down for the faith that suits you. This is where one must
amplify what is involved in description in this context.

The description of a faith or of an aspect of it--for
instance of the Catholic Mass or the experience of grace--
cannot, to be successful, just be "flat" and "external."
It needs to be evocative, to bring out the "feel" of what
is being talked about. By the same token the essential
seriousness of life-choices has to be conveyed. This is
of course a matter of feeling and attitude, not just a
matter of information. Thus in an important way the study
of religion must transcend the informative.

By a paradox, in Britain the more conservative kinds
of curriculum, Biblically based, tend towards a woodenly
descriptive and merely informational character, for it is
easy to treat the Bible as a kind of textbook which is to
be mastered and examined formally. The paradox lies in
this: that evangelical premisses have unspiritual
conclusions.

Of course, not all conservative argumentation has
precisely evangelical roots. Many who favor the limitation
of religious education in the U.K. to the Christian tradition (except for those students who on conscientious
grounds opt out) think of Christianity as the basis of
morals, and they think of religious education as the best
version of moral education. Others see Christianity as
the dominant moulding force of British culture in the past
and so its transmission is an important ingredient in the
general transmission of cultural values.

To take the second point first: there is no doubt
that Christianity has had a major role in British history.
But just as we would not on analogous grounds limit the
study of literature simply to British literature (or in
America to American literature), so however prominent a
place Christianity might have in the curriculum it would
not exclude treatment of other traditions, including both
Judaism and humanism, themselves vital for the understanding of Western culture. Since in any case education should
be planetary in scope, the appreciation of religious and
ideological traditions must likewise be planetary. Thus
the argument about the importance of Christianity tends to
resolve itself into the argument that great weight should
be placed upon it in a Western curriculum (though conversely in Sri Lanka greater weight would naturally be
placed upon Buddhism).

Naturally once we begin to approach religions plural-
istically, certain questions emerge. How far do all men
share a similar religious morality? Can one see similarities in the patterns of worship as between differing
faiths? Why do some faiths use images and others abhor
them? What is the holy? Who is the holy man? Is there a
similarity between religious and in particular mystical
experience the world over? Why do some religions believe
in reincarnation? What are the origins of belief in the
gods?

Now many such questions are difficult ones, and I am
not suggesting that they all have to be treated directly

in the course of a religion curriculum in a high school,
still less of course at the primary level. But the curriculum needs to bear them in mind. Take the last
question. The answer we give will relate to the issue
between religion and science. Consider the following line
of reasoning which may indeed be at the back of many
people's minds on this subject.

> "Men first of all thought of nature as
> animated, but so to speak broken up into
> many animated aspects: the wind was one
> god, the sun another, the ocean another,
> love another, a mountain another . . . Then
> they came to think of nature as a unity,
> and animated or controlled by one God. In
> either case it was important to make sac-
> rifices, or to say prayers--to communicate
> with the spirits of Spirit who controlled
> our environment. But now we can explain
> the operations of nature without recourse
> to a Soul or souls. Science replaces
> religious faith, and technology replaces
> prayer."

There is partial truth in this line of reasoning, and
it helps to explain some of the ways in which modern religion has evolved. However, since there is little doubt
that a kind of popular scientism is fairly pervasive, even
if often only fragmentarily articulated, the answer we give
to the question about the gods has existential force,
directly or indirectly in the classroom.

Implicit Religion and Existential Concerns

This is where we make the bridge from the plural,
evocative character of the study of religion to the problem
of the existential condition of the student. This of
course is in part a matter of empirical research. But it
is fair to say that there are some recurrent themes which
belong to human experience in a modern society to which
education, and religious education in particular, should
relate. Questions about the nature of the individual,
attitudes to death, the character of living in community,

race questions, the nature of luck and fate, the meaning of
love, the possibility of altruism, the relation between
science and other knowledge--such existential concerns
relate to religion (and ideology). Such issues have sometimes been referred to as implicit religion: i.e., an
area where religion is implicit rather than explicit, and
this is a way of saying that to them explicitly religious
teachings and activities are relevant. It is also a
shorthand way of indicating the educational need to tie
the exploration of religion to the social and personal
condition of the student.

In addition to what here is called "implicit" religion
one may also point to elements of life which somewhat ad-
ventitiously are culturally existential--kinds of sport,
certain brands of SF, astrology, pop music, sexual mores:--
these may command intense interest among young people, e.g.
at the secondary level. The relation of religion to such
themes is not unnatural, for these are surface manifestations of deeper existential concerns. To some degree sport
is a refinement of aggression, while the inhabitants of
science fiction are modern substitutes, up to a point, for
the gods. The use, however, of such entrances into religious education belong to the tactics of syllabus-construc-
tion.

So far, then, we have argued for a paradigm of
religious education which is plural, aimed at generating
understanding of religions and other practically-oriented
worldviews, but which aims also at relating to the
implicit elements in life, not to mention those culturally
determined particular enthusiasms of young people which
have relevance to religious and analogous claims.

The balance between implicit and explicit religion is
to be harmonized with the feasibilities arising from the
stages of psychological and intellectual development in
young people. It is also as I have indicated to be harmonized with the particular cultural experience of the
environment.

Dimensional Analysis

Within the treatment of religion and religions it is
also necessary to reach towards a balance of another sort.
Many curricula, whether at tertiary or secondary level, in
the field of religion are too much bound up with teaching
and too little with practice. It is too easy in a school
context to mistake what is in books for living realities.
As a method of providing a kind of checklist, so that we
can see how far our approach to religious phenomena is a
rounded one, my doctrine of the six dimensions of religion
has a certain use.[4] Broadly it divides religion into
three dimensions which have to do with belief and three
which have to do with practice. (But they have to be
understood rationally with one another, as we shall see:
and this represents a vitally important observation for
the whole of religious education.) The belief trio are
what I have called the doctrinal, mythological, and ethical
dimensions. Thus in Christianity there are certain
doctrines--the dependence of the world on the creative
activity of God, the Trinity doctrine and so on--which
afford a framework in which certain other beliefs and
values are to be understood. Thus not only do they tell
us something of the structural relations between the world
and God, but they also form the background against which
the central stories of the faith are apprehended--stories
such as the history of Israel, Christ's birth, death, and
resurrection, and so on.

I refer to this story-aspect of faith as the mythological dimension: naturally, I mean the term descriptively
and analytically: by a myth is meant a story about the
divine or the transcendent in relation to human beings,
etc. Whether such a story is true or false, to be taken
literally or metaphorically, is a further matter about
which men may well differ. In brief, by "myth" I mean a
certain kind of story, not a false story as popular par-
lance often has it (this being so, there is some doubt as
to whether the term can easily and profitably be used in
the educational context, since so many misunderstandings
have to be moved out of the way).

The belief-trio has as its third member what I call
the ethical dimension--the moral and social values which a
religion tends to inculcate. Insofar as, to understand a
religion in a rounded way, it is necessary to look among
other things to its moral aspect, it follows that there is
a manner in which religious education overlaps with moral
education. However, the geography of religious education
is much broader and its aims rather different (that is,
from those commonly conceived under the head of moral
education).

It is clear that the belief-trio is interconnected.
After all, in the case of Christianity, doctrines of
transcendence and creation themselves stem from reflection
upon the stories, and likewise the Trinity doctrine is a
way of systematizing what is implicit in various historical and revelatory episodes. Nevertheless, and conversely,
the mythic aspect of religion is misunderstood unless it's
conceived as the Power behind the whole universe. The
ethical teachings and values of a faith may in part stem
from the general moral perceptions of humanity, but their
special flavor derives from the whole context of belief
and practice. Thus Christian humility is reinforced and
molded by the example of Christ himself, who divested
himself of divine pomp, and met death as a despised out-
cast. Conversely, human love is considered in Christianity
as providing insight into the nature of God.

The practical trio of dimensions I have described is:
the ritual, the experiential, and the social or institutional. Thus in the first instance religion typically
involves rituals such as those of worship, the sacraments,
etc.: symbolic acts in which the individual or group
establishes communication or relationship with what is
transcendent or with what is the subject-matter of the
mythic dimension. In some religions the rites are inter-
iorized and may in effect take the form of techniques of
meditation and the purification of consciousness. But it
is always possible to make out, in the religious context, a
practical dimension which involves certain characteristic
transcendentally-directed activities.

Second, there is what I have called the experiential
dimension: that is, the aspect of religious life in which
men experience the divine being or other foci of their
faith. Clearly, religion is not only believed, but also
felt, and there is necessarily an expectation that the
referents of the doctrinal and mythological dimensions are
capable of entering into the living experience of individuals and groups. In other words, there is an existential aspect of religious teachings, which means in turn
that it is not possible to learn doctrines and spiritual
stories as though they are merely propositions to be
memorized: their relationship to feeling has to be
appreciated. This means that empathy is an ineluctable
component of religiateness.

Third, in the practical trio there is the fact that a
religion typically expresses itself in a social way: as
the activity of a community, for instance. The way in
which a faith relates to social facts and its institutional
embodiment are its social dimension. The intertwining of
the practical three is obvious in such an event as a
solemn sacrament such as a marriage in which ritual, feeling, and social relations are equally vital.

And the practical trio has to be interpreted in relationship to the belief triad. Thus the worship of Vishnu
(ritual related to a mythic representation of the transcendent) expresses _bhatki_ or devotion (a feeling of love and
awe) typically within the context of Indian society, so
that devotion reinforces social solidarity, and ties into
various perceptions of the individual's ethical obliga-
tions. Or to put matters another way: the belief triad
supplies the phenomenological objects for the intentionality of the practical triad.

This six-dimensional analysis of religion applies with
modification to the more "existential" ideological systems,
such as Maoism. Naturally certain dimensions are, for
certain religious or other movements, less important than
others (Quakers stress the ethical and experiential
dimensions rather than the ritual and doctrinal, though

the latter are not utterly absent; conversely, some religious
traditions such as Orthodoxy, are much more ceremonious).

Empathy and Freedom

One may now restate the criteria for a balanced
program of religious studies. It is one which is plural,
pays some attention to the cultural context of the student,
relates explicit religion to implicit or "existential"
issues, and in its treatment of religion and religions
makes use of something like a six-dimensional analysis,
this serving as a checklist to ensure a rounded view of
religions. Thus even the "explicit" side of religious
studies deals not just with external facts but the inner
feelings and values which animate belief.

For one of the recurring puzzles about pluralistic
education, and not merely in the field of religion, is
how it is that we manage to convey various, sometimes
conflicting, viewpoints and feeling-stances with empathy.
For it is important for a person contemplating Islam to
have at least some inkling of what it feels like to be a
Muslim: and he must have this inkling even if consciously
he rejects Muslim ideas. This is often a hard task, but
its necessity is shown by the terrible lessons which come
from not understanding other people's points of view.
(Incidentally, this is where media such as literature and
television are important: consider the insights into
another world provided for the Westerner by such novels as
Narayan's The Guide or Forster's A Passage to India, or
the educative impact of such series as The Long Search.)
So we need to add: explicit religion too must be exis-
tential--it must be taught with empathy.

These criteria of a balanced program say nothing
about the questions of ultimate, or even of intermediate,
truth. While it is the province of the religious organization, such as the church, to promote evangelization and
so catechetical schooling, it of course does not follow that
issues concerning the truth of the content of religion are
or ought to be excluded from the educational operation.

This is, however, where we come to the problem of how we
deal with the question of the ideology of freedom itself.

For it is inevitable that where religious education
is primarily aimed at presenting a plural understanding of
the great systems and at enhancing existential sensitivity
there can be no overall imposition of conformity in attitude or in practice (beyond the limits necessarily imposed
by education itself and the requirements of social existence). This presupposes an ideology, which can be
expressed roughly as follows:

Our society is an open one in which so far as possible
men are free to have diverse opinions. Such openness is
important for the pursuit of science and learning and so in
general the discovery of truth. Indeed truth often emerges
through the elimination of what is false, and for this
reason people should be allowed, indeed encouraged, to
take up critical attitudes. It is true that they may come
to the conclusion that in some matters, for instance in
religion, it is necessary to put oneself or one's group
under authority--of guru, Bible, or Church: but even so
this acceptance of authority is in our society something
freely arrived at. A total freedom willingly limited
differs from a limited freedom unwillingly accepted. Our
society therefore is one in which absolute authority is in
some degree limited. Since conduct is also a matter of
debate, for what is right and wrong in part depends upon a
worldview, and we are committed to a sort of pluralism of
worldviews in principle, since any worldview can ultimately
be subject to criticism--acceptance or rejection--, it
follows that our society is one in which men are entitled
to differences in conduct. This holds, provided however
that they can live together without causing one another
grievous harm: if a man wishes to pray five times daily
to Allah, that is his concern; and if liberty is restricted
because a kind of conduct is condemned as grievously
harmful, that too can be a matter of debate.

This does not mean that our society is relativistic.
It only means that it is pluralistic and that it recognizes

that on serious matters serious persons seriously differ.
We therefore encourage in our young an attitude of empathy,
so that they can see that other man have meaningful yet
different creeds and mores; while at the same time we
encourage them seriously to weigh the truth and value of
what they encounter, whether in religion, economics,
technology, science, or whatever. They should be open
without being superficial, show empathy without sacrific-
ing their own standards, be critical without carping,
desire truth without hounding heresy, and should understand
the implications of freedom.

The merit of this ideology lies partly in its respect
for the dignity of the individual and partly in its con-
gruence with scientific and other truth-seeking methodology.
It however may have the disadvantage of failing to realize
that not all societies are yet in a position to adopt such
an outlook. A degree of social commitment and conformism
may be necessary at certain stages. Only strong revolutionary impulses could reshape China in the disastrous
aftermath of Western intervention and the collapse of the
old imperial order. Maoism thus was needed in China. In
many countries abject poverty implies that priorities
point towards stomachs not heads. But ultimately conformism
is not a necessity, and it is to this stage of human
evolution that the ideology speaks.

It follows that our ideology, though higher-order,
because it is about the ways of arriving at conclusions
rather than the conclusions themselves, is nevertheless in
conflict with certain conformist ideologies, such as Islamic
theocracy and most Marxist socialism. It is even in conflict with Christian establishmentarianism, mild though
this is in its Western manifestations. But it is thus in
conflict primarily because it looks to truth from an educational point of view. This is where the very conception
of religious education (as distinguished from instruction)
has a plural flavor.

It is open to folk (Marxists, say) to argue that a
different model is to be applied. But their revolution is

a revolution in education and in appreciation of the truth.
It may be that sometimes social change, or defence of one's
people, loom larger than research, creativity, and education. But they can only do so, I think, temporarily. Thus
the criteria which I have mentioned in regard to the
framing of a religion curriculum have a lasting relevance.

To put things a little differently: in a numinous
universe and on a plural planet, who can fail to feel the
beginning of a new age of creativity in religion?

NOTES

[1] "Schools Council Working Paper 36," Religious Education in Secondary Schools (London: Evans Methuen, 1971)
and Discovering an Approach (London: Macmillan, 1977).
Though both these publications were written by teams, they
substantially express the thinking and work of Donald
Horder and Julian Frost, respectively.

[2] Ronald Goldman, Religious Thinking from Childhood to
Adolescence (London: Routledge and Kegan Paul, 1964).

[3] The Phenomenon of Religion (Second Edition, Oxford,
England: Mowbray and Company, 1978).

[4] Chapter 1 of The Religious Experience of Mankind
(New York: Scribners, 1976).

CHAPTER EIGHT

CURRICULUM DESIGN IN
PUBLIC EDUCATION RELIGION STUDIES

William E. Collie

This chapter addresses the educational questions
which the teacher should consider when he or she begins to
design a unit or a course on religion studies for public
education. Since this remains a highly controversial
subject area in many parts of the United States, it is
imperative for such teachers to follow their profession's
highest standards when they design and teach such units
and courses.

Those involved in public education religion studies,
whether approaching religion studies from within as a
teacher educator, public school teacher, or curriculum
developer or from related areas such as the academic study
of religion in higher education, must understand the educational terminology in order to work effectively within
the educational system and to be able to communicate with
others in the system. While the specialized language of
education often is regarded as jargon by the outsider, to
the extent that educators share common understanding of
this terminology it becomes a facilitative communications
vehicle.

In this chapter the term "curriculum" is used to refer
to the end result of the instructional process, that is,
the goals of instruction. "Instruction" refers to the
methods and techniques, activities, and content selected
to achieve the goals of instruction. "Curriculum design"
designates the integrative process of concurrently examining curriculum and instructional needs with the ultimate

William E. Collie, Ed.D., is Associate Professor of Education and Codirector, Public Education Religion Studies
Center, Wright State University.

aim of producing an instructional entity which has internal
consistency and interrelatedness among its component parts.
Curriculum design in this context, then, means examining
the various elements of curriculum and instruction to
clarify their particular function within the overall
design or plan and to determine their impact on the other
components.

Within the field of curriculum development in education, there has been increasing emphasis and general
consensus that curriculum design should be regarded as a
wholistic process, since the components have such a complex,
interactive relationship. Thus, for example, one cannot
select the content or subject matter of instruction.
Likewise, curriculum materials used for instruction may be
appropriate for one instructional setting but not for
another due to any number of contributing factors, such as
the ability levels of the students, the amount of prior
knowledge needed for the study, or the level of understanding being attempted in the particular segment of instruction.

The ultimate outcome of viewing curricular and instructional design in such an interrelated, systematic fashion
should produce benefits for all concerned in the actual
instructional implementation phase. For the teacher,
clearly knowing what he/she is about allows for more
appropriate instructional decision-making both in the
initial design of instruction and in the subsequent revision of instruction.[1] The student benefits from systematic
planning if the goals of instruction are clear, the content
is appropriate, the instructional activities actually
facilitate learning, and the methods of evaluation
actually reflect the intent and actual results of instruction. A full- articulated plan for instruction also allows
the administrator/supervisor to more accurately determine
if appropriate instruction indeed is taking place. Likewise, clearly articulated curricular and instructional
plans in writing enable school officials to better communicate their programs to parents and other community
members concerned about both what and how the school
teaches their children.

There are several ways in which the curriculum can be organized and articulated for instructional purposes. A course of study usually is a description of the content and, sometimes, the objectives to be covered for a given subject at a given grade level. A resource unit normally is a collection of possible instructional activities and resources from which a teacher can plan a segment of instruction for longer than one class period. A teaching unit generally is a particular plan of instruction developed by one or more teachers for a period of instruction in excess of one classroom period. The most specific plan is the lesson plan which provides a fairly detailed instructional plan for a single classroom period.[2]

In order to provide concrete examples of how the different components of instructional decision-making may be described, this chapter will utilize material from the Teacher's Guide for Level 1 by Joan G. Dye prepared for the Learning About Religions/Social Studies program developed by the Religion-Social Studies Curriculum Project at Florida State University.[3] The LAR/SS material is used for a variety of reasons. It is commercially available and thus potentially widely used. It is written for religion studies at the elementary grades, a level for which it is difficult to prepare appropriate materials. Much that is done at this level is concerned with an excessive emphasis on memorization and recall of factual data about religions. However, LAR/SS makes a commendable attempt to encourage students to operate at higher levels of thinking but in a manner and with a sophistication that is in keeping with their experiential and conceptual development. Finally, because the LAR/SS program does clearly delineate the varied components of the instructional program, it exemplifies how such a detailed program of studies provides to the person(s) making curricular and instructional decisions within a given instructional setting sufficient information about the program to make intelligent, informed conclusions about the materials' appropriateness.

In planning curriculum and instruction for public
education religion studies, one should clearly articulate
how the following components interrelate: the introductory
rationale for the study; the content, including the main
concepts and generalizations to be studied as well as the
specific subject matter to be examined; a clear statement
of goals and objectives expected for students to achieve
as a result of the study; a description of the varied
instructional activities to be used to facilitate learning;
a plan for evaluation which demonstrates that the intended
learning has taken place; and finally, a list of instructional resources to be utilized. Each of these areas is
examined in further detail using Level 1 of LAR/SS as the
examplary materials. However, the components considered
similarly might be part of other kinds of instructional
plans such as teaching units or lesson plans.

Rationale

Any program of study, whether a unit or a course,
should be defined within the overall context of the curriculum of which it is a part. For example, why should
students study "World Religions" as a part of the
secondary social studies program? What unique contribution
does this unit make to the objectives of the program? How
does the particular study fit into the sequencing of instruction? When in the course or sequence of courses will
the study take place? What would students have studied
before this unit? Is there any necessary prerequisite
knowledge that students must have before studying the
unit? To what age, grade level, subject and ability level
is the unit aimed? How long will it take to complete the
unit? This rationale is of extreme importance since it
justifies to the reader the appropriateness of including
the study in the curriculum.[4]

The Learning About Religion/Social Studies material,
for example, provides an overall programatic rationale
that justifies the appropriateness of teaching about
religions in elementary social studies, stressing the

unique contributions religion studies makes to the social
studies program. At the same time the rationale supports a
primary goal of elementary social studies: "educating
children to become thinking, feeling citizens whose
judgments will be based on factual analysis and sound
reasoning, tempered with empathy and compassion."[5] In
addition each unit within a particular level has a section
entitled "Conceptual Framework" which not only provides a
rationale for the given unit but also provides a more
focused rationale for the particular unit, such as Unit
One built around the concepts of "Story and Way."[6]

Content

As curriculum is developed for public education
religion studies, it is important to look beyond the
specific content being taught in a given unit of instruction to identify what larger ideas or generalizations
about religion such a study contributes. In the LAR/SS
program, for example, twelve generalizations (which are
referred to as "Main Ideas") are identified and serve as
the organizing intellectual underpinning of the curriculum.
Such main ideas are identified as "The religious dimension
is both a personal and a community experience." And
"[R]eligious experiences and expressions change over time."[7]
Related to these generalizations are general concepts such
as "story or world view," religious concepts such as
"sacred literature" and "traditions," and such social
studies concepts as "acculturation" and "group."[8]

Additionally, it is helpful to include a specific
subject matter outline which identifies the particular
content to be used as the vehicle for teaching the
generalizations and concepts. The distinction between
concepts and generalizations and the actual subject matter
utilized for instructional purposes is significant, because
it is quite possible that the teacher could select any of a
variety of specific subject matter examples to teach the
same idea. For instance, in the LAR/SS Level 1 Unit Two on
"Sacred Space," Lesson 7, emphasizing that "a home is a

place for a family's special way," uses the example of a
Japanese home.[9] Later lessons have the students consider
their own homes as well as the homes of an Atoni family in
Indonesian Timor.

The selection of subject matter to illustrate a concept is a conscious decision which is made for a variety
of reasons. The choice may be determined by the teacher's
own value judgment about the worth of the particular subject matter. Selection of subject matter often is based
on the pragmatic factor of adequacy of resources available
on a given topic. Thus the teacher might develop the same
topic, if he or she were designing the instruction without
the LAR/SS resources, choosing a Spanish home for an
example simply because he/she had been there for a summer
and therefore had the personal experience, knowledge, and
resources to make the study worthwhile. Both a sense of
teacher competency and adequate available resources are
appropriate considerations in selecting specific subject
matter for instructional purposes.

Since the LAR/SS Teacher Manual format more
appropriately parallels a teaching unit rather than a
resource unit, it describes the content of instruction in
the particular unit and lesson plans. In a short,
simplified narrative form the content of the overall
program is outlined for each of the three levels that have
thus far been produced along with a brief indication of
the content for levels 4-6. Lack of a specific content
outline forces the teacher to have to read carefully
through the LAR/SS materials to see how the ideas are
developed.

A chart of concepts and organizing ideas keyed to the
topic of each lesson is helpful but still does not provide
adequate information. For example, the chart indicates
that in Unit Three on "Sacred Times" there are five
lessons with the titles "Birthday," "Perahera," "Passover,"
"Tradition," and "Diversity of Traditions." Though the
chart indicates that Lesson 13 on Passover focuses on the
concepts of story and celebration and on the organizing

idea that "[e]ach celebration has a story," the prospective
teacher still does not know what information about Passover
is taught specifically.[10] Even after turning to the lesson
outline, the content or the "what" of instruction is known
only by reading through the entire lesson and by examining
the suggested instructional resources. A content outline
would have made understanding the instructional program a
much simpler process.

Goals and Objectives

It is so easy to become committed to specific bodies
of content that one can lose sight of what it is one is
ultimately after. Pursuing the question of "what should
students know" is a selective one, because there are so
many things in our complex, sophisticated world worth
knowing. Certainly using that question alone as the
criterion for establishing curriculum leads only to frus-
tration: we simply cannot squeeze all the worthwhile
things in a mere twelve or thirteen years of elementary
and secondary education! And certainly those of us eager
to increase the attention given to religion studies have
vast content areas to add to the already overcrowded
curriculum.

Fred Wilhelms, using systems analysis terms, suggests
that too often input is confused with output. That is,
one views informational content, what is "put across," as
input, and what the student learns and retains as the output. In fact, much of the content detail that is "put in"
is soon forgotten and thus the output is nil. The actual
effect, then, is that the teacher is goal-less. Wilhelms
suggests the curriculum emphasis needs to be put back
where it belongs, that is, on the purposes to be achieved,
with subject matter selection serving an ancillary role.[11]

Identifying the goals for a particular unit of
instruction are more understandable when seen within the
broader context of the generalized goals for public
education religion studies. For example, five general
goals for public education religion studies are identified

by Nicholas Piediscalzi and William Collie in Teaching
About Religion in Public Schools.

   ...to develop a broad and discerning understanding of:

   1. the religious dimension of human existence
       and the many and diverse ways in which it is
       embodied and expressed in historical groups
       and individual lives;

   2. the way in which religions function in history
       and culture, with special emphasis on how re-
       ligions influence institutions and in turn are
       influenced by them;

   3. the meaning and significance of making a reli-
       gious commitment and living by it;

   4. the numerous different ways in which religion
       may be studied;

   5. the difference between practicing and studying
       about religion.[12]

   The LAR/SS materials might be examined in relation to
these goals. Utilizing these goals or some set of criteria
provides the teacher with guidelines for instructional
decision-making. While there may be a wealth of things
that possibly could be taught about, if the content
selection is made in terms of some set of purposes the
specific instruction is supposed to serve, the range of
appropriate content is somewhat narrowed. Thus one can
examine a particular segment of instruction, in this
exemplary case the LAR/SS program objective statements, to
see if they are consistent with general goals for public
education religion studies. Because such statements often
are broad statements and not behaviorally stated, one
actually must look at specific statements of student
behavioral objectives to see if the stated intent is
actually fulfilled and, if so, at what level of sophistication.

   While the LAR/SS general program objective includes
developing the main idea that "the religious dimension
has to do with the world view and life style," one has to
look at the behavioral objectives for particular lessons

to ascertain actually the level of understanding expected
of the student.[13] What one finds is that lessons throughout the three units of Level 1 contribute to this understanding. For example, the first lesson in Unit One on
"Story" contributes to the development of this idea at a
very simple level appropriate to first graders by expect-
ing the student to be "able to tell something about
his/her own story verbally or in picture form."[14] Other
lessons in Level 1 and the subsequent levels are designed
to broaden the students' understanding of this idea.
When the broad goals are examined in detail along with the
specific objectives and the learning activities of
particular lessons, the actual approach implemented in
the LAR/SS program appears to be consistent with the
public education religion studies goals identified in
Teaching About Religion in Public Schools, particularly
goals one and two.

Thus, while it may be useful to state broad goals for
a unit of study, in order to judge the appropriateness of
the other components of instructional design and for overall clarity of intent, it is helpful also to include
particular performance objectives one ultimately has for
students. Given the potential for misunderstanding when
dealing with religion, it is imperative that the teacher
fully articulate the behavioral expectations of students.
This information should be shared with students and should
be available in written form for any concerned person to
examine.

Selecting appropriate educational objectives,
particularly when stated in behavioral terms, is not an
easy task. Those involved in the curriculum design process
should consider what intellectual or *cognitive* behaviors
the students will be expected to be able to exhibit as a
result of a given unit of instruction. Also what *affective*
behaviors, what values, what feelings, what attitudes are
the students to exhibit as a result of the study? Are
there particular *psychomotor* objectives, physical/motor
behaviors, expected? Usually units on religion studies

emphasize cognitive and affective concerns. Taxonomic
analyses of these domains can serve as useful tools in the
design of objectives at differing levels of the cognitive
and affective domains.[15] Additionally there may be
specific skill objectives which might be distinguishable
from the areas dealt with in the three domains.

The discussion of goals has shown how the LAR/SS
material in Level 1 Unit One develops the concept of story
as a part of building understanding of the idea that the
religious dimension has to do with world view and life-
style. The objective from Lesson One, "the child will be
able to tell something about his/her own story verbally or
in picture form," is concerned with the cognitive domain,
since the ability to draw on what is taught in the lesson
and to apply it to one's own situation is essentially an
intellectual task.[16]

While LAR/SS identifies attitudes to be developed for
the overall program and particular lessons, it does not
specifically identify behavioral objectives for those
attitudes. This is, no doubt, in part due to the difficulty in defining appropriate measures for the affective
domain, but it can be done. For example, in the same
lesson one attitude stressed is "[f]eeling free to make
appropriate references to and statements about one's own
feelings, values, world view, life-style, and religious
and/or secular tradition."[17] Building on the cognitive
objective stated previously, an affective objective could
be stated as "the child is willing to tell something about
his/her own story verbally or in picture form." Other
attitudinal concerns may be shown in patterns of behavior
which can only be observed over a time span greater than
the particular unit of instruction entails. It is to the
instructor's benefit, despite the difficulties, to try to
delineate what his/her affective expectations of students
are since the topic of religion is so amendable to affective impact. Failure to state affective goals or objectives may only be taken to mean that they are present in
the program but hidden or unexpressed because they are of
questionable validity.

Skills in the LAR/SS program are listed along with the general objectives of the program and tend to be a mixed bag. Nine skills are identified. Number 2 "[p]articipating in a real experience through sense experience, simulation, field trip" is hard to classify. It sounds more like an experiential objective than a specific skill to be developed. Some "skills" such as "attaining concepts" and "applying generalizations and interpretations to make judgments" could be classified as cognitive operations, while such "skills" as "internalizing the learning" and "working effectively with others" might be regarded as affective objectives. The skill, "[d]eveloping and testing concepts, generalizations, and interpretations by stating and checking hypotheses ..." could be viewed as a decision-making skill.[18]

Regardless of whether or not one would agree with the classification of the categories as skills, the fact is that the LAR/SS developers have so designated them. In each lesson the skills being stressed are indicated alongside the description of particular instructional activities. Thus, in Unit One, Lesson 1 on "Story" the follow-up to showing a filmstrip suggests that the teacher show the filmstrip again without sound and ask the children to tell what is happening and encourage them to tell about similar events in their lives. The margin note indicates the skill emphasis is on analyzing information.[19] While one might quibble with terminology, or even seriously argue about the actual skill being stressed, the specificity of the instructional design clarifies the intent so that at least it is discussible. Sadly, most instructional plans are debatable for the opposite reason, that is, that they are so vague no one knows what they mean.

Possible Activities

Description of a variety of possible learning activities the teacher might provide inside or outside the classroom that would enable the students to attain the goals and objectives of the unit helps clarify the means

the teacher will use to achieve the instructional ends.
The listing of activities as "possible" indicates that
the means to the desired ends may follow multiple paths
and the activities listed are only some among many ways
the actual instruction could take place. Such a delinea-
tion of activities provides the prospective teacher with
concrete suggestions on how to implement instruction while
retaining the prerogative of the teacher in a given setting to actually make the final instructional decisions.
For the concerned citizen wondering what students
actually will be doing as they study about religion, the
written instructional plan provides exemplary activities.
Especially for the layman unaccustomed to the educational
phrasing of goals and objectives, what the students
actually will be doing may, indeed, be his/her real
concern.

As the curriculum designer plans instructional
activities, the sequencing of activities may be seen as
falling roughly into three phases. What possible
initiatory activities might be used to begin the
unit? What kinds of pre-assessment might be conducted
to determine what students already know as they approach
the study? What kinds of activities might be used early
in the study to establish interest and to clarify the
purposes of the study? In the second phase, once the
students have become involved, what developmental activities can be utilized which will enable the students to
learn? Finally, what windup or culminating activities
might the students do which would bring the bits and
pieces they have studied into a meaningful whole? Are
these activities which can at the same time encourage
students to continue study on the basis of their own
interests?

In the LAR/SS teacher's manual, a section entitled
"Using The Teacher's Guide" describes the format for each
lesson. Even at this specific level of particular lesson
plans, a section labelled "Introduction" suggests activities the teacher can use to focus student interest on the

area of inquiry. The section on Development is concerned
with the major portion of the lesson and includes activities which may even extend over a period of days if the
teacher wishes to expand the lesson. This section also
includes culminating activities as well. In addition
there are other suggested extending experiences which are
used for enrichment and individualization.   This kind of
detail, even though it retains instructional flexibility,
is vital if the instructional plan is expected to provide
real assistance for the teacher. Provision of only
statements of goals and indication of content to be
studied are insufficient to guide instruction and thus are
no guarantee that the instructional program in any way
will be carried out in an appropriate manner. Public
education religion studies curriculum designers should
beware of such inadequate planning if they expect their
programs to be justifiable or defensible.

Evaluation

In terms of actual impact, the way the instructional
program is designed to evaluate learning reveals the
educational "bottom line" of what appears to be significant in the unit of instruction. Particularly for the
students, the evaluation is what the instruction is all
about. They usually could care less about the teacher's
grandiose goal statements. They interpret the ultimate
significance of the program based on the kinds of information wanted and the way they are required to perform
when being evaluated. Correct or not, this programatic
response comes from years of experience in which evaluation
is used for establishing grades. Thus for the students'
sake, the means of evaluation should closely correlate with
the statement of goals and objectives or else the intent of
instruction will be lost. How many of us in our own
student days have not had the experience similar to the
following situation: The teacher indicates that the
purpose of the study is to "understand" the first Thanks-
giving, but when test time comes the examination is a

matching exercise that is a "who was there" type approach.
Obviously the level of understanding required is not very
sophisticated. After several experiences of this type,
the students learn what the instruction is really all about!

A more educationally oriented rationale for designing
evaluation measures which clearly reflect the stated
objectives is simply that if the evaluation does not
accurately measure the intent of instruction, the instructor has no way to adequately judge whether the intended
learning actually has taken place. Without this kind of
feedback, the instructor also cannot evaluate the adequacy
or the appropriateness of the instruction that has been
conducted. Without this kind of data on pupil learning,
the instructor has no clearcut guidelines on which to
revise or adapt instruction.

A helpful instructional plan, then, needs to detail
the procedures to be used to determine if the objectives
have been met. If an essay exam is to be used, sample
questions should demonstrate that the objectives are to be
evaluated appropriately. Sometimes, the activities which
are conducted within the unit of study also serve as
evaluation tools. All evaluation certainly does not have
to be in the form of a paper-and-pencil test given at the
conclusion of instruction.

The LAR/SS program includes a section on evaluation
for each of the lessons. The goal of consistency between
objectives and evaluation is illustrated in Unit Two of
Level 1 concerning the concept of "Sacred Space," Lesson 7
on "Homes." The lesson deals with the idea that a home is
a place for a family's special way. The stated objective
for the lesson is that "through participation in role play,
the child will be able to demonstrate comprehension of the
use and meaning of space in a Japanese home." Activities
include discussion and use of an activity book that provides the necessary information to do the role play
activity which serves as the evaluative measure. The
lesson plan in the manual outlines teacher directions to
give for the role play as well as follow-up discussion

questions leading to the generalization that both the
students' families and Japanese families live in their
homes in their own unique family ways.[20] Based on the
information provided in the LAR/SS manual, the teacher
thus knows how to determine if the instructional objectives have been achieved.

Instructional Resources

The final aspect of curricular and instructional
design is the listing of instructional resources which
help the teacher actually implement instruction. Particularly when curriculum design is occurring at the local
level for specific schools, it is important that resource
listing be realistic. What practical good does it do for
a teacher to have a list of twenty-five films on a topic
if the films are not available in the school district and
are obtainable only by paying high rental fees the school
cannot afford? For more widely used curriculum designs,
such as commercially prepared materials like the LAR/SS
program, listing of appropriate resources may serve as a
buying guide for local school districts if the purchasing
source is indicated.

The listing of resources can be as inclusive as the
curriculum designer can provide. There may be reference
works for teachers and listings of textual or reference
resources for students. Other resources for the unit of
instruction might fall into a variety of categories such
as films, filmstrips, transparencies, tapes, pamphlets,
charts, maps, resource people, and community agencies. In
each case detailed bibliographic data is most helpful.

The LAR/SS program provides the kind of detailed
information we have suggested. In the teacher's manual
for each level, the lesson plans include a section on
resources. The program itself includes a kit of material
for each level that includes student activity books,
student readers, filmstrips, audio cassettes, and a
teacher's manual. Some kits also contain additional
activities material. In the teacher's manuals the lesson

plans list specific resources. For example, in the Unit
Two, Lesson 7 on "Homes," the Resources section includes
the text of a poem and a list of songs to use including
the book reference and publisher's address. Similar data
is provided for the other resources listed plus an
annotated description of the subject of the material. The
resources listed includes books to use with students, one
film, two filmstrips, and a record.[21]

Materials selection for religion studies in the public
schools is certainly an area for sensitive, thoughtful
consideration. This is particularly true since most of
the available commercial materials dealing with religion
were designed as religious education materials for use
with a particular faith community or from a faith perspective. While such materials may be developmentally sound
for use with children, they are not educationally sound
for use in the public school context. Utilization of
criteria for materials selection, such as the Public
Education Religion Studies Center's "Criteria for Evaluating Curricular Materials," may help the curriculum
designer consider aspects about the materials' appropriateness that otherwise can easily be overlooked in the rush
to find usable instructional resources.[22] In addition,
the ability to report that materials selection has taken
place only after thoughtful review based upon agreed upon
criteria indicates that responsible educational procedures
have been utilized by the curriculum developer as a part
of the total curriculum design process.[23]

Summary

One of the indications of teacher competency for
dealing with religion studies in the public school setting
is that teachers demonstrate their pedagogical soundness
by using the same procedures for planning, developing, and
evaluating curricula as are employed in designing other
academic programs. Since the aspects of curricular and
instructional design outlined in this chapter are generally
accepted within the educational community, curriculum

designers for public education religion studies must
address the issue of how their programs of study deal with
each of these areas. The PERSC "Guidelines for Teacher
Competency" suggest that the design issue is one of five
significant foci to consider in determining pedagogical
competency. Additional considerations have to do with
utilization of appropriate teaching methods, selection of
teaching materials which includes appropriate methodological techniques for instruction, design of instruction
which reflects knowledge of the conceptual developmental
levels of the students being instructed, and the knowledge
and ability to use a wide variety of print and non-print
media. Competency also includes curricular and instructional implementation which reflects the non-confessional,
pluralistic approach required by the legal context in which
public education religion studies may take place.[24]

   Curriculum design for public education religion
studies, then, is no simple task. It is made even more
complex by the fact that what constitutes appropriate
public education religion studies at the elementary and
secondary levels is not clearly understood by the general
public, educational administrators, or teachers. Stung
by innumerable instances of having religious practice
conducted in the schools under the guise of appropriate
academic instruction, both the public and the educational
community are wary of moving into this potentially explosive area. It is incumbent, therefore, upon those desiring
to foster the implementation of appropriate public education religion studies to use the strictest standards of
educational probity in the design of curriculum and
instruction or, in the case of the adoption of commercially prepared instructional programs, to utilize those
same standards in selecting such materials.

NOTES

[1] Systematic Instructional Decision-Making (Los Angeles: Vimcet Associates, 1967). This is one of series of film-strips which is widely used in teaching curricular and instructional design and which advocates the wholistic process approach.

[2] Teaching Units and Lesson Plans (Los Angeles: Vimcet Associates, 1969).

[3] Joan G. Dye, Teacher's Guide for Level 1; Learning About Religions/Social Studies (Niles, Illinois: Argus Communication, 1976).

[4] Hollis L. Caswell, "Editorial: The Realities of Curriculum Change," Educational Leadership, 36 (October, 1978) 29. Caswell argues that a changing attitude among curricular workers to no longer equate change with progress may mean less willingness to accept new programs without rigorous examination. He suggests the changing attitude bodes well for curriculum change in the future.

[5] Dye, Teacher's Guide, 6.

[6] Ibid., 23-25.

[7] Ibid., 7-9.

[8] Ibid., 9.

[9] Ibid., 92-96.

[10] Ibid., 18-19.

[11] Fred T. Wilhelms, "Priorities in Change Efforts," Curriculum: Quest for Relevance, ed. by William Van Til (Boston: Houghton Mifflin, 1974) 303.

[12] Nicholas Piediscalzi and William Collie, eds., Teaching About Religion in Public Schools (Niles, Illinois: Argus Communications, 1977) 16.

[13] Dye, Teacher's Guide, 7-8.

[14] Ibid., 27.

[15] Selecting Appropriate Instructional Objectives (Los Angeles: Vimcet Associates, 1967).

[16] Dye, Teacher's Guide, 27.

[17] Ibid.

[18] Ibid., 9-10.

[19] Ibid., 23.

[20] Ibid., 92-94.

[21] Ibid.

[22] "Criteria for Evaluating Curricular Materials,"
Religion Studies in the Curriculum: Retrospect and
Prospect, 1963-1983, ed. by Peter Bracher, et. al. (Dayton,
Ohio: Public Education Religion Studies Center, 1974)
86-88.

[23] P. Kenneth Komolski, "The Realities of Choosing and
Using Instructional Materials," Educational Leadership 36
(October, 1978) 41-50. Komolski discusses the impact of
curriculum materials on actual instruction.

[24] "Guidelines for Teacher Competency," Religion
Studies in the Curriculum: Retrospect and Prospect, 1963-
1983, ed. by Peter Bracher, et. al. (Dayton, Ohio: Public
Education Religion Studies Center, 1974) 91-93.

SECTION II

IMPLEMENTATION

This more pragmatically oriented section analyzes
various approaches and strategies used in establishing
public education religion studies programs. The value,
limitations, and application of survey research results in
this process is illustrated by Henry Hoeks, Michael McIntosh, John Leahy, and William Collie.

The issue of teacher certification in the field is
evaluated by Frank Steeves and Joseph Forcinelli in terms
of the present situation and existing certification
approaches. An analysis by Paul Will of specific certification paradigms in Michigan addresses theoretical and
practical questions regarding the actual curricular composition of such teacher education programs.

The last chapter examines a variety of strategies that
have been used to implement public education religion
studies. Paul Will reviews both public awareness and
teacher education program possibilities. Specific examples
of differing statewide tactics provide readers with a
variety of usable approaches.

Chapter Nine

RELIGION STUDIES IN MICHIGAN SECONDARY SCHOOLS:
PREVALENCE, PRACTICES, AND PROPENSITIES

Henry J. Hoeks and Michael H. McIntosh

The Council on the Study of Religion in Michigan
Schools (CSRMS), composed of representatives from private
colleges and state universities interested in or committed
to teacher education in public education religion studies,
periodically surveys the state's public secondary schools
to obtain statistical information on this area of the
curriculum. Such a survey was commissioned by CSRMS in
1977-78. This chapter summarizes the data received from
respondents and presents some conclusions drawn from the
data.

The objectives of the survey were twofold: (1) to
determine the actual number of courses and units on reli-
gion(s) taught in the state's public secondary schools
(grades 7-12), and (2) to discern some trends, as perceived by departmental chairpersons and principals,
regarding curricular offerings in religion studies as well
as the apparent interest, or lack thereof, among teachers,
students, and their communities with respect to religion
studies.

Procedure

An explanatory cover letter and a two-page questionnaire were devised and subjected to limited field-testing.
Then a cover letter and questionnaire accompanied by a
self-addressed but not postpaid return envelope were bulk-
mailed in November, 1977. The first mailing was addressed
to both the social studies and English department chairpersons in each of 1,270 secondary schools in Michigan.

Henry J. Hoeks, Ed.D., is Professor of Religion and Education, Calvin College, and Michael H. McIntosh, A.B., is a
graduate of Calvin College.

Council members thought that chairpersons would have
greater interest than principals in religion studies and
thus higher motivation to return the questionnaires. The
names and addresses of the schools were obtained from the
1975-76 Michigan Education Directory.

The first mailing, therefore, was directed to 2,540
potential respondents, and 13.5% (341) of the chairpersons
responded. 218 of these, almost two-thirds, were from
departmental chairpersons in senior high schools (grades
10-12) while 121, somewhat over one-third, were from
junior high schools (grades 7-9). There were returns from
both the social studies and English department chairpersons
of 23 senior high schools and 11 junior high schools.
Usually, however, one chairperson per school responded.
These returns represented 307 of 1,270 secondary schools.

A follow-up mailing had been planned for all those
chairpersons who neglected to respond within a month but
the cost became prohibitive. Instead, increased coverage
was achieved at a lower cost by means of a single mailing
to principals of the schools from which a reply had not
been received by January 1, 1978. This second bulk-
mailing, which contained a revised cover letter, a questionnaire, and a self-addressed but non-stamped envelope
was sent to principals of 965 schools. From this mailing,
245 additional replies were received for a follow-up
return of 25.3%. 136 (55.5%) of the replies were from
senior high school principals; 109 (45.5%) were from
junior high school principals.

In total, then, data was received from 552 schools,
or 43.4% of all Michigan secondary schools. Of this total,
331 (60%) were reports from senior high schools and 221
(40%) from junior high schools. This rate of return provides a sufficiently representative sample to warrant the
following analysis of the responses and the accompanying
conclusions.

Analysis of the Data

In view of the overall response, it is probably
correct to surmise that the incidence of religion studies
in Michigan secondary schools is not significantly higher
than the figures which will be cited below, even though
the rate of return is less than fifty per cent. This
statement is based on the assumption that chairpersons of
departments which do offer units or courses in religion
studies are probably more likely to respond to such a
questionnaire because they have something positive to
report than chairpersons whose schools do not have offerings in religion studies.

The first question sought to determine the respondents' awareness of the Academic Study of Religions as a
certifiable teaching minor in the State of Michigan. Of
the 586 returns, only 194 persons indicated such awareness,
even after reading the rather rhetorical question; 133 were
senior high chairpersons or principals and 61 were junior
high chairpersons or principals. It is probably appropriate to assume that lack of awareness among those who did
not return the questionnaire is considerably greater than
among those who did respond. An obvious conclusion is
that there remains a widespread and pervasive lack of
awareness regarding the availability of religion studies
as a certifiable teaching area. If broader interest in
religion studies is positively correlated with increased
awareness of its certifiable status, then efforts in
promoting teacher and principal awareness of this field of
study in whatever ways are appropriate and effective must
be increased.

Clues to the prevalence of religion studies in
Michigan public secondary schools were gained from the
replies to the question: "What are your departmental
offerings regarding studies about religions?" Of the 552
schools represented in the responses, 267 taught some type
of unit (1-8 weeks) and/or course (9-18 weeks) and 200 of
these were senior high schools. Regarding the curricular

offerings reported in junior high schools, the preponder-
ance were units (55); there were few courses. While
replies were received from less than one-half of the
schools, we would venture to say that no more than 25% of
all public secondary schools in Michigan have curricular
offerings in religion studies.

A wide variety of departmental or subject matter
areas embracing religion studies were found in the 267
junior and senior high schools which did provide education
in religion studies (see Table 1). The totals exceed that
of the number of schools reporting curricular offerings,
since these schools often noted more than one unit or
course in religion studies as defined by the questionnaire.

TABLE 1

Scope of Religion Studies Reported in 1977-78

Departmental Areas	Only Units S.Hi.	Only Units J.Hi.	Only Courses S.Hi.	Only Courses J.Hi.	Both Units and Courses S.Hi.	Both Units and Courses J.Hi.
History	38	12	20	4	8	0
Literature	18	15	61	5	17	0
Psychology	5	0	1	0	2	0
Sociology/Anthropology	14	4	5	1	4	0
Social Studies	14	33	31	6	13	0
Humanities	9	2	12	0	4	0
	98	66	130	16	48	0

The pattern of curricular offerings shown above is
similar to that reported in the 1975 CSRMS survey and in
other statewide and national surveys. Courses having to
do with religion(s) are typically taught under the rubrics
of literature (American, World, Biblical, Mythological)
and history (American and World). However, a surprising
number of units, judging from the individual responses,
are taught in the humanities and in sociology--especially
on the senior high level. There also continues to be a
tendency to include the academic study of the Bible or
world religions within standard courses, although an increasing number of schools now offer full courses in both
of these areas.

Some observations should be made regarding those returns which reported no unit or course offerings in religion studies. This category includes 131 of 331 (39.5%) of senior high schools and 152 of 221 (68.4%) of junior high schools. In all probability the actual percentages for the absence of religion studies of any kind are probably higher than these survey figures indicate, although there may be instances in which 1-8 week units on religion(s) are offered by teachers about which the department chairpersons or principals are unaware.

The most common reasons given by respondents for the absence of curricular offerings in religion studies in their schools were "lack of student interest" and "no one qualified to teach it." Other reasons were given by a small minority of respondents, such as "school board disapproval" and "community disapproval." A few respondents also mentioned financial restraints and the erroneously assumed illegality of teaching religion studies in public schools. Eleven junior high school respondents said either that offerings were simply not considered or that religion studies are the curricular concern of the senior high school.

It was apparent from the responses to the question regarding how many teachers in a department were involved in teaching about religion that in most schools which offer religion studies, generally one or two teachers per department are involved. Many senior high departments have two teachers. Of the 331 senior high schools teaching about religion(s), 107 reported one teacher involved in religion studies; 38 have two teachers; and 28 have three or more teachers assigned to this subject area. Hence, religion studies involve relatively few teachers throughout the state because this area of studies continues to be a minor part of the curriculum.

Six questions in the questionnaire were designed to ascertain present trends regarding religion studies in the schools. Table 2 summarizes the data regarding changes in curricular offerings and Table 3 addresses changing interests with respect to religion studies.

TABLE 2

Additions and Deletions of
Religion Studies Offerings

		Sr.High		Jr.High	
		Yes	No	Yes	No
Q.4	New Offering in Past Two Years	36	302	9	209
Q.5	Discontinued Offering in Past Two Years	45	?	5	?
Q.6	Proposed New Offering in 1978-79	17	323	6	209
Q.7	Proposed Dropping an Offering in 1978-79	12	288	4	183

The significance of the data in Table 2 is found in
the "yes" columns. Speaking positively, there are signs
of increased activity in some schools regarding recent or
proposed introduction of curricular offerings in religion
studies. Negatively, however, a significant number of
senior high school department chairpersons and principals
reported that curricular offerings in religion studies
were being dropped. The question marks in the "no"
columns under item 5 are due to an inadvertent typographi-
cal omission of the "no" option on the first questionnaire
mailed. Many gave a "no" answer in writing. It is our
judgment that the "yes" answers apparently were largely
unaffected by this omission.

The "yes" responses to questions 4 through 7 were
further studied with a view toward ascertaining whether
those who reported recent or proposed additions in religion studies were the same persons, and hence schools, who
reported recent or anticipated dropping of offerings or
vice versa. Such a correlation was found to be true in
merely ten cases. Most of those who indicated offerings
were or would be dropped also reported that they had not
recently introduced new units or courses. It appears,
therefore, that some "established" units or courses are
being dropped in secondary schools. Very few persons
whose departments introduced new offerings in religion
studies in the past two years anticipated the introduction
of more units or courses. Thus our survey seems to indicate that religion studies in the state is in a period of
slight overall decline.

The data concerning trends which respondents discerned
with respect to student interest, community interest, and
the impact of the "Back to Basics" emphasis with respect to
religion studies were mixed.

TABLE 3

Changing Interests and Impacts Regarding
Religion Studies

	Sr.H. Response			Jr.H. Response		
	Inc.	Dec.	Same	Inc.	Dec.	Same
Q.8 Student Interest	53	31	232	32	15	140
Q.9 Community Interest	21	20	256	22	12	158
Q.10 Impact of "Back to Basics"	2	36	244	0	15	155

Almost twice as many department chairpersons and
principals discerned an increase in student interest in
learning about religion(s) than those who perceived a de-
crease. The vast majority of respondents believed that
student interest is remaining about the same. Yet
several respondents who reported recent or anticipated
deletions in unit or course offerings cited decreasing
enrollments and/or declining student interest as the
reason for discontinuing some offerings.

The majority of respondents discerned little net
change in community interest with the exception of a minor
rising interest in junior high school offerings in religion studies. Thus, the slight increase in religion
studies may reflect the "temper of the times" in the
United States, especially the rise in prominence of the
evangelicals.

The early wave of the "Back to Basics" emphasis was
regarded by a significant number of respondents (51) as a
cause for decline in unit or course offerings, although
about 90% regarded this movement as having no current
impact upon religion studies offerings. However, if this
movement gains in impetus, one could expect that religion
studies ordinarily would not be regarded as "basic" in the
public school curriculum and probably would be regarded by
many as an expendable area of an already crowded
curriculum.

TABLE 4

Special Preparation in Religion Studies

	Sr.H. Yes	Response No	?	Jr.H. Yes	Response No	?
Q.11 Some Preparation in Religion Studies	74	203	62	31	131	52
Q.12 Interest in Regional Workshops	166	140	--	84	110	--
Q.13 Interest in CSRMS Newsletter	195	---	--	89	---	--

When asked whether their colleagues who are teaching
religion studies had received any special training in this
discipline, chairpersons and principals reported that about
one in four teachers participated in pre- or in-service
education in religion studies. The potential helpfulness
of regional workshops was affirmed by 250 respondents, an
encouraging figure for those who plan to offer workshops
and those who already do.

There also was a large number of persons who requested
that the CSRMS Newsletter be sent either to them or to
their departmental colleagues. On the basis of these two
final items, there appears to be at the present time a
significant interest in learning more about religion
studies on the part of departmental chairpersons and
principals. There also seems to be a readiness to explore
the possibility of introducing religion studies in the
schools. Many of the comments written on the questionnaires indicate that the survey itself may have contributed
to developing an increased openness to including religion
studies in Michigan schools as a vital part of the secondary curriculum, though some still disbelieve or doubt the
legality of religion studies in public schools.

Conclusion

The greater prevalence of religion studies curriculum
offerings, especially at the senior high school level is
heavily dependent on the interest of teachers and chairpersons. Their involvement is related directly to efforts
to disseminate information about certification

opportunities, availability of curricular materials, and instructional methods in religion studies. Therefore, a high priority should be given to making teachers and administrators aware of how the introduction of religion studies contributes to the development of a complete education and a well-rounded curriculum.

At the present time, there seems to be a relative balance in Michigan between the introduction of new courses and the discontinuation of certain curricular offerings in religion studies. What remains to be explored is whether there is a correlation between particular school districts where courses and units are being introduced and their proximity to teacher education institutions which recently have offered regional workshops in religion studies.

The survey indicates that vigorous efforts must be continued by statewide organizations, teacher education institutions, and other agencies concerned with public school religion studies. These are needed to offset the potential decline in curricular offerings produced by recent calls to return to "the basics" in combination with student, teacher, and community ignorance or apathy regarding the the basic importance of religion(s) in cultural and humanistic studies.

CHAPTER TEN

ILLINOIS RELIGION AND PUBLIC EDUCATION SURVEY:
BACKGROUND AND ANALYSIS

John T. Leahy

Officials in the state of Illinois have replied in-
consistently to surveys seeking to determine the extent
of certification programs in religion studies. For
example, in response to a 1969 Michigan Department of Education survey, authorities in Illinois replied that
"religion is a certificating area for secondary teachers."
The survey concluded that "inquiry dealing with an official
position or statement regarding religion, revealed that
Florida, Idaho, and Illinois have officially taken positions which recognize religion as an appropriate preparation area for teachers."[1] A more recent survey of 50
state departments of education published in Liberty
magazine states about Illinois: "The State Office of
Public Instruction has no ready data on religion courses
that may be taught in Illinois public schools, nor is there
any record of a survey ever having been taken on which
schools offer such courses."[2]

The 1976 issue of The Directory of Approved Programs
for the Preparation of Educational Personnel in Illinois
Institutions of Higher Education lists two secondary programs (6-12) in Theology, one at Concordia Teachers
College and the other at Mundelein College. Both program
notations are prefaced by an asterisk that reads: "This
program was approved on December 30, 1968, and July 10,
1969, but does not lead to Certification for teaching in
recognized Illinois public schools."[3] The following year,
the Directory reproduced the same note as above for Concordia Teachers College but no listing was included for

_John T. Leahy, S.T.D., is Associate Professor of Religious
Studies, DePaul University._

Mundelein College.[4] Thus at present, there is one approved
secondary program in Theology but no certifiable secondary
program in religion exists in any Illinois teacher education institution.

Given the ambiguous situation of public education
religion studies in Illinois, the Illinois Religion and
Public Education Survey was conducted in 1977 with two
goals in mind: 1) to provide educators and interested
citizens with current and perhaps the sole data about the
status of the academic study of religion in Illinois
junior and senior high schools, and 2) to determine the
feasibility of the certification of religion as a teaching
area in Illinois. The study was announced in the Bulletin
of the National Council on Religion and Public Education
and encouraged by a "Consultation on Religion and Public
Education" called by the Illinois Council of Churches in
March, 1976.

The Survey Tool and Procedures

Since this was the first state-wide survey undertaken
to determine the status of the academic study of religion,
in Illinois public schools, an exploratory methodology was
selected.[5] The study used preformed groupings and selected
educators whose professional organizations have access to
knowledge about the constitutionality of an objective study
or religion and are leaders in providing educationally
appropriate materials and training for teachers. Educators
so targeted were principals, social studies teachers, and
English teachers. Their respective national professional
organizations are the American Association of School
Administrators (AASA), the National Council for the Social
Studies (NCSS), and the National Council of Teachers of
English (NCTE).

The survey instrument was pretested for its clarity
and comprehensiveness by eighteen educators in six junior
and senior high schools. The educators were asked seven
questions with which to evaluate the instrument. Their
comments were helpful in the revision of several questions.

Each instrument included a letter explaining the background and purpose of the study which was sent from the
School of Education, DePaul University. The letter
reported that the State Superintendent of Public Instruction endorsed the survey and contained his affirmation that
the information "would be very beneficial in planning for
the future educational needs of Illinois students." Information about the Schempp case and a definition of public
education studies also were included.

The Survey forms were color-coded according to the
respondent's position in the school. The first mailing was
sent March 30, 1977 with a request for return by April 14.
A second complete mailing was posted on May 1, 1977 with a
request for return by May 15. All responses were received
by the first week of June, 1977. These mailings were sent
to schools designated junior (510) or senior (760) high
schools in an official state document.[6] In total, questionnaires were sent to 3,810 educators in 1,270 Illinois
junior and senior high schools. Responses were received
from 38.3% (487) of the schools and 23.1% (882) of the
educators (398 principals, 236 social studies teachers, and
238 English teachers.)

TABLE 1

Respondents: Educators (882/3810) = 23.1%

Principals	45.1%	(398/882)
Social Studies	26.7%	(236/882)
English	26.9%	(238/882)

The survey instrument was divided into three parts.
The first section sought to obtain data on the respondents'
awareness of the certification of religion in some states;
whether their schools offered separate religion studies
courses, units, or other informal approaches; the grade
level at which they were offered; the titles of any textbooks or materials used; whether teachers had academic
preparation for such work; the existence of written
guidelines for teaching about religion in a school's
district; and the number of hours per semester spent on

teaching about religion through courses, units, and other
approaches. The second section measured on a scale from
one to four the attitudes of professional educators in
social studies, English, and school administration toward
the academic study of religion in the public schools:
a) as a separate subject or as a unit of another discipline
such as social studies or English, b) as an appropriate
minor or major certificating area in Illinois, and c) regarding the competent authority to decide about the
inclusion or exclusion of the academic study of religion
in the public schools. The third section provided demographic information about the respondents: the relative
number of respondents from each grouping, the grade level
at which they work, the age of the respondents, their sex,
and the number of school districts that responded.

Results of Present Practice

This study attempted to identify three different ways
of teaching about religion: as a separate course, as a
unit, and other informal approaches. Educators responded
to questions about these three ways of teaching about
religion, teacher preparation, and guidelines for the
academic study of religion.

When asked whether they were aware that religion was
a certifying teaching area in some states before receiving
the survey form, 49.2% of the educators answered in the
affirmative. An almost identical number did not have such
knowledge. In regards to religion studies offerings,
separate courses on religion are taught in 9.5% (46) of
the schools in Illinois and are clustered in the departments of English and social studies, although a few are
also offered in other departments.

In 60.9% (28) of these schools, the English department
offers separate courses. Half of these are full or complete courses, and 39.3% are mini-courses. No identification as to the actual nature of the course offered was
received from 10.7% of the schools. The social studies
department provides separate courses in 28.2% (13) of

these schools. There were five complete courses, six
mini-courses, and two unidentified. In seven of the
schools reporting courses, five complete and two mini-
courses are offered outside the English and social studies
departments. Nineteen different course titles were identified through the questionnaire. Some titles were
repeated in a number of schools, e.g., "Bible as Literature."

Units about religion are taught in 10.5% (51) of the
487 responding schools. In 43.1% (22) of these, the
English department offers the units, in 52.9% (27) the
social studies department provides the units, and in 7.8%
(4) of the schools, some other department offers units
about religion.

Other informal approaches to religion listed on the
questionnaire were guest speakers, explanations of holi-
days, field trips, and other. These approaches to the
study of religion are held in 25.5% (124) of the schools
that responded to the survey. The English department
provides these approaches in 41.9% (52) of the schools and
the social studies department in 45.2% (56). In 26.6% of
the schools (33) other departments study religion in this
manner. Thus, the total number of schools teaching about
religion as separate courses, units, and through informal
approaches is 35.55% (173/487).

Guidelines and Teacher Preparation

There are written guidelines for teaching about religion in 4.31% (21/487) of the schools. The percentage of
schools with guidelines which engage in the academic study
of religion is 61.9% (13/21). The percentage which does
not is 38.09% (8/21). In schools teaching separate
courses about religion, 8.7% (4/46) have guidelines. There
are guidelines in 9.8% (5/51) of the schools which teach
units about religion. Finally, guidelines are found in
11.29% (14/124) of the schools which have informal
approaches to study about religion. 87.08% of the responding individual educators report that there are no

guidelines in their districts; 3.51% affirm the presence
of guidelines; and 9.41% make no response to this question.

The 83 responses on the grade level offering for
public ecucation religion studies report larger percentages at the higher grade levels: grade 7 - 4.9%, grade
8 - 4.9%, grade 9 - 6.1%, grade 10 - 12.2%, grade 11 - 35.4%,
and grade 12 - 36.6%.   In regards to teacher preparation,
62 of 882 teachers or 7% had attended courses or workshops
on teaching about religion in the public school and 24 of
487 schools or 4.9% had such staff members.

Educators' Attitudes

In the attitudinal part of the survey instrument, the
882 educators expressed their professional opinions on the
place of religion in the public school curriculum.   They
were given four possible responses: three may be considered
positive and one negative.   These options ranged from definite agreement to definite disagreement.   The reasoning for
providing these four options was to determine how many educators would be positive even with reservations and how
many would be strongly negative given the novelty of public
discussion about religion in Illinois public schools.   In
general, educators in Illinois are positive about public
education religion studies while having significant reservations about required courses, a major certification area,
and religious institutions making curricular decisions.
The questions and responses in percentages are found in
the accompanying table.

TABLE 2

Attitudes of Illinois Educators About
Religion in the Public School Curriculum

    1 = definitely agree
    2 = somewhat agree
    3 = willing to permit on a trial basis
    4 = definitely disagree

	Percentages			
	1	2	3	4
7.0 the inclusion of the study about religion in public school curriculum	27.21	27.89	27.66	15.64
8.0 the requirement of a basic course about religion in junior or senior high school	7.82	10.43	18.14	63.03
9.0 the availability of an elective course about religion in junior or senior high school	35.68	27.32	26.19	9.75
10.0 an objective presentation of religions whenever they occur in the curriculum	58.61	24.03	10.31	5.44
11.1 the academic study about religion in English or Social Studies as a full course	11.56	10.88	18.02	38.54
11.2 the academic study about religion in English or Social Studies as a mini-course	14.39	24.94	22.33	17.00
11.3 the academic study about religion in English or Social Studies as a unit or units	31.76	27.27	18.96	10.54
12.1 certification of the academic study about religion as a minor teaching area	16.21	28.11	18.42	29.47
12.2 certification of the academic study about religion as a major teaching area	9.75	14.51	17.46	43.65
13.1 decisions about religion in the public school curriculum are to be made by the local school board	62.92	20.52	4.30	7.25
13.2 decisions about religion in the public school curriculum are to be made by the teaching staff	32.31	30.95	8.04	16.43

(Table 2--continued)

	Percentages			
	1	2	3	4
13.3 decisions about religion in the public school curriculum are to be made by the parents	33.33	29.02	7.82	16.66
13.4 decisions about religion in the public school curriculum are to be made by the students	19.38	28.57	11.45	26.30
13.5 decisions about religion in the public school curriculum are to be made by local churches and synagogues	12.81	16.55	10.31	43.99
13.6 decisions about religion in the public school curriculum are to be made by the school administration	38.43	31.17	7.14	12.24

Conclusion

Demographic information based on responses shows that 41.2% were junior high school educators and 51.7% senior high educators. The percentage of the 882 respondents according to age were: 21.1% in the 20-32 year bracket, 41.9% in 33-45, 29.8% in the 46-56, and 6% in the 56 plus category. The survey was completed by 214 women and 653 men. There are 182 school districts represented in the survey.

In 1977, the Illinois Religion and Public Education Survey of junior and senior high schools was undertaken to provide the first accurate information on religion studies in public education and to inquire about prospects for the certification of religion studies as a teaching area. Responses were received from 38.3% (487/1270) of the schools and from 23.1% (882/3810) of the educators. The total number of schools teaching about religion as separate courses, units, or informal approaches is 35.55% (173/487). The survey also revealed that 16.1% of the teachers favored certification of religion studies as a minor teaching area, while 29.47% definiately disagreed. A lower percentage, 9.75%, favors certification as a major teaching area while 43.65% strongly disagreed.

NOTES

[1] Michigan Department of Education, Survey of Certification Practices with Regard to Religion in the Fifty States, 1969.

[2] Liberty, 69/5 (September-October, 1974), 22.

[3] 11 and 33.

[4] 3.

[5] I wish to acknowledge my indebtedness to the sponsors of similar surveys in Michigan (Henry Hoeks), Minnesota (Gerald C. Farenholtz), and New Jersey (Donald Wimmer) who graciously permitted me to borrow from their work in the formation of the Illinois survey instrument.

[6] Fall Enrollment and Teacher Statistics, Illinois Public Schools, 1974-1975 School Year, Circular Series A, Number 34.

CHAPTER ELEVEN

THE EXTENT AND EFFECT OF PUBLIC EDUCATION RELIGION
STUDIES IN THE SCHOOLS: RESEARCH FINDINGS AND
THEIR IMPLICATIONS

William E. Collie

Formal and informal reports from numerous parts of
the United States point to a growth pattern in public
education religion studies since 1963. However, attempts
to obtain accurate information on the extent to which
religion studies currently is included in the curriculum
of elementary and secondary schools or the effect such
study has upon students produce incomplete results.
Several factors limit the identification by survey research
of the extent and content of religion studies in the
schools. In the first place, schools are sometimes reluctant to reveal what they do in this area. They either may
not be sure what they are teaching is actually legal or
appropriate or they may not trust the integrity of an
"outsider" asking such questions. Second, because the
conduct of religion studies may be integrated into the
existing curriculum, it is sometimes difficult to pinpoint
where or if religion studies is included, particularly by
an administrator who does not know the details of what is
taught in each course. Finally, problems in conducting
this research parallel difficulties generally encountered
in similar types of research and data collection in other
areas.[1] The cautious implications which may be drawn from
such surveys point to the rather urgent need to develop
more sophisticated research instruments since such findings
only provide incomplete and fragmented information about
either the extent or the effect of public education religion studies.

*William E. Collie, Ed.D., is Associate Professor of Educa-
tion, and Codirector, Public Education Religion Studies
Center, Wright State University.*

This chapter reports two research efforts conducted in
the spring of 1976 by the staff of the Public Education
Religion Studies Center and a faculty member at Wright
State University, Dayton, Ohio. The projects sought to
determine the extent to which the academic study of religion was included in the schools of Ohio and the effect of
religion studies on students' attitudes.

Religion Studies in Ohio Schools

Preliminary to the conduct of the study, the Ohio
Department of Education was contacted to identify those
courses they considered as religion-related. The 1974-75
staff and student counts were under three categories:
Bible Literature with 86 teachers and enrolling 3,679
students, Bible History taught by 3 teachers and enrolling
49 students, and Religion taught by 30 teachers and
enrolling 1,043 students.[2] It is worth noting that the
categories identified by the Department of Education were
limited and did not include the most commonly taught
religion studies course within social studies, i.e., world
religions, and they only identified courses, not units of
instruction.

After this task was completed, a one page questionnaire was mailed to 1,054 Ohio secondary school principals
of both public and private institutions in an attempt to
identify the number of programs in the academic study of
religion, as distinguished from sectarian instruction.
Of that number 249 schools responded with 209 responses
identifiable as from public schools, 26 from private and
parochial schools, and 14 with no identification. Analysis
of these responses was published in the journal of the
Ohio Council for the Social Studies.[3]

Of the 249 schools responding, 68 indicated that the
school board had a specific policy or regulation regarding
teaching or study about religions in the curriculum. No
policy was indicated for 136 schools, while 33 respondents
said they did not know if a policy existed.

Asked if the school had a unit of a course, a full
course or a mini-course which teaches about religion objectively, 105 respondents indicated "yes" while 133
responded "no." Of the religion studies offerings, 45
schools taught units, 33 taught full courses, and 37 taught
mini-courses about religion.

Units about religion are most commonly offered at the
upper secondary level with the number of units increasing
with grade level. By grade, units were taught in the
following grades: 7 - 12, 8 - 13, 9 - 33, 10 - 53, 11 - 77,
12 - 81. Religion-related units are offered in a variety
of subject areas but generally are found in literature and
history or social studies courses. Units about religion
were identified for the following subject areas: literature - 77, history - 40, social studies - 45, humanities - 18,
sociology - 17, philosophy - 8, art - 5, music - 6, others - 14.
School representatives indicated that 346 teachers teach
units in which religion studies is included.

Full or mini-courses about religion also tend to be
most commonly offered at the upper secondary grades.
Courses were identified for the following grade levels:
7 - 4, 8 - 6, 9 - 21, 10 - 36, 11 - 61, 12 - 66. The results
clearly indicate that religion-related courses are taking
hold at the upper levels where students have more freedom
to take elective courses.

An analysis of the particular courses described shows
that English classes have been particularly open to
restructuring as mini-courses with "the Bible as Literature" by far the most popular single course. Of the 46
English courses specifically identified by title, 39
utilized variations of this title, occasionally listed as
"Bible Literature" or as "Literature of the Old Testament
and New Testament."

Social studies course offerings listed by specific
title by respondents also indicated a preponderant trend
for one course. While 55 social studies courses were
identified, 46 were specifically listed and of those 25
were called "World Religions" and 8 were entitled

"Comparative Religions." In our experience, the two
titles are used interchangeably but both usually examine
major world religions. In addition, 4 schools listed
courses simply as "Religion" while 2 listed "History of
Religions." In addition .there were a variety of singular
titles, including "Man's Search for God" and "We Believe."
Private and parochial school offerings which were indicated
as being non-sectarian were listed under such course titles
as "Ecumenism," "Bible Culture," "Morality," "Other Christian Religions," "Eastern Religions," and "Life's Dimensions."

To the extent that this survey is indicative of the
inclusion of the academic study of religion in the
secondary schools of Ohio and to the extent that practice
in Ohio is similar to that in other states, several conclusions may be drawn:

From the notes on several of the responses, it is
apparent that many school officials misunderstand court
rulings and erroneously believe that religion cannot be
studied legally in a public school setting. Evidently
many school districts have neither examined the issue
carefully nor established clear policies or guidelines
regarding religion studies. It would seem appropriate for
schools to establish school policy for this potentially
explosive issue in which schools would articulate their
support for the academic, objective inclusion of the
study of religion in the curriculum but, in the case of
public schools, firmly oppose any attempts to include
sectarian or so-called "interdominational" religion
classes which more appropriately belong in a church
setting. The objectives of religion studies as an academic
study should quite clearly be distinguished from religious
education which is conducted by religious institutions.

The results of this survey reflect the difficulty in
determining the extent of the inclusion of religion
studies in the curriculum. If the study is naturally included where appropriate as a part of other courses such
as "World Culture" or "World Literature" it is a part of

the curriculum not identifiable in and by itself. Thus
while the listing of courses with religion-related titles
is instructive, the quantification of such courses alone
does not accurately reflect what actually is being taught
in this area.

Where religion-related units of study have been
identified, it appears clear that religion studies has
found its curricular "home" in English and social studies
offerings. While the potential exists for the inclusion
of the religious dimension in other subject areas such as
humanities, art, and music, in practice this does not seem
to be the case in secondary schools.

In English, all religion-related courses were in the
area of literature. The total dominance of the offerings
by the one course, "The Bible as Literature," indicates
that there has been ready acceptance in this one area.
Certainly the popularity of the mini-course format has
facilitated this inclusion. Other potential areas of
study appear to be almost totally lacking, however. Moreover, while courses on the scriptures and religious literature of non-Western traditions are possible, they
apparently have not been introduced. Furthermore, there
is a vast body of religious literature within the Jewish
and Christian traditions in addition to the Bible which is
worthy of examination. The quest for the meaning of life
by self-proclaimed atheists and agnostics reflects a world
view which might be contrasted with that held by individuals within the more conventional religious traditions but
such an approach has not been found in practice.

Within social studies, Ohio respondents indicate
"World Religions" is the most common religion studies
curricular vehicle. Often such courses tend to examine
the historical development and major tenets of the "great
religions" of the world. Certainly there is educational
value in examining religion as one of many factors which
have impact on culture. While an examination of our own
American culture is greatly enhanced by a study of the
religious dimension, not a single offering was listed for

such possible courses as "Religion in American Life" or
"Religious Issues in American Culture." World history
courses provide innumerable opportunities for exploration
of the impact of religion. From the "missionary motives"
for the European expansion in Africa to the Christian
conscientious objectors of Vietnam, from the "Holy Wars"
of Islam to the Nazi Holocaust, religion has played a
significant role in shaping world events, sometimes for
the good and sometimes for the bad.

Religion Studies Students' Attitudes

An additional question which has been answered mainly
by either intuition or speculation rather than specific
research efforts seeks to determine the effect of the
academic study of religions on students' attitudes. In an
effort to address this need, the author of this chapter,
along with a colleague in the College of Education at
Wright State University, conducted a survey of students
enrolled in secondary education religion studies courses
to ascertain their evaluation of the instruction they had
received. The findings were subsequently published in an
educational journal.[4]

The information was gathered during the Spring of
1976 when requests were sent to teachers in 239 schools in
Indiana, Kentucky, Michigan, and Ohio asking them to
administer an anonymous, pencil-and-paper attitude scale
to their students. The list of teachers known to be
teaching religion studies courses was obtained from the
files of the Public Education Religion Studies Center.
The courses surveyed were at the secondary level and
offered under a variety of titles but generally were a
part of either the language arts and English or social
studies curriculum. Thirty-nine schools, 30 public and 9
parochial, participated in the survey. In each case,
regardless of whether the schools were public or parochial,
the teachers participating agreed that the courses as they
were taught were consistent with the PERSC guidelines for
the academic study of religion and, therefore, appropriate

for a public school setting. The number of useable student
questionnaires returned was 1,227.

The survey instrument was a 30 item, 5 point Likert
Scale ranging from "strongly agree" to "strongly disagree"
and was completed anonymously. Areas surveyed included
those aspects emphasized in the PERSC guidelines for religion studies goals, teacher education, and teacher competency - objectivity, tolerance, and teacher preparation as
well as personal evaluation of the impact of the course,
student motivation for taking the course, and the student's
own degree of religious involvement.

Basic to instruction in religion studies, as in any
subject, is sound planning for instruction. Students
generally felt their religion studies teacher was well-
prepared with 84.4% of the students checking the "strongly
agree" or "agree" categories.

The context of instruction, however, is probably the
greatest concern of those who stress the importance of
objectivity in religion studies. To tap student attitudes
on this vital issue, a number of questions related to objectivity were posed. In response to the direct statement,
"The teacher was objective and fair in dealing with differing religious beliefs," 86.1% of the students chose the
"strongly agree" or "agree" categories. When the statement
read, "A person belonging to a religious faith other than
Christian would feel comfortable in our class," only 65.8%
chose the two positive categories. At the negative extreme,
however, note that only 2.3% strongly felt that a non-
Christian would be uncomfortable. When asked about the
comfortableness of a person with no religious belief, those
choosing the positive response categories dropped to 60.3%.

Continuing to explore the class atmosphere, students
were asked whether they agreed with the claim (which religion studies educators support) that "studying religion and
religious belief in school is different from what is done
in church or temple." 83.6% responded positively with only
5.3% actually negative. To determine if this response
might be related to classroom experience, students were

asked if their own class was too much like a church or
temple class. Only 4.9% agreed it was while 88.5% either
"disagreed" or "strongly disagreed."

     In such a sensitive area as religion studies, what
should the teacher do about expressing his or her own
beliefs? When students were asked the degree of their
agreement with the statement,"Teachers of religion studies
courses should indicate clearly their own particular religious beliefs," opinion was divided but the general tendency
was toward non-agreement with 51.1% of the responses in the
"disagree" or "strongly disagree" categories.

TABLE 1

Class Atmosphere for Religion Studies

T = 1,227   ( ) = Adjusted Frequency

	Strongly Agree	Agree	Unde- cided	Disa- gree	Strongly Disagree
1.Teacher objective and fair in dealing with different religious beliefs.	536 (43.9)	515 (42.2)	101 (8.3)	43 (3.5)	25 (2.0)
2.Person of faith other than Christian would be comfortable in class.	168 (13.7)	637 (52.1)	213 (17.4)	177 (14.5)	28 (2.3)
3.Person with no religious belief would be comfortable in class.	147 (12.0)	590 (48.2)	181 (14.8)	230 (18.8)	75 (6.1)
4.Studying religion in school is different from what is done in church or temple.	371 (30.5)	646 (53.1)	132 (10.9)	51 (4.2)	16 (1.3)
5.This class was too much like a church or temple class.	23 (1.9)	36 (3.0)	81 (6.7)	512 (42.1)	565 (46.4)
6.Religion studies teachers should clearly indicate their own particular religious beliefs.	107 (8.7)	248 (20.3)	239 (19.6)	370 (30.4)	255 (20.9)

In summary, an examination of the responses to questions related to the issue of objectivity indicated that students completing religion studies courses generally felt that the teacher was objective and fair. At the same time the class atmosphere leaves room for improvement if students who are of faiths other than Christian or are nonreligious are to feel comfortable. Students generally recognized that study about religion in school is different from religious education in church or temple and that, indeed, in practice in their own classroom the distinction is maintained. Perhaps cognizant of the impact of teacher influence, students generally opposed teachers revealing their own religious beliefs in a class setting.

Several questions in the attitude survey attempted to determine the impact of religion studies on both the understanding and attitudes of the students. 67.5% of the students "agreed" or "strongly agreed" that their religion studies courses had helped them achieve an objective and fair understanding of belief systems different from their own. When asked if the course resulted in their having more respect for different religious faiths 63.6% responded positively.

While not all of the courses surveyed dealt with the student's own religious faith, the survey asked the student to respond to "I understand better my own religious tradition as a result of taking this course." Even under the conditions described, 63.2% agreed that the course did have this effect. This being the case, one may ask, did the course help the student better understand his or her own personal religious attitudes better? Positive responses of 65.5% indicated religion studies does have this impact whether intended or not. Does what students learn and experience in a religion studies course cause them to become more committed to a particular religious faith? When asked if the course they took had this effect on them, only 35.2% responded positively, while 43.5% responded negatively. Interestingly, when asked to respond to "This course helped strengthen my moral and spiritual values," 51% responded positively.

TABLE 2

Impact of Religion Studies
Instruction on Students

N = 1,227   ( ) = Adjusted Frequency

	Strongly Agree	Agree	Unde- cided	Disa- gree	Strongly Disagree
1. Helped me look at different religious beliefs more objectively and fairly.	211 (17.3)	613 (50.2)	258 (21.1)	116 (9.5)	22 (1.8)
2. Have more respect for different religious faiths.	253 (20.8)	522 (42.8)	265 (21.7)	138 (11.3)	41 (3.4)
3. I understand my own religious tradition better.	236 (19.4)	534 (43.8)	202 (16.6)	214 (17.6)	32 (2.6)
4. I understand my own religious attitudes better.	298 (24.3)	494 (40.3)	221 (18.1)	170 (13.9)	38 (3.1)
5. I feel more committed to a particular religious faith.	116 (9.5)	313 (25.7)	260 (21.2)	397 (32.6)	133 (10.9)
6. Helped strengthen my moral and spiritual values.	173 (14.2)	449 (36.8)	360 (29.5)	187 (15.3)	57 (4.2)

When viewed as a composite, religion studies in
current practice as reflected by the responses to this
survey appears to encourage tolerance, and indeed, respect
for differing religious beliefs. Religion studies appear
to help a number of students better understand both their
own religious tradition and personal beliefs. The course
itself does not appear to have the effect of leading students toward a stronger particular faith commitment. This
fact is consistent with general goal statements for
religion studies and the emphasis on objectivity. While
religion studies educators have emphasized that the intent
of the academic study of religion is distinct from moral
and values education, the results of this survey indicate
that students felt that religions studies had a positive
impact on their values.

Several other questions attempted to determine student attitudes on a variety of religion-related issues. When asked to respond to the statement, "religious beliefs strongly influence a society's culture," 80.3% of the students responded positively. "People who have religious faith are better people than those who don't have religious faith" received only 24.5% agreement, while 48.6% of the students disagreed. The statement, "religion study better prepares a person for responding to a changing world," received positive support from 67.6% of the respondents. When given the related statement, "public schools should teach about religion," 64.1% of the students agreed.

Overall reactions of students to the religion studies courses they took were generally positive. An overwhelming 79.9% of the students either "agreed" or "strongly agreed" that they "learned a lot in this class." Similarly, 77.7% responded positively to "I am glad I took this class."

What is the religious background of students who en-roll in religion studies courses? Of the respondents, 70.3% responded positively to the statement, "I am a religious person." Membership in a religious organization was claimed by 71.1% of the students. Regular attendance at religious services received a 69.5% positive response. Only 9.7% of the respondents indicated positive interest in a religious vocation. Parental membership in religious organizations was reported by 70.5% of the students while regular religious service attendance by parents was claimed by 64.4% of the students. Since religion studies courses are generally elective courses within the curriculum, it is not surprising to see that students taking religion studies courses generally are from religious backgrounds.

Parental influence may well have encouraged enrollment in the religion studies course. When asked to respond to the statement, "my parents were in favor of my taking this class," 63.8% responded positively with 23.8% strongly agreeing and 40% agreeing with the statement. This broad survey of the attitudes of students enrolled in secondary

religion studies courses indicates student interest and
positive value attached to the experience of studying
about religion in school. Future studies will need to
examine discreet subject areas in order to evaluate more
closely the impact of particular programs of study.

Conclusion

Both surveys point toward the additional efforts
greatly needed to systematically monitor and evaluate the
inclusion of the academic study of religon in elementary
and secondary curriculum. While survey instruments such
as those reported in this first part of this chapter can
identify at what points in the curriculum religion study
currently is taking place, the far more crucial next question of what happens to students when it does occur
largely remains unanswered. To a populace wary of religion studies in the public schools, proof must be presented
that such study indeed can be conducted in ways that contribute positively to the development of their children's
understanding and attitudes without violating individual
religious conscience. Thus, while the survey research
attempting to identify where and in what ways religion
study is done in schools is useful, additional research
indicating the impact of religion studies on students as it
now is practiced may be the most significant key to the
further integration of religion studies in the elementary
and secondary curriculum. If skeptical parents, administrators, and teachers can be shown that students actually
do benefit from such instruction, then the opportunities
for religion studies in elementary and secondary schools
will expand.

NOTES

[1]Another factor which possibly limited responses to the survey was the statement that teachers identified in the study would be contacted for further information. Some administrators may have been hesitant to complete the forms in order to avoid further questions.

[2]Ohio Department of Education, Letter to the author, October 9, 1975.

[3]William Collie, "Religion Studies in Ohio Secondary Schools: Present and Potential," The OCSS Review, the Journal of the Ohio Council for the Social Studies, 13 (Spring 1977).

[4]William E. Collie and Madeline H. Apt, "Attitudes of Secondary School Students Toward Religion Studies Courses," Educational Leadership, the Journal of the Association for Supervision and Curriculum Development, 35/7 (April 1978).

CHAPTER TWELVE

CERTIFICATION PROGRAMS FOR PUBLIC EDUCATION
RELIGION STUDIES

Frank L. Steeves
Joseph Forcinelli

During the academic year 1972-73 one of the writers
of this chapter investigated the status of teacher certification in the study of religion. The investigation was
based upon information furnished by all state departments
of education and by many persons working in state-approved
programs. Later published as a reprint by the Public Education Religion Studies Center, the report was accepted as
accurate through mid-September, 1973.[1]

Now, six years later, the present chapter represents
an effort to update the earlier work where changes have
occurred, to repeat the earlier findings where there have
been changes in state policy, and to modify interpretations
and recommendations on the basis of the situation in 1979
and the perspective gained in the interim.

Eight states provide for some form of certification in
religion studies. Even though only approximately one-fifth
of the state departments of education in the United States
license teachers in this subject area, it is inaccurate to
conclude that there is a lack of interest in the subject.
Many strong and divergent points of view surface during any
consideration of the topic by educators, religionists, or
the general public. And, as documented in other parts of
this volume, religion studies in public education has a
distinguished history, considerable support, a rich literature in curriculum and methodology, and an extensive

*Frank L. Steeves, Ed.D., is Professor of Education, Mar-
quette University, and Joseph Forcinelli, Ph.D., is Director and Lecturer, Program on Religion and Education,
Harvard Divinity School and Member of the Faculty, Harvard
Graduate School of Education.*

pattern of school courses and programs in actual practice.
Consequently, our descriptive summaries of the state programs which provide for teacher certification should not
be interpreted as an emerging national pattern but, rather,
as useful models for study by those contemplating the
introduction of certification programs in their states.

Certification Programs

The 1973 study found that Michigan, Wisconsin, and
California were the only states that approved college
teaching majors or minors leading to certification for
teaching religion studies in the public schools. Each
program was relatively new with those in Wisconsin having
started in 1971 and those in California and Michigan in
1972. Because there are significant differences in the
general approach to certification among the patterns
established in Michigan, Wisconsin, California and,
recently, Massachusetts, each is reviewed separately.

Both Michigan and Wisconsin permit certification in
the subject area of religion. Wisconsin recognizes what
it terms "Religious Studies" as an academic major. Michigan approves academic minors for what it calls the "Academic Study of Religions." Thus, the student graduating
in Wisconsin with a major in Religious Studies may be
certified to teach in that area alone. The student
graduating in Michigan must have some other academic major
in order to earn the degree. However, the state does not
specify the related subject field; it is selected by the
student. Typically, the minor in Michigan is taken in
conjunction with an English or social studies major,
although a variety of major-minor combinations have
developed as new programs have been approved.

When approving new programs, Wisconsin treats Religious Studies as one among 85 subject areas in which
teachers may be certified. A college seeking approval of
its curriculum in any of these areas must submit a detailed
statement of objectives; a listing of each required and
elective course, including credit hours and course

descriptions; and a statement describing facilities and
qualifications of staff. Approved programs in Michigan
must fulfill the requirements contained in a statement of
standards issued in 1972. This document sets specific
standards for institutional eligibility, qualifications
for instructional staff, program components, and instructional resources. A separate statement developed at the
same time supplements the state standards and assists
institutions developing new programs. Development of
programs based on these exacting standards, followed by a
formal review by a Committee of Scholars, typically
involves a three-year period from initial proposal to final
approval.

An examination of developments in these two states
from 1973 to 1979 reveals a significant increase in the
number of approved programs. In 1973 Wisconsin had three
state-approved programs in Religion Studies--at the University of Wisconsin-Whitewater, Edgewood College, and
Marquette University. By 1979 the programs at these
institutions still existed and nine additional programs had
been approved for a total of twelve. The new programs include academic minors at the University of Wisconsin
campuses at Eau Claire, Oshkosh, and Stevens Point;
academic majors at Cardinal Stritch College, Mount Mary
College, and Lawrence University; and major-minor combinations at Alverno College, St. Norbert College, and Viterbo
College.

In 1973 only the program at Calvin College was
approved by the Michigan Board of Education. At that time,
however, four other applications were under consideration,
and by 1979 six new programs had come into being for a
total of seven. The new programs are located at Western
Michigan University, Michigan State University, Hope
College, Alma College, Central Michigan University, and
the University of Detroit.

About ten students per institution are enrolled in
the Michigan programs. The situation in Wisconsin is
similar. Students in eleven of these programs are required

to have a separate teaching major as their prime teaching
responsibility, so it is difficult to know how many
graduates have found actual job placements in religion
studies. Moreover, a public school rarely hires someone to
teach religion studies full-time.

Teacher certification includes structural prerequisites
and standards that operate regardless of the subject field.
Such structures are part of a teacher preparatory program
because of their inherent value to the teaching arts.
State and institutional standards supporting this point of
view thus become the starting point for an understanding of
the manner in which any subject field, including religion,
becomes part of the training program approved by a state
department of education.

The decade of the 1970s was the occasion of a timely
conjunction of interests in religion studies as a certifiable subject field with a restructuring of certification
standards and requirements in the states of California and
Massachusetts.[2] This coincidence of interests afforded
one of these writers an opportunity to participate along
with numerous others, at the state committee level in both
states, in the formulation of a basis for accommodating
standards of certification in religion studies within the
structure of new teacher education laws in these states.[3]
Thus a description of certification policies in religion
studies for California and Massachusetts can best be
understood in relation to the procedures for institutional
program approval required by these states.

In California and in Massachusetts, new legislation
put the administration of teacher certification standards
under the authority of a Commission headed by an executive
secretary or director and placed the responsibility for
final approval of commission recommendations in the hands
of the state board of education, the superintendent or
commissioner of education, and, ultimately, the citizenry
through public hearings.[4] Therefore, proposals for
certification in the study of religion submitted by state
educational institutions must undergo successive reviews
by these groups responsible for granting approval.

We have alluded to the procedural similarities for certification which these two states follow. There is a major difference existing at the control level of the structural design for the content of certification standards and requirements. Both states have legislated broad guidelines for teacher certification. However, Massachusetts prefers to locate the control of the structural content within the function of the State Bureau of Certification which is responsible for monitoring teacher preparation institutions seeking approval under the requirements. California requires the teacher preparation institutions themselves to submit to the state licensing commission a proposal for the authorization of their training program.

While the distinction may seem slight, it is significant. Although both states have legislated statutes for regulating certification standards, California reasoned that design and content should reflect the educational philosophy of the institution, whereas Massachusetts preferred to retain control of teacher preparation at the state level. The implications are more clearly seen in a separate look at each state.

California has a large number of private and state colleges and universities which offer teacher education degrees.[5] Most, if not all, of these institutions contain departments or divisional studies in history, social science, humanities, arts, religion, philosophy, and psychology, all of which are germane to the study of religion. Therefore, in approving a certification proposal in religion studies from a college or university, the Teacher Certification and Licensing Commission expects that the content of the proposal will meet state requirements in the subject field and in student teaching as well as an integration of religion with particular subject field(s) specified by the institution. A certification proposal for social science/religion or for English/religion would be common examples.

In 1973, the University of California at Santa Barbara
and California State University at Northridge offered
approved subject matter programs in religion studies, both
under the designation of social studies. These two programs continue to exist in 1979. No new institutional
programs have been added since 1973. However, it should
be noted that California has developed and is still refin-
ing a broad, complex system of teacher certification. This
effort has taken a priority over the development of new
programs.

Under the California legislation a student receives a
provisional credential in the fourth year but does not
receive a full credential until the end of a fifth year
that involves graduate work. There are no written requirements for a credential in religious studies. At the University of California-Santa Barbara, a student pursuing
this area is expected to complete a full religion major
which provides a broad and concrete background in religion
studies. This should include study in related fields such
as psychology, history, geography, etc. If the student
successfully fulfills the religious studies major requirements and the education requirements proscribed by the
UCSB faculty, the single competency examination is waived.
California State University, Northridge offers a program
that requires 6 lower division and 30 upper division units
in religion, 30 units in the social sciences, and 27 professional education units including student teaching.

Massachusetts, under the direction of its Advisory
Commission, conducted state-wide studies through Professional Advisory Groups assigned to the diverse subject
fields to make recommendations for content and practicum
requirements for teacher certification. The question of
certification in religion studies was reviewed by the
Professional Advisory Group on the Social Sciences, which
recommended that psychology, philosophy, and religion be
certifiable under the rubric of social science. After
public hearings and final deliberations, the Massachusetts
State Board of Education voted to exclude philosophy as a

certifiable subject; to certify psychology under a new
certificate designation as "teaching in the behavioral
sciences;" and to include "the study of religion" in the
new certification for social studies. This new certification law became effective in September, 1980.

The Harvard Program on Religion and Education conducts
a two-year graduate program based on this plan. The program design meets the requirements for a major concentration (30 semester hours each) in both social science and
religion, as well as for a practicum (16 semester hours).

Neither California nor Massachusetts include religion
as a single subject certification area for teachers, rather
they provide a means for professional educators representing both academic and teacher training fields to recommend
certification standards for integrating religion studies
within the social sciences and the humanities, and with
obvious cognate areas--history, literature, psychology,
and philosophy.

Several other approaches to certification in religion
studies were noted in the 1973 report and continue in 1979.
For example, a provision in the Indiana certification requirements allows regularly licensed English teachers to
teach Biblical Literature. Pennsylvania permits the
teaching of religious literature, literature of the Bible,
and other religious writings, as elective courses in literature in public secondary schools. Florida's certification in Bible permits the teacher so certified to teach
Bible history or Bible literature within grades 7-12; in
addition, certified English teachers may also teach Bible
literature. Tennessee's certification area in Bible
requires a minimum of 18 quarter hours in literature of
the Bible. These courses may not be in theology, doctrine,
ethics, or dogma.

The 1973 report treated these forms of certification
as somewhat peripheral to the subject of religion and as
efforts in other directions. In retrospect, however, all
four of these forms of certification seem to recognize
that religious themes are intrinsic to the subject areas

named. Within the parameters of these subjects--Bible,
English, and literature--the four states are relying upon
the certification process as a means of approaching
clearly defined religious topics. Therefore, these states
are now perceived to have a form of certification for
dealing with religious topics and themes.

Common Elements and Differences

Even though this chapter focuses on the processes of
certification and does not compare or contrast specific
institutional programs, it is appropriate to point out that
programs approved by the several states share common
elements as well as differences. All of the programs
examined by the authors share the following common elements:

1. The programs are interdisciplinary. Although a
department of religion or theological studies may provide
a core of course work for the major or minor, the programs
often include extensive requirements apart from formal
religious studies courses. These include preparation in
areas such as philosophy, history, classics, English,
literature, sociology, psychology, anthropology, and
archaeology. Even in institutions where the department of
religion offers all of the required courses, interdisciplinary offerings constitute a part of the program.

2. The programs are non-sectarian. Even the
theological components of these programs are broadly
conceived to include a far-reaching range of religions
both contemporary and ancient as well as different
approaches to the study of religion, including the
historical-critical method. Furthermore, the programs may
include such diverse topics as studies of humanism,
agnosticism, atheism, witchcraft, occult phenomena,
mysticism, human sexuality and religion, and the religious
implications of death.

3. All programs include the same professional preparation required for teachers in other subjects at the
institution and in the state where they are located.

4. All programs require the major or minor in religion studies to meet the core curriculum or general education requirements established by the institution for its degree programs.

5. The programs give careful attention to the legal aspects of the area, to special methodological problems, and to the many problems and restrictions inherent in the nature of the subject even when legality may not be at issue. Plainly, the practice of any particular religion is distinguished from the study of religion as a significant force in the lives of human beings.

Despite such important common elements, there are many differences. These often take into account differing institutional strengths and emphases. For example, the resources of a strong department of anthropology or sociology may be called upon to bolster the major or minor in religion studies in one institution, whereas another may take advantage of a strong unit in psychology. Distinctions also result from the preferences of the department in which the religion concentration is located. Thus, one program may emphasize historical interpretation because this is the approach favored by the religion faculty, yet another may stress literary approaches and implications. Beyond this, core curricula vary from college to college. Professional education requirements vary among states and institutions. The end result is that the four-year program at one place is never precisely the same as that at another.

This diversity is to be expected and encouraged. All of these programs are less than nine years old and are, therefore, still undergoing refinement and development. Even where the structural content is perceived as a state responsibility, as in Massachusetts, some diversity because of institutional differences can be anticipated.

Opposition and Frustrations

While the authors neither wish to overemphasize existing opposition to the inclusion of religion studies

in public education nor to dwell upon the frustrations
experienced when trying to obtain accurate information
about certification in different states, these problems
nevertheless must be noted because the fabric of educational thinking as it has developed in this country
includes a strong pattern of antipathy toward religion in
the public school. It follows that any consideration of
teacher certification in the area arouses historical and
contemporary arguments about the appropriateness of the
proposal.

Dr. Fenwick W. English, formerly Associate Secretary
of the American Association of School Adminsitrators,
after identifying himself as an advocate of studying about
religion in public schools noted that when anyone with this
in mind "...approaches the public schools, there is and has
been a continuing history of avoidance behavior cultivated
by public educators in this area. You will not be enthu-
siastically greeted for the most part."[6]

This avoidance behavior ranges from indifference to
hostility. It results, at least in part, from the training
received by most school administrators, curricular specialists, and other educators, which traditionally has centered
upon what cannot and should not be done in the area of
religion and not on what is possible. It reflects a long
history of a determined effort to remove religious divisions from public education and to maintain the public
school as a neutral institution.

At least two additional factors add to this problem.
First, the branches of large state education bureaucracies
do not always know what other branches are doing. Second,
writers and researchers sometimes confuse the effort of
voluntary groups and individuals or the interest of
university personnel, with official action by a state
department of education. Thus, while preparing the 1973
report, the investigator received three letters from one
department of education stating categorically that the
state did not certify teachers in religion studies. Yet
at the same time, the state had published its standards

for program approval in religion studies. Another state
was reported to be receptive to the idea of certification
in the area. Ultimately it was learned that the effort
was centered in a single college. Only one unproductive
meeting with the state's department of education personnel
had been held. There have been persistent reports that a
New England state is among those that certifies teachers
in religion studies. Working independently, both of the
present authors verified that this state does not and that
all of the reports stem from the unsuccessful efforts of a
group of university professors. As recently as July, 1978,
a Midwestern state was reported to be involved in developing a certification plan. So far, the involvement of the
state is minimal as the effort has been initiated by a
voluntary group of people from several universities in
cooperation with others interested in the topic. Eventually
the work may lead to official state consideration and action. In the meantime, it is premature to suggest that the
state is actively involved.

The se examples, although frustrating for those trying
to determine the facts, are neither discouraging nor interpreted as evidence of opposition by those in positions of
authority on the state level. On the contrary, the involvement of state officials is seldom possible until
voluntary groups have established their own positions. As
noted below, the entire religion studies movement, and
certainly any move toward the certification of teachers,
must be multi-faceted if it is to succeed.

A Multi-Faceted Approach

Organizing strategies for public education religion
study are discussed elsewhere in the volume and need not
be repeated here. However, it may be well to re-emphasize
that certification of any sort does not result from
unilateral action by state education departments. Typically, certification programs require a process of extended
discussion and compromise among a wide variety of individuals and groups. These include university teachers,

teachers and administrators at elementary and secondary
levels, churches and their related organizations, clusters
of associations and interested citizens, and state officials. The process is open to all. Certification occurs
neither in a vacuum nor in secret.

Moreover, teacher certification is only one aspect of
a task which includes at least two other major facets.
Certification merely identifies a teacher who may be
capable of teaching particular subjects at particular grade
levels. However, in order to become certified, the teacher
must have completed an approved program. This process
involves accreditation of college programs by each state.
The teachers who successfully complete these programs are
certified not only to teach in a specific area but to
improve instruction in the elementary and secondary
schools. Hence, standards for school programs must be
developed. Work in all three of these areas is necessary
to establish a coherent and unitary program. And, although
separate factors are being considered in one form or
another in many states, seldom does one come across an
approach which involves all three. An exception may be
California which, when planning for teaching about religion
during the early 1970s, produced documents which include
specific standards for public schools and teacher preparation as well as guidelines for the approval of university
programs.

More typical, however, is the situation in many other
states where large numbers of courses related to religion
now are taught in the public schools but where state
involvement has stopped short of establishing certification
standards for teachers in this area. A reverse situation
exists in Wisconsin. Here, the state has certified teachers
and maintained approved college programs in religion
studies since 1971. Courses are taught in the subject in
public schools throughout the state. However, guidelines
for such study in the public schools only now are in the
process of development.[7]

Sooner or later all of these issues must be faced. A marked increase in the activity of state departments of education may be expected during the decade ahead as they move to establish some form of certification, accredit university programs, and issue standards or guidelines for public schools in religion studies.

Recommendations

1. New institutional programs in religion studies should adhere to the common elements in existing programs. Public school expectations demand that the programs be interdisciplinary and nonsectarian. They should include the same professional preparation and general education requirements required for other academic majors and minors at the preparing institution. They should give special attention to the particular legal and methodological problems of study about religion. At the same time, institutional diversity of internal program components should be expected and encouraged.

2. State departments of education should consider seriously the question of some sort of certification for teaching religion studies. This may take the forms followed in the four states described herein, in which direct certification is possible in religion studies, either as a single subject, with a correlated subject, or as a component of another subject. Or, certification may follow patterns described for other states where certified teachers with proper training may teach specific courses related to religion. Whatever the model adopted, it seems unwise to permit extensive public school teaching in the subject without statewide standards for the preparation of teachers and for implementation of the programs in the schools.

3. In states where certification is not available but where courses in religion studies are taught in the schools, employing officials should make certain that teachers have completed appropriate workshops, institutes, or courses. An obvious problem is that proponents of particular religious viewpoints may find their way into schools as teachers.

Such persons are less likely to be objective, to be
sensitive to differing viewpoints, to appreciate legal
parameters of the subject, or to know the facts about
faiths other than their own.

4. Employing officials should also be aware that
"major" and "minor" are academic distinctions which have
meaning only within the institution issuing the degree.
One college's academic minor may be the equivalent of
another's major. The only way to ascertain the depth of a
prospective teacher's preparation is to examine the
teacher's transcripts.

5. Writers, speakers, researchers, and reporters
investigating the subject should take unusual care that
their reports actually identify what official state
agencies are doing when states are named. Too often, the
effort of voluntary groups and individuals has been confused with that of state departments of education.

6. Those interested in certification programs in
this area should be prepared for extended involvement with
a wide variety of people and organizations. Having established their own positions, sponsors should approach state
officials with an open-minded expectation of further
analysis and refinement. The subject should not be
treated as inherently controversial and need not be if
models and factual data now available are built into
proposals.

7. Although not emphasized in this chapter, the
writers strongly recommend that employees of state departments of education, universities, other institutions and
organizations, and individuals concerned with religion
studies in public education, join appropriate associations
and attend the meetings of these groups.

8. Most divisions of education or religion studies
should consider programs short of full scale academic
majors or minors. This is not to protect existing major/
minor programs from competition. It is merely a recognition of the existing job market. A real need exists for
presently certified teachers, largely in English and social

studies, to be trained in religion studies. This need can
be met by most institutions in their geographic areas with
sequences of courses, institutes, and workshops adding to
something less than the typical academic minor. Of course,
this recommendation does not apply in states where certification expectations are now specified--except in Massachusetts, where allowance is made for programs which
contain less than an academic minor.

NOTES

[1]Frank L. Steeves, State-Approved Curricula in Religious Studies, (Dayton, Ohio: Public Schools Religion
Studies Center, 1973).

[2]In California, Section 13147 of Education Code (1972)
and in Massachusetts, Chapter 847 of the Acts of 1973.

[3]Joseph Forcinelli served on the Moral Guidelines and
Implementation Committee, California State Board of Educa-
tion, 1973, and the Professional Advisory Group in Social
Science for the Advisory Commission, Bureau of Teacher
Certification and Placement, Commonwealth of Massachusetts,
1978.

[4]In California, the Teacher Certification and Licensing Commission; in Massachusetts, the Advisory Commission
of the Bureau of Teacher Certification and Placement.

[5]Patterson's American Educational Directory (1977),
lists fifty-nine such institutions in California and
thirty-seven in Massachusetts.

[6]Keynote Address, annual meeting of the National
Council on Religion and Public Education, St. Louis,
Missouri, November 19, 1977.

[7]The task has been charged to the Subcommittee on
Religious Studies of the State of Wisconsin Social Studies
Curriculum Study Committee, Department of Public Instruc-
tion, Madison, Wisconsin; Thomas E. White, University of
Wisconsin-Oshkosh, Chairperson.

CHAPTER THIRTEEN

MICHIGAN'S CERTIFICATION PROGRAMS:
PHILOSOPHICAL AND PRAGMATIC PARADIGMS

Paul J. Will

In the relatively new academic area of public education religion studies, the teacher is the factor crucial
to a successful instructional program. An instructor
without a basic knowledge of the world's religions and
their sacred writings, a sensitivity about the problem of
objectivity in a pluralistic society, and the ability to
evaluate critically curricular materials is severely
handicapped in this undertaking. Without systematic
teacher training based on clear objectives and standards,
plans for the successful implementation of the academic
study of religion will invariably go aglimmering.
Fortunately, an increasing number of professional leaders
in various states are dealing with this problem.

The State of Michigan has been a leader in the field
of public education religion studies certification, both
in terms of defined standards and number of approved programs. Seven institutions of higher learning were approved
for an initial five-year provisional period to prepare
teachers for certification in the Academic Study of Religions. Calvin College was approved in April 1972, Western
Michigan University and Michigan State University in
January 1974, Hope College in May 1975, Alma College and
Central Michigan University in November 1976, and the
University of Detroit in January 1978.[1]

The initial impetus for the certification program in
Michigan came from Calvin College, a private four-year

_Paul J. Will, Ph.D. candidate, teaches in the Department of
Religion, Central Michigan University. This chapter is a
revision of a paper presented at the annual meeting of the
American Academy of Religion in Chicago, November 1975._

denominational college in the western portion of the state.
In 1967 an inquiry was made to the state about the propri-
ety of preparing teachers for certification in the area of
religion. In 1969 Calvin College formally requested the
State Board of Education to approve certification of a
major and/or minor in "the history and literature of
religion." This request resulted in a study of constitutional considerations, existing courses in Michigan
schools, and practices in other states.[2] An advisory
committee of professionals was established to recommend a
course of action to the State Board.[3]

The outcome of these deliberations was that in April
1970 the Michigan State Board of Education approved the
Academic Study of Religions as a minor for elementary and
secondary certification purposes with a 20 semester hour
minimum requirement. In addition to the requirements for
the minor, students must complete those for education,
usually 24 to 32 hours, and a major of 30 credit hours.
In the case of the elementary curriculum three minors may
be substituted for the major/minor sequence. Usually
students select a religion minor to complement an English,
history, or social studies major, although the religion
minor has been linked to a wide variety of majors including
music, biological science, and home economics. Yet most
distinct courses as well as units on religion in the public
schools are found in English and social studies departments.

State Guidelines

At the same time the Board approved the minor it
adopted a set of standards which established a framework
for evaluating institutional requests for approval. First,
the college must be approved in three other certification
areas to be eligible. It must show that the instructional
staff have appropriate earned academic degrees, hold membership in learned societies, and make contributions to
scholarly advancement through research. The program must
be based on a comprehensive curriculum in the structure
and history of religions. A rationale for the program

must be provided. The relationship to other departments
and professional educators, including plans for student
teaching, must be defined. Finally, it must be shown that
there are adequate library resources and instructional
materials appropriate to the academic study of religions.[4]

To supplement these formal standards, a set of more
specific program development suggestions was prepared by
the advisory committee. These suggestions do not have
official State Board approval but contain a number of
specific recommendations. There should be a systematic
curriculum with required core offerings making up at
least one-half of the proposed minor. All the major
religions must be represented, including required offerings
in Eastern religions. An introductory course to provide a
common orientation in methodology and ontology is needed.
Consideration should be given to a course on the contemporary American religious situation. The inclusion of
electives from related academic disciplines is encouraged.
There also must be a program administrator, provision for
a file of teaching materials, adequate budgetary support,
and a system of program review.[5]

These two documents serve as practical guides for
institutions preparing their proposals for review and
State Board action. If the proposed program meets basic
requirements regarding the form of the application, it is
submitted to a Committee of Scholars for review.[6] This
committee is appointed by the State Board of Education.
Its membership varies but has included professors of religion and education from both public and private colleges
as well as representatives from the Michigan Department of
Education. This committee reviews each proposal and makes
recommendations. At least one visitation to the campus of
the institution seeking approval is part of the committee's
standard procedure.

In reviewing these proposals the committee has focused
on a number of problems. A major concern in most cases is
that the program components provide a balanced coverage of
the major religious traditions and do not reflect a

particular religious orientation. Usually schools are
asked to clarify the relationship between the proposed
program and the departmental committee structure of the
school by including an organizational chart and program
review procedures. The committee sees a need to assign
responsibility for advising students and supervising
directed teaching experiences. Formulation of a policy
regarding the transfer of credit from other academic
institutions is often another recommendation. Schools are
questioned about the extent of teaching materials germane
to the field that would be available to students.[7]

The Committee of Scholars is increasingly reluctant
to recommend approval of a specific minor for elementary
teachers in view of the need for broad, general preparation
for the self-contained classroom situation. Apparently
this attitude developed after the minor was initially
adopted. The result is that Calvin College is approved
for both elementary and secondary certification but the
other programs are validated only for the secondary level.

Given these guidelines and suggestions there is still
diversity in the programs approved by the State Board of
Education. This leeway allows for the implementation of
differing philosophies and techniques. A critical evaluation of the individual teacher-training curricula spot-
lights this divergence.

Calvin College

Since Calvin College had no initial model to follow
in designing a program, its proposal, in some ways, is the
most complex paradigm of all of the approved applications.
A student is required to take 31.5 semester hours, significantly above the state minimum of 20 semester hours for a
teaching minor. Although defined as an interdisciplinary
group minor, the curriculum still relies heavily on Department of Religion offerings. Presently, six courses are
required of all students: Introduction to Religion
Studies, World Religions, Contemporary American Religious
Situation, Historical and Theological Foundations of

Religious Education, and two half courses, Readings and
Research and Senior Seminar in Interpretation of Biblical
Literature.[8]

Calvin has introduced changes in its program based on
actual experience. The original proposal as approved in
1972 had a slightly different format. Before the final
application was submitted to the state, Religion and
Theology 205: World Religions was restructured and made a
300 level course. Then Philosophy/Religion 205 was created
as Ethics (Religio-Ethical Systems) and was designed to:

> . . . provide a methodology and ontology
> which are valid both descriptively and
> analytically for the academic study of
> several major world religions. The axio-
> logical structure of this required course
> also recognizes that the program of con-
> centration to which it is an introduction
> is a teaching minor. Thus the axiological
> approach is appropriate because of its
> similarity and ready transfer to the study
> of religions in secondary and elementary
> schools where the prevailing motivation
> and context for such study is heavily
> oriented toward value education.[9]

This focus proved unmanageable and was replaced with one
that includes methodology and stresses legal and curricular emphases. The course was renamed Introduction to
Religion Studies. Religion 301 also underwent a transformation from Christianity and Culture, which covered the
cultural impact of the religious traditions coming out of
the Reformation, to the present Contemporary American
Religious Situation. Interestingly, the Christianity and
Culture course initially designated for use in the program
was itself a modification of an earlier existing offering
entitled Calvinism.

To further clarify the role of religion in education
there is Historical and Theological Foundations of
Religious Education, which "...is designed to give the
student an understanding of how the various social

institutions in society, such as home, church, school, government, etc. have organized themselves and their curriculum and teaching to meet their goals in a way consistent with existing religious values and within the legislative, judicial, and social limits placed upon each institution in various times, places, and religious traditions."[10] The half course in Reading and Research, an independent study-tutorial course, fills in any gaps left in the student training especially in the areas of methods and professional attitude.

The remainder of the Calvin program involves four elective courses. Two courses must be taken from eleven offerings in Religion/Philosophy. These include theology, Biblical literature, and philosophy courses. Finally, two courses must be elected from among three groups (History, English/Fine Arts, and Sociology/Psychology). Each group has four courses for selection, and no more than one course may be chosen from any one group. The stated intent of this interdisciplinary requirement is to give students further exposure to non-Western religions.[11] A careful analysis of these offerings reveals that they barely touch, if at all, on Asian religion, and they have only a cursory religion component in general. The result is that most, and probably all, students would have only the one required general course in World Religions as their basis of knowledge about non-Western religions. This clearly is a weakness in the program.

I would also question the inclusion of theology courses in a minor in the academic study of religion approved by the state for the secular classroom. From a literal standpoint theology implies a sectarian view and while some courses under the rubric of theology have no denominational focus and utilize a descriptive approach, I believe that it is clearly advisable in constructing a minor of limited scope to exclude theological studies. And although I can conceive of situations in which actual theological training could be utilized, its broad application and usefulness in the elementary and secondary

settings is questionable. The State Board apparently does
not share this concern, for the approved programs often
contain such courses and the official standards state:
"Religion as an academic discipline describes, interprets
and compares sacred writing, creeds, theologies, mythologies, and cultic practices of a culture or cultures."[12]
If theology is to be included in teacher preparation, a
clearer definition of what is involved is necessary. Unfortunately it is difficult enough to convince educators
in the public sector of the validity of teaching about
religion without introducing such complications.

Thus, elimination of both peripheral and purely
theological courses from the list of program electives
would be an improvement. Clearly the major strength of
the Calvin certification minor is the combination of a
required core of over half the courses and an interdisciplinary component. There is evident concern with the
appropriate methodology and attitude toward the subject
matter. The willingness to change course content as the
program evolves is laudable, and the direction of this
metamorphosis is in line with the unofficial program
development suggestions distributed by the state.

Western Michigan University

In some respects, the plan of Western Michigan University's Department of Religion is the most intriguing. This
22 semester hour minor is based on the department's structure and its underlying philosophy that religion is an
autonomous discipline with its own identifiable perspective
and methodology. From the inception of the certification
idea Western Michigan's faculty argued that this viewpoint
should be the rationale for the teaching minor in Michigan.
Even before any proposal gained approval they suggested
particular criteria to the state for this new certification
area. These were eloquently advocated and philosophically
compelling in many ways.[13] While the State Board did not
formally adopt Western Michigan's ideas in toto, some of
their logic and even specific suggestions were incorporated

into the official standards. For example, the requirements
that an applying institution must be approved in a minimum
of three other certification areas and that instructors
must hold academic rather than professional seminary
degrees may be attributed to Western's influence.[14]

Western Michigan's approved program embodies this
particular ideological perspective. Two of the six
courses in the curriculum are required of all students:
Introduction to Religion and The Teaching of Religion in
the Public School. The latter two-credit class represents
a clear recognition of the special pedagogical problems
in this field. Subsequent applications from other colleges
to the state generally have adopted the idea that there
should be a specific requirement in the methodology of
teaching about religion in the elementary and secondary
schools. The remainder of the minor provides for a series
of choices within certain designated areas. Students are
to select one course in primitive religions and one in the
Christian, Jewish, or Islamic religious traditions within
the departmental category of Historical Studies. Finally,
another course either in Historical Studies, other than
those areas previously specified, or in Methodological
Studies must be elected.[15] The absence of a required content course in Asian religions is a serious problem.
Western Michigan's proposal recognized this lack but claimed
that knowledge about Eastern religions was implicit in its
requirements:

> Moreover, the rationale of the present proposal
> is such as to lead the student to investigate
> the nature and function of religion and the
> religious experience, or consciousness, as such.
> Consequently, the widest possible familiarity
> with religious phenomena is encouraged and heavy
> emphasis is placed on morphology and phenomen-
> ology both of which presuppose such broad
> familiarity.[16]

Despite the disclaimer, this still is a deficiency. Most
teachers fail to have even a rudimentary understanding of

the Asian traditions. Under Western Michigan's program
students can elect to avoid even a single offering on
Eastern religions, although they are required to have a
course on primitive religions.

It should be noted that the other disciplinary exami-
nations of religion available under Methodological Studies
are taught by religion department faculty and not professionals from those fields. However, the department has
excluded from the certification options part of their
regular curriculum entitled Constructive Studies, which
includes courses on theology. Certainly, the experiences
of those prepared by this unique program will be particularly valuable in determining the type of teacher-training
model that is most viable.

Michigan State University

Michigan State University's minor of 30 quarter hours,
the equivalent of 20 semester hours, envisions a liberal
elective system from the Department of Religious Studies'
offerings. Three courses are required of all students:
Understanding Religious Man, Introduction to Western Religions, and Introduction to Eastern Religions. Four
elective courses must be taken in Western religions, with
at least one in Judaic or Islamic studies. Three elective
courses on Eastern religions complete the requirements.[17]
Elective courses must be planned with the department's
Teacher Certification Program Administrator. Under this
scheme students have the chance to concentrate on either
textual or historical studies, depending on their teaching
goals, e.g. religious literature or history of religion.
A number of theology courses are available as departmental
electives. The program has no methods course and no
interdisciplinary offerings.

The strength of this curriculum is its balance between
Western and Asian traditions, thereby insuring substantial
coverage of the non-Western area. However, there is a
disparity in course offerings, with twenty in Western
religious traditions versus six in Asian religions, and

two of these latter are offered only in alternate years.
Moreover, this balance was achieved only after the
Committee of Scholars recommended that the department
revise its original plan. That first proposal, which was
based on a slightly different departmental curriculum,
called for two introductory courses, Introduction to
Christianity and Comparative Religion, and nine credits in
Biblical Studies. Students were to select another nine
credits from the field of either World Religions, Religion
and Culture, Religious History, or Ethics and Theology.
They also were to take six credits of electives in the
Department of Religion.[18]

The simplicity of the officially approved Michigan
State program, with its stress on departmental content
offerings, raises the issue of how specific and diversi-
fied the requirements for a teaching minor in religion
should be. Some will argue that a minor is inadequate to
the task and that a major concentration is needed. However, the State Board of Education has expressed its
concern about the placement of these newly prepared
teachers. Since it is unlikely that they will be teaching
only courses dealing with religion, preparation in another
academic area is essential. For the Michigan situation a
minor accreditation seems to be the most practical. Thus
the real issue for the present remains how many areas the
minor can and shall cover and how to delineate them in the
curriculum.

Hope College

Given this concern, Hope College's minor seems to be
the result of a careful analysis of the state's program
suggestions and of a survey undertaken by Professor Lambert
Ponstein in 1973. He found that the actual courses in
religion offered in the high schools were almost equally
divided between Bible as Literature and World Religions/
Comparative Religions.[19] The Hope program therefore calls
for an introductory course in the phenomenology of religion,
two courses in the Western religious tradition, two

sequential courses in Asian traditions, one interdisciplinary course, one course in Religion in America, and an
education course entitled Teaching of Religion in
Elementary and Secondary Schools. Provision is made for
several possible course substitutions. Literature of
Judaism and Christianity can be replaced by Religion in
Society or Intertestamentary History. Religion and
Psychology and Religion and Sociology can be substituted
for Philosophy of Religion. Contemporary Religious Thought
can take the place of Religion in America.[20] The minor
consists of 21 semester hours with the additional methods
course of two hours.

Additional Programs

Hope College's program followed the state advisory
committee's guidelines more closely than any of the
preceding ones. Subsequent applicants for state approval
also found it useful to adhere to these unofficial guidelines since the trend is for the Committee of Scholars to
use them more consistently in evaluating applications.
Alma College's program is similar to that of Hope College.
Given the typical curriculum offerings of most private
liberal arts colleges, this model may become quite widespread.

Central Michigan University's original proposal,
since modified, required courses in primitive religion,
approaches to the study of religion, and an orientation to
public education religion studies. Presently, only the
latter two are required. The remainder of the 23 semester
hour minor is divided on an elective basis between different cultural areas, with at least one course in both
Eastern and Western religious traditions; Biblical studies;
and religion as related to other disciplines or issues.
This is an attempt to include both core-required courses
while retaining a degree of flexibility in student
selection within a broad framework.[21]

The University of Detroit also followed the suggested
format in their 24 semester hour minor. The required

portion seems tailor-made for the state guidelines with an
introductory course, two offerings on major world religions,
a study of religion in America, and an education methods
course. Students then are allowed to elect three classes
in one or all of three broad fields: textual studies,
history of religions, and historical and cultural studies
in the Western tradition. This elective component provides
for a realistic concentration in the actual area of expected
teaching, e.g., literature, world religions, etc. Interestingly, the first Detroit application had to be amended
because in the Committee's opinion it lacked a required
course in the Western religious tradition and thus was not
balanced.[22] In fact, most applications were not readily
accepted by the Committee and required either program
alterations or further documentation. This in turn
resulted in a delay of several years between the time
applications first were filed and, then, finally accepted.

Conclusion

At this time, the full ramifications of certification
are not being tested. What would be the repercussions if
the state required those already teaching religion studies
courses to have minor certification in the field? There
are over 200 such instructors with virtually no formal
training in the academic study of religions teaching in
Michigan schools. Most school districts expect their
teachers to have only a background college course or two.
North Central accreditation which calls for six semester
hours preparation in similar fields (e.g. sociology,
psychology, and anthropology) also sets an informal
standard. There is a realization that there is a very
limited number of preservice religion studies minors
available. In addition, few schools specifically hire
someone in the field; rather they tend to look to members
of their present staff to teach these courses.

All of the approved programs are housed in full departments of religion or religious studies. Whether a
truly interdisciplinary proposal would gain approval is

uncertain. In general, the teaching minor programs
reflect the particular departmental philosophies of each
college and their ability to staff the offerings. Yet, in
many cases a few specialized courses were created just for
the minor.

The State of Michigan has thus established general
standards but no rigid criteria for the undergraduate
certification minor. The more specific program component
suggestions are not literally adhered to and remain unofficial. All approved colleges include an introductory
course for orientation in the discipline of religion and
the religious dimension in human experience. However,
this is the only suggested course subscribed to by all
schools. Only the private colleges meet the recommendation
of having at least one-half of the courses required of all
candidates. Apparently, there is little interest in including courses from related disciplines. Most schools
have a course on religion in America included.

The inclusion of courses on Asian religions as required core offerings often is minimized. Philosophic
polemics temporarily aside, one could argue for their
adoption on pragmatic grounds, for half of the religion
courses taught in Michigan public high schools are in
world religions. But if an Asian religions course is
required in the certification minor not on the basis of
theoretical comprehensiveness but because of its appropriateness to existing classroom situations, then the same
logic would justify requiring a college course on Bible as
Literature.[23] Perhaps the real question is whether high
school curricular offerings should dictate the form of the
teacher preparation program or whether the colleges should
concentrate on preparing teachers in a theoretical and
methodological understanding of religion and its role in
human culture, thereby letting high school courses evolve
out of this context. No consensus regarding this problem
has emerged among professionals in religion and education
nor is one likely soon.

Finally, one can ask to what extent these programs are useful not only for current teacher preparation but as models for future developments. Has the state been too lax or too restrictive? Or has it struck the golden mean that allows for a fair degree of experimentation within a sound academic and pedagogical framework? Perhaps the major contribution of the Michigan certification programs, which range from 20 to 30 semester hours, is in providing a variety of actual curricular paradigms rather than abstract theoretical structures to analyze. The teachers produced by these programs and their experiences in the schools as well as the reactions of those administering the departmental teaching minors may provide the real verdict on their value.

NOTES

[1] Adrian College's proposal was evaluated in Fall 1979 and subsequently approved in 1980.

[2] A 1969 Survey of Certification Practices with Regard to Religion in the Fifty States conducted by the Michigan Department of Education found that only 24 of 44 responding states had consistently negative reactions to four questions concerning the appropriateness of religion as a teaching area.

[3] Department of Education, State of Michigan, Preparing Teachers for the Academic Study of Religions, September 30, 1970.

[4] Department of Education, State of Michigan, Standards for Approval of the Academic Study of Religions for the Certification of Teachers, n.d.

[5] Department of Education, State of Michigan, Program Development Suggestions for Teaching Minor in the Academic Study of Religions, n.d.

[6] Usually the application is filed using the official form, Request for State Board Approval Amended or New Teacher Education Program, available from Teacher Education and Certification Division, Bureau of Higher Education, Department of Education, State of Michigan.

[7]Department of Education, State of Michigan, Report of Committee of Scholars Regarding Michigan State University Request for Approval of a Teaching Minor in the Academic Study of Religion, November 30, 1972; Report of Committee of Scholars Regarding Western Michigan University Request for Approval of a Teaching Minor in the Academic Study of Religions, November 30, 1972; and Report of Committee of Scholars Regarding Hope College Request for Approval of a Teaching Minor in the Academic Study of Religions, n.d.

[8]Request of Calvin College to the State of Michigan Department of Education to Add the Academic Study of Religions as a Certifiable Teaching Minor in its Secondary and Elementary Teacher Education Programs, October 20, 1971.

[9]Ibid., p. 11.

[10]Ibid., p. 12.

[11]Ibid., p. 13.

[12]Department of Education, State of Michigan, Standards for Approval of the Academic Study of Religions for the Certification of Teachers, n.d.

[13]Department of Religion, Western Michigan University, Suggested Criteria for the Training of Public School Teachers in the Discipline of the Academic Study of Religions, (Revised as of September, 1970), and Guntram G. Bischoff, "Toward the Academic Study of Religions in the Public School? Reflections Occasioned by Recent Developments in Michigan," Bulletin of the Council on the Study of Religion, 2 (April 1971) 3-10.

[14]Bureau of Higher Education, Michigan Department of Education, Minutes of Meeting of the Committee on Religious Education, February 19, 1970. Their recommendations were adopted by the State Board of Education in April 1970.

[15]Department of Religion, Western Michigan University, Request for State Board Approval of an Amended or New Teacher Education Program, n.d.

[16]Department of Religion, Western Michigan University, Response to the Document, "Program Development Suggestions for Teaching Minor in the Academic Study of Religions," issued by Department of Education, State of Michigan and received at the Department of Religion, Western Michigan University on April 24, 1972, n.d.

[17]Department of Religious Studies, Michigan State University, Request for Authorization to Offer a Teaching Minor in the Academic Study of Religions, n.d.

[18]Department of Religion, Michigan State University,
Request for Authorization to Offer a Teaching Minor in
Religion, n.d.

[19]Untitled summary of the survey on the teaching of
world religions in the public schools of Michigan,
October 12, 1973. The results showed 104 courses distributed as follows: World Religions - 22, Comparative Religions - 22, The Bible as Literature - 42, History of
Religion - 6, Great Western Religions - 1, Bible History,
Old Testament - 3, Bible History, New Testament - 3,
Humanities, Discussion of Religions and Religious Beliefs -
3, Religion in America - 1, and History of the Bible - 1.

[20]Request of Hope College to the State of Michigan
Department of Education for the Purpose of Adding the
Academic Study of Religions as a Certifiable Minor in its
Elementary and Secondary Teacher Education Programs,
January 31, 1973.

[21]Department of Religion, Central Michigan University,
The Teaching Minor in the Academic Study of Religion, n.d.,
and subsequent annual reports submitted to the State Board
of Education.

[22]Department of Religious Studies, University of
Detroit, Request for State Board Approval of Teacher Education Program Changes, September 26, 1974 and subsequent
revisions.

[23]The use of the designation, "Bible as Literature,"
may be an inaccurate description for some high school
teaching situations. I find the title used in Pennsylvania,
"Religious Literature of the West," often more representative and useful.

CHAPTER FOURTEEN

STRATEGIES AND PROGRAMS FOR PUBLIC AWARENESS
AND TEACHER EDUCATION IN RELIGION STUDIES

Paul J. Will

No formula exists for the successful introduction of
the academic study of religion in public school systems.
The nature and extent of the particular program envisioned
as well as the specific climate of the local situation
actually determine what approach to utilize. However, in
any undertaking the academic integrity of public education
religion studies should not be sacrificed for expediency.
Those who maintain that one should use any rationale or
means to initiate a religion studies program, regardless
of whether such strategies are legally or educationally
sound, are in error. Such approaches will rebound negatively not only on the individual employing them but on
the entire undertaking.

General Strategies

Certain carefully conceived strategies based on sound
principles are appropriate regardless of the actual focus
of the program. Seventeen years after the Schempp decision ignorance about the constitutionality and feasibility
of public education religion studies among educators and
the general public still is widespread. A 1976 attitudinal survey in Wisconsin, a state actively involved in the
field, revealed that 62% of the school administrators
questioned said that Supreme Court rulings did not encourage the study about religion in public schools. However,
the survey also showed that they felt objective study of
comparative religion (60%) and the Bible (41%) was

*Paul J. Will, Ph.D. candidate at the University of Michi-
gan, teaches in the Department of Religion, Central Michigan University.*

desirable. The 808 educators believed that public education religion studies was a valuable academic endeavor
(53%) that could be done objectively (70%) and favored
studying religion in separate courses (34%) and where it
is relevant in other subject areas (72%).[1]

The education of colleagues, elected officials, and
the general public remains a continuing need and is part
of any strategy for implementing public education religion
studies. Familiarity with the legal basis of religion
studies derived from judicial decisions and individual
state statutes is a prerequisite before undertaking any
specific program. The exact language of the state's constitution and laws as well as the department of public
instruction's directives generally have a direct bearing
on what form teacher education and school programs take.

Clarification of terminology can resolve many educators' concerns and anxieties. Religion studies must be
distinguished from traditional religious education. The
distinction between education for specific religious formation and teaching for general religious literacy or
awareness provides a useful contrast in this regard. Any
rationale for the study of religion in the public schools
is more firmly based on an educational concern for understanding the academic importance of the religious dimension
in a humanities curriculum than on a narrow focus stressing
values orientation. This is not to negate the inevitable
ethical component that religion study involves but to put
it in proper perspective. The raison d'etre for public
education religion studies is not values education. In
some sense, the same types of misunderstandings about the
focus of the academic study of religion experienced on the
college level are present with public school personnel
considering religion studies programs.

Since each state exercises autonomy in determining
its own educational standards, early contact with the
educational establishment is advisable in order to ascertain their attitude and gain their approval. Common

misunderstandings and general avoidance of special interest
groups may color their initial reaction to plans for
teacher education and curricular programs. Considerable
effort in educating department of public instruction personnel, professional educational organizations, curriculum
specialists, and local school district leadership thus is
needed. Concrete information about the existing extent of
religion studies in the state's schools provides a powerful, persuasive tool in this regard. In most cases, only
a specific survey will yield this particular information
since official reporting documents rarely record religion
courses but subsume them under English and social studies
categories. Yet, experience in state after state shows
that there are 50-100 high schools already offering distinct courses in religion studies and that the educational
authorities are unaware of the fact.

A 1975 survey of all Oregon school districts, for
example, uncovered 130 public school courses, usually under
the rubric "Bible as Literature" in the English curriculum
and "World Religions" in social studies. The survey also
revealed that only one-third of the teachers instructing
in such courses had significant college preparation, i.e.
more than one course in religion studies. Another third
had minimal exposure to the academic study of religion and
the remainder had no academic preparation at all. A 1976
survey of administrators of large school districts in the
Pacific Northwest produced similar results.[2] Such information supports the argument for programs designed to train
teachers in an objective, pluralistic approach to religion
studies. In most states, a case can be made for in-service
programs based on the existing situation and need rather
than as an attempt to implement new curriculum.

Since most public education religion studies programs
are dependent on collegiate leadership, chances for success
are enhanced if the School of Education as well as the Department of Religion takes an active interest. Professors
of education act as a liaison with the state authorities
and education professionals in the field and are conversant

with the official terminology and standard procedures for implementing programs within the educational framework. In some cases, only they can initiate action with state agencies. Unfortunately, usually there is little initial positive response from School of Education personnel who are invited to consider establishing teacher education programs in public education religion studies. However, hard statistical evidence on the extent of religion studies in the schools and the opportunity to co-sponsor educational programs are two effective ways of arousing their interest.

To have a significant impact on the state level, experience suggests that the formation of a broad coalition is advisable. It may be called a committee, council, or task force, and its particular focus may vary. Existing state committees differ widely in their actual composition. Membership typically is some combination of professors of religion and education, state education officials, school board members, administrators, teachers, or representatives of the public and religious groups. Rarely are all of these groupings represented. Formulating a sound plan of action and a thoughtful rationale is easier with such a coalition. Gaining the support of state authorities and professional organizations is more likely when they are approached by a group rather than a single individual or institution. In addition, such cooperative arrangements tend to replace or at least defuse competition for leader- ship. Some of the most successful state efforts began initially with a well-planned awareness conference and for- mation of a state committee, subsequently followed by teacher education programs.

Program Possibilities

Regardless of the particular organizational framework, there are a variety of programs or practical goals that can be sought. (Representative program designs are found in the Resources Section of this volume.) Sponsoring awareness conferences for the public or professionals is a frequent

approach which not only creates general understanding but
also enlists support for specific school programs. Careful planning is a prerequisite for success. Program
planners need to include a variety of speakers. Educators
and teachers already involved in religion studies in their
own schools are a particularly valuable addition to any
such conference. Information on the historical and legal
background of public education religion studies, available
curriculum material, and possible instructional options
generally are part of the program format.

School board members, administrators, curriculum
specialists, and teachers can be targeted as a potential
audience through official mailing lists maintained by the
state or their respective professional organizations. Many
colleges maintain such a compilation of contact people in
area schools. Professional journals and newsletters are a
frequently overlooked vehicle for publicity. Usually
direct contact with principals and chairpersons of English
and social studies departments of every school within
driving distance of the conference site increases attendance.

Many of the specifics of pre-service undergraduate
certification programs in the field of the academic study
of religion are covered in previous chapters in this
volume. However, some basic strategic considerations
should be noted. An essential preliminary step in establishing such programs is to have the state designate
religion as an approved certification area. Only after
this is achieved can individual colleges apply to have
their programs approved.

Advocates of certification in religion studies must
ascertain whether the state specifies majors (usually 20-30
college semester hours), minors (15-20 hours), or broad-
based competency areas (as social studies and humanities)
in which religion can be a component. Then a rationale
and proposal as to the place of religion studies in the
overall state certification pattern can be formulated. It
would seem that the best justification for religion studies

is as a minor field or a specialization in a competency
area rather than a major which holds little opportunity
for employment. Usually religion studies courses are
offered as electives and very few schools have enough
classes to justify a full-time person. In fact, teachers
are hired for their academic expertise in a discipline
other than religion studies. Thus religion studies courses
are offered typically by professionals trained primarily in
another discipline.

State education officials should be involved at an
early stage as political considerations may weigh as
heavily as programmatic ones. Approval can be a long process with creation of standards, hearings, and bureaucratic
and/or legislative approval. Whether religious organizations should be involved directly in certification efforts
is debatable. Such a strategy probably is undesirable due
to the confusion that would result over the real purpose
of such academic programs.

As the K-12 school population base shrinks and the
number of new personnel entering the teaching profession
declines, plans for implementing religion studies will
focus increasingly on the interest and skills of experienced teachers. This will necessitate providing more
in-service school district programs to upgrade their
qualifications. Increasing emphasis is being placed on
this type of effort with over fifteen colleges offering
appropriate summer workshops in the past few years.
Components in such programs include clarification of the
legal basis for religion studies, strategies for school
district adoption and implementation, appropriate methods
for the subject matter, discussion of the question of
objectivity, evaluation of current curricular materials,
development of teaching lessons, content information on
common misunderstandings and difficult concepts, and
available resources such as films, field trips, and outside
speakers.

In a typical three-week workshop, like one offered at
the University of Detroit, one-third of the time is

scheduled for academic content information on the workshop
theme, e.g. world religions. An early focus is given to
the legal aspects and general orientation to public education religion studies and later emphasis is placed on
developing individualized curricular materials.

Not to be overlooked is the possibility of one-day
academic seminars, such as those conducted in Michigan
where teachers react to presentations on specific academic
content material and methodology. They also have a unique
opportunity to meet with others who teach religion
studies. These seminars are structured either on one
theme, such as Utopias or American religion, or tracked so
that there are different offerings for English and social
studies teachers.

On a larger scale, a few universities have developed
graduate programs in public education religion studies.
They represent another attempt to provide graduate training for practicing teachers. The existing programs at
University of Kansas, Western Michigan University, and
Wright State University require 30 semester hours or its
equivalent divided roughly equal between religion and
education courses. Typical of programs that lead to a
Masters degree in education, they provide a balance between
content and curriculum development, including a curriculum
project and/or a methods seminar. The education component
is determined by the School of Education while the religion
section is planned by the Department of Religion. The
Harvard Program on Religion and Education conducts a two-
year graduate program for seminary students who wish to
obtain teacher preparation and a Master of Theological
Studies degree. All of these graduate programs enroll a
small number of students, suggesting a limited appeal for
this option.

In-service opportunities provide a means of establishing continuous contact among teachers, curriculum
specialists, and administrators which is not accomplished
by efforts directed at state officials. The state educational bureaucracy is usually too removed from the

classroom situation to affect directly curricular changes
or individual teachers. The results of all such programs
are reflected not only in the classroom but also in clearer
understanding among school officials and the public regarding the feasibility and nature of public education religion
studies programs.

Examples

Most of the sustained statewide activity in public
education religion studies is centered in the Mid-West
Many of these states have active groups that are directly
affecting the education programs in their area and maintaining liaison with the state department of education.
Varying local situations have fostered different strategies and programs.

In Michigan, a formal organization for public education religion studies was created in 1972 as the result of
a statewide conference of college professors. The Council
on the Study of Religion in Michigan Schools consists of
representatives from fourteen public and private institutions of higher learning and regional teacher groups. An
annual dues structure allows the Council to provide modest,
but important, services. Among these are successive surveys of the public schools to determine the extent of
religion studies. Through these surveys the dramatic
growth in distinct semester courses about religion from 96
(1973) to 115 (1975) to 178 (1977) can be documented. This
information was shared, in turn, with the Michigan Department of Education at a time when it was determining whether
a need for teacher training programs in public education
religions studies existed.

A mailing list of over 600 educators involved in the
field resulted from these surveys which encouraged the
Council to publish a semi-annual newsletter. This publication contains evaluations of curricular materials,
announcements of in-service offerings, and updated information on the field as well as creates a sense of identity
among religion studies teachers throughout the state.

Other publications underwritten by the Council include a bibliography of available audio-visual aids and an extensive handbook on the legal basis and methods for religion studies in Michigan schools.

Several years ago, the Council followed the suggestion of Guntram Bischoff to create distinct regional religion studies teachers' organizations that meet in annual day-seminars to review and develop new academic approaches to the study of religion. These programs are particularly successful in improving established school programs and creating a sense of professional identity. They also draw educators interested in innovating programs in their schools and provide a setting for them to interact with experienced colleagues. Day-seminars held in the Western and Central regions attract between 20-40 participants each. Colleges in the respective area host the meetings and a budget of approximately four hundred dollars covers the cost for mailing, publicity, materials, and facilities. A nominal registration fee is also charged. With the inauguration of an Eastern region in 1980 there are now three regional groups of approximately 50-70 educators each. A steering committee of teachers is in charge of planning programs and carrying on the work of each respective regional group.

Approaches by the Council to the secondary principals association as well as individual school districts proved relatively unsuccessful and the present commitment is to encourage the regional concept and thus achieve direct contact with teachers. These regional groups send representatives to the Council's meetings and give a grass-roots dimension to the Council's work.

The Council tries to enlist professors of education in their work but is not too successful. In the beginning, it consciously chose not to involve the Council of Churches, believing that this would confuse the purpose of the organization and distract it from the urgent need to assist the some 120 teachers who were already teaching about religion. Recently, the Detroit area Council of Churches expressed

interest in public education religion studies and issued a
positive position paper. Liaison between the organizations
now is established. All this cooperative activity in the
state complements the efforts of individual colleges, many
of which have approved certification programs in this
field.

In contrast to the Michigan strategy, Minnesota's
striking record of success is directly linked to the work
of the state's Council of Churches. Its Committee on
Religion and Public Education under the effective leadership of Gerald Fahrenholz consistently seeks to make an
impact on public education in the state. In the mid-1960's
the Minnesota Council distributed to pastors throughout the
state a booklet containing the recommendations of the American Association of School Administrators concerning the
study of religion and public education. Simultaneously,
the state Commissioner of Education mailed them to every
superintendent in the state and conversations between
clergy and educators in local areas based on the document
were encouraged.

Building on this effort, two statewide awareness
conferences for school administrators and religious
leaders to discuss the legal aspects and present situation
of religion studies were held in 1967 and 1969. A third
conference in 1970 was conducted for professors of religion and education in order to encourage them to offer
college courses in public education religion studies. A
number of universities responded and both summer and
semester offerings were forthcoming.

The committee hosted a series of one-day consultations
for educators. The last two were co-sponsored by the
Minnesota State Department of Education, and each drew
100-200 persons. Their latest joint effort was a unique
weekend religion studies planning workshop. Ten different
school districts were invited to send school personnel,
school board members, and community representatives to
work together in planning public education religion
studies strategies.

Another outcome of the involvement with state
officials was the creation of a special committee to
develop guidelines for public education religion studies
in Minnesota. These were officially reviewed by the State
Board of Education. Rather than adopt these guidelines
officially, the Board delegated responsibility to local
districts for developing their own policy and implementation strategies. The committee's guidelines provide an
unofficial model for local use.

Kansas provides yet another approach and highlights
the point that often the real impetus for public education
religion studies centers around one particularly active
individual or institution. Lynn Taylor, Dean of the Kansas
School of Religion and Professor of Religious Studies at
the University of Kansas, inaugurated a program that was
carefully linked to an in-service summer graduate course
for teachers. At the outset, cooperation was established
with the University of Kansas School of Education and
awareness conferences for the general public were conducted throughout Kansas. Starting in 1972 with one site and
five students, the summer program grew to four sites with
over a hundred teachers involved. Much of this work was
done on volunteered time and a modest budget. Some outside foundation support underwrote the project, eliminating
much of the cost to the participants, who included a significant number of elementary school teachers. Additional
incentives were the state requirement for continuing professional development and the opportunity to explore a new
field.

The Kansas Center for Public Education Religion
Studies located in Lawrence grew out of these endeavors.
It serves as a repository for the curricular materials
created through these summer programs as well as a sponsor
of teacher training and public awareness programs. Hun-
dreds of teachers in Kansas teaching religion studies now
have a focus for their interest and are being brought into
the work of the Center in increasing proportion. More
recently, the Midwest Center for Public Education Religion

Studies of the National Council on Religion and Public
Education was located at the Kansas School of Religion.
It was created to assist and coordinate similar efforts
among eight Middle Western states (North Dakota, South
Dakota, Iowa, Kansas, Nebraska, Missouri, Oklahoma, and
Colorado).

Other state committees have employed different strategies. The Council on Religion Studies in Iowa Schools,
formerly the Iowa Educators' Task Force on Teaching about
Religion in Public Schools, with both institutional and
individual representation from all levels of public education, received a state humanities public programs grant to
sponsor a series of regional awareness conferences. These
featured as speakers a lawyer, educator, humanist,
theologian, and historian and drew mixed, limited response.
The Council has held ongoing consultations with state
officials regarding certification possibilities.

The Ohio Committee on Public Education Religion
Studies has close ties to the educational establishment
by stressing that each collegiate institutional member
have two representatives, one each from education and
religion. With this support base, the Ohio committee
studied the possibility of certification, agreed on common
guidelines for teacher education and certification proposals, and helped members design certification proposals
according to these guidelines for submission to the Ohio
Board of Education. It encourages member institutions to
offer in-service programs and is seeking state humanities
funding for a series of one-day regional conferences.

While all of these endeavors in public education
religion studies are time-consuming and demanding, they
enhance the public school curriculum in a long neglected
area and enable collegiate religious studies programs to
provide a new outreach. The need, opportunity, and
techniques for continuing involvement in elementary and
secondary education are present and only await a bold,
determined effort based on viable individualized
strategies.

NOTES

[1]Wisconsin Council of Churches and Department of
Philosophy and Religious Studies, University of Wisconsin-
Eau Claire, Attitude Survey of Clergypersons and School
Administrators in Wisconsin on the Study About Religion in
the Public Schools.

[2]James L. Ash, Jr. and John Phillip King, Public
Education Religion Studies in the Pacific Northwest; A
Proposal to Develop Teacher Training and Certification
Programs at Oregon State University, 1977.

SECTION III

RESOURCES

This section provides a selection of materials useful
in developing public education religion studies. It follows the Implementation Section where the actual utilization of these materials is discussed. A representative
selection of guidelines adopted officially by professional
organizations includes both general education directives
and specific program standards. Sample education program
formats, including pre-service, graduate, in-service, and
public awareness offerings, reflect the variety of
approaches introduced throughout the nation. A bibliogra-
phical listing of relevant books and films completes this
compendium of resources.

TEACHING ABOUT RELIGION IN THE PUBLIC SCHOOLS
EDUCATIONAL RESPONSIBILITIES OF SCHOOL PERSONNEL

Officially Adopted by the
California State Board of Education
January, 1973

1. Teaching about religion in California
   The California State Board of Education stated in 1963
   that "our schools should have no hesitancy in teaching
   about religion. We urge our teachers to make clear the
   contributions of religion to our civilization. . . ."

2. Teaching about and practicing religion
   A legal and logical distinction exists between teaching
   about religion and practicing religion. Public schools
   may not sponsor the practice of religion; but it is
   legally permissible and educationally responsible to
   ensure that study about religion is carried on in the
   public schools.

3. Teaching about and instructing in religion
   To teach about religion is not to instruct in religion.
   Teaching about religion embraces the study of various
   religions; appreciation of the nature and variety of
   religious experience historically and currently; information on past and present sources, views, and
   behavior of religious persons or groups; and the
   influence of religion on cultures and civilizations.
   Instruction in religion, by contrast, is to seek
   acceptance of and commitment to a particular religion,
   including a non-religion like secularism. Freedom to
   instruct in a religion is a treasured part of the
   American heritage. Instruction is carried out in the
   home and in the churches. Although instruction in
   religion may help a person to achieve a deeply meaningful life, it is prohibited in the public schools.
   Teaching about religion is not, however, prohibited.
   The only commitment intrinsic to teaching about
   religion is a commitment to learn, to study, to seek
   to understand, and to communicate. To learn about
   religion is to understand religious views and values,
   to recognize the immense importance of religion to the
   American heritage, and to realize that religion continues to permeate both Western and Eastern cultures.

4. School personnel to ensure teaching about religion
   School authorities should see that students are taught
   about religion and that teachers are adequately prepared
   to teach it. Teaching about religion can take place
   in an entirely separate course, in an appropriate part
   of another course, or in an enrichment program. School
   personnel are obliged to help students develop an

informed understanding and appreciation of the role of
religion in the lives of Americans and the people of
other nations. Teachers should seek to encourage
students to become aware of their richly diverse and
complex religious traditions and to examine new forms
of religious expression and insight.

5. Subject matter
    The subject-matter areas mentioned here are only
    suggested; the list is in no sense exhaustive.
    a. Religion in America. Study about religion in
        America is fundamental to understanding and appre-
        ciating the American heritage. America is a land
        of many races, cultures, languages, and religions.
        Students should learn about the contributions of
        religion to America. They should study about
        principal religious figures, groups, issues, and
        trends; fundamental beliefs contributing to the
        growth of democracy and the democratic process;
        the background of the First Amendment to the U.S.
        Constitution; the problem of religious persecution;
        and the value of religious freedom. They should
        recognize and seek to understand the diversity of
        religious expressions that have helped to shape
        this country; they should appreciate problems of
        conscience in relation to historical and contem-
        porary issues of religious freedom; and they should
        become aware of the historical, cultural, and social
        conditions contributing to religious pluralism and
        diversity.
    b. World religions. An educational imperative is to
        seek to understand ourselves, others, and the
        world. Religion has been a decisive factor in the
        development of civilizations. Students should
        comprehend the religious ideas that have helped to
        shape Western and Eastern cultures and civilizations;
        they should become aware of the influence of
        religion on life-styles (work, prayer, devotion,
        ritual, worship, meditation) and on the development
        of ideas. The teacher should assist students to
        understand religious views that can be quite un-
        familiar in the United States. Care should be
        taken, however, to avoid emphasizing unusual
        religions or religious practices so that respect
        for religion will not be undermined. Of importance
        in Western religious thought and practice are the
        various formative periods of Western civilization.
        To become educated in Western religious thought
        and practice, students should be exposed to the
        major religious heritages of Judaism, Christianity,
        and Islam. Similarly, students should study the
        major Asian religions.
    c. Classical religious texts. The study of represen-
        tative portions of the classical sources of major
        religious traditions is appropriate in public edu-
        cation. These religious documents have contributed

to the major cultures, to the personal lives of countless persons, and to self-understanding. A knowledge of biblical literature, for example, is necessary to understand Western literature, history, and the values underlying the United States and many of its laws. In accord with appropriate grade levels, the study of biblical sources should include an understanding of fundamental approaches to the examination of the texts; an awareness of the historical, cultural, and geographical context and the languages; a scrutiny of the literary forms and images; and a consideration of themes, events, basic ideas, and values.

d. Development of courses. Other courses or parts of present courses can be developed in the study about religion. Examples of courses that can be developed are Religion and Society, a study of the influence of religious views and values on the social, economic, and political aspects of society; Religion and the Arts, a study of the influence of religion on art, music, literature, dance, architecture, and sculpture; and Man's Religious Experience, a study of the effects of religion on the lives of men.

6. Guidelines for teaching about religion
Religion should be discussed with sensitivity. Conflicting points of view are to be expected and considered; open discussion is a proper method for truth searching in study about religion; religious indoctrination is to be avoided.

a. Need for factual accuracy. The need for factual accuracy is paramount in teaching about religion. Careful and balanced examination of sources is requisite for informed judgment. As much as possible, teachers should use primary sources and should encourage students to use them. Secondary sources are useful for overview and clarification. Students should be helped to identify, compare, assess, and communicate ideas and viewpoints. Teachers should be thorough in studying the sources and related materials; they should also recognize and admit their limited knowledge or understanding in a specific area.

b. Need for empathy. Teachers should also seek to understand the points of view of different religions. They should empathize sufficiently with the view of an adherent of a particular religion to grasp the significance of that view for the one who holds it. This empathy helps one to understand why the view is held and why it is valuable in the life of the one who holds it. One must first seek to come to an understanding of a religion within its own historical context rather than solely from one's own viewpoint.

c. Problem of oversimplification. In teaching about religion, one must avoid the tendency to convey a

false impression of the subject by oversimplifying
it. Teachers should explain the extent to which a
particular religion or religious view is to be
considered in class. Students should be made fully
aware of the limitations imposed on their study
about and, consequently, their understanding of a
religion. Further, the diversity within religions
as well as among religions should receive careful
attention. In addition, the teacher should state
why certain sources, selections, historical periods,
themes, and issues have been selected for study.

d. Need for sensitivity. In teaching about religion,
the teacher should be sensitive to the diverse
views, levels of sophistication, and critical
ability of students, parents, and members of the
community. School administrators and teachers
should be sensitive to the possible problems involved such as misunderstandings and misconceptions.

e. Avoidance of ridicule and prejudice. Ridicule and
prejudiced statements must be avoided in the study
of religion and religious practices whether from a
historical or contemporary viewpoint. Ridicule is
rooted in an anti-educational attitude; it is the
product of failing to be sensitive or empathic.
It results from a callous disregard for the views
of another person or group.

CRITERIA FOR EVALUATING CURRICULAR MATERIALS

Developed By
Professional Advisory Council
Public Education Religion Studies Center
May, 1973

A. Is the material educationally sound and pedagogically
    effective?
Curricular material should always be usable and appropriate
in terms of subject matter, of the abilities of students,
and of the competence of teachers. Information, concepts,
illustrations, and the reading level of the material should
be suited to the students who will use it, and the general
presentation should be in keeping with their abilities.
Material should reflect a sophisticated awareness of educational methodologies and incorporate appropriate pedagogical
techniques. Material should also be presented in ways suited
to the skills and training of the teachers who will use it.
In addition, it should provide adequate guidance to reference,
research, and supplementary material and help in lesson preparation, including suggestions for the use of the material.
Finally, material should--where appropriate--encourage and
assist teachers to use audio-visual materials and other non-
book resources.

B. Does the material reflect an academically responsible
    approach?
Curricular material should be based on sound scholarship
in the field of religion. If possible, it should employ
primary sources or follow them faithfully. If secondary
sources are used, they should be recognized as academically
responsible, as faithful to original sources, and as avoiding
bias by presenting alternative viewpoints. Content should
be non-confessional, pluralistic, balanced, comprehensive,
and factually accurate, distinguishing historical from
confessional fact. Material should reflect an awareness
of scholarly definitions of religion and a concern for the
relationship of religion and culture. It should also reflect both formal and institutional as well as informal
and personal religious phenomena and the many ways in
which they are expressed. Thus material should help
students achieve religious literacy and an awareness of
diverse religious phenomena.

Although the basic approach should be critical and analytical, material should seek to combine the scholar's
"outside" view with the adherent's "inside" view. It
should avoid onesidedness by presenting traditional as
well as contemporary academic interpretations of religions
and their scriptures. Similarly, material should avoid
reductionist approaches (for example, purely psychological
or sociological ones) that limit the perspectives from

which religion is studied. While curricular material need
not be interdisciplinary, religion studies are not limited
to the confines of traditional academic disciplines. Thus,
material may be interdisciplinary in its approach to religion study. While it must be academically responsible,
curricular material which assumes a high level of scholarly
aptitude by either teacher or pupil should be carefully
evaluated. Material should always reflect a scholarly
competence that is appropriate to those who will use it.
Finally, it should be noted that while no single piece of
curricular material is likely to meet all of these criteria, it is essential for the teacher to select that
material which comes closest to meeting them and to compen-
sate for its deficiencies.

C. Is the material sensitive to the religious and
    political problems of America's pluralistic society?
Because of the social and political reality of divergent
viewpoints in American life, curricular material should be
non-confessional, making a pluralistic, not positioned,
presentation of content. Such a goal can be achieved in
part if material is presented not solely from an analytical, scholarly point of view. It should also reflect the
point of view of the people who have experienced it,
preserving the integrity and authenticity of their
particular religious commitment. In this way material can
be sensitive to the views, beliefs, and concerns of religious minorities. In addition, material should be open-
ended, seeking not consensus but understanding and
appreciation of the values that lead to different religious
commitments in both the broad and narrow sense, especially
with the object of breaking down the stereotypes that lead
to religious prejudices and discrimination and of helping
students to accept the validity of other religious experiences than their own.

D. Does the material reflect a non-confessional and
    interfaith perspective?
Although it is not essential that curricular material be
developed jointly by people of different religious faiths,
it should certainly reflect the non-confessional perspective such interfaith development produces. Ecumenical
teams should contribute to the development of material as
authors, consultants, or field testers so that in the
course of the process divergent points of view are
reflected. Materials carefully developed in light of the
criteria discussed in sections B and C above are likely to
achieve the objectivity and pluralism of viewpoint that an
interfaith perspective is meant to assure.

E. Does the material reflect and has it been written
    within the parameters of the major Supreme Court
    decisions?
Although curricular material which meets the criteria laid
out in sections B and C above will probably be legally
appropriate, it is important to make sure that it is as

objective as possible and does not exclude, favor, or
derogate any particular religious group or sect. Material
must be non-proselytizing. If the use of material which
does not meet these criteria is unavoidable, it may be
necessary to use materials representing many positions and
beliefs to achieve a legally appropriate balance and objectivity. However, it should be stressed that the
legality of curricular materials is best assured by careful attention to the guidelines in the preceding criteria.

F. Has the material been field tested?
The success of any curricular material in the classroom
depends to a considerable extent upon the degree to which
it has been field tested. An adequate testing program in
actual classroom situations should involve students and
teachers of varied backgrounds, abilities, and faiths and,
in the case of teachers, of varied academic and pedagogical
preparation as well. Curricular material should be evaluated
as fully as a determination of these matters permits.

In summary, curricular material for teaching about religion
in the public schools should be pedagogically sound,
academically responsible, sensitive, non-confessional,
legally appropriate, and field tested. These general
criteria imply material that is appropriate as to subject
matter, age level of students, and teacher competence;
material that is pluralistic, balanced, and comprehensive
in content; material that employs objective data and an
analytical but empathetic approach; and, finally, material
that encourages awareness of and respect for each person's
religion whether traditional or secular.

242   Resources

GUIDELINES FOR TEACHER EDUCATION PROGRAMS

Developed By
Professional Advisory Council
Public Education Religion Studies Center
May, 1973

The following guidelines are recommended for the use of
colleges, universities, and professional schools in
developing or conducting pre- and in-service teacher
education programs in religion studies.

Teacher education programs in religion studies should

1. be jointly planned and taught by members of the
    education and religion faculties;

2. make clear that religion studies teachers use the
    same tested methods employed in other disciplines
    to plan, design, and develop programs;

3. provide substantial grounding in

    a. U.S. Supreme Court decisions pertaining to
        religion studies in public education;

    b. method of studying religion, e.g., phenomeno-
        logical, sociological, psychological,
        anthropological, as well as philosophical and
        theological;

    c. history of religions, literature of religious
        thought, religion and culture, religion and
        ethics, and religion in America; and

    d. relating the insights of developmental
        psychology to teaching about religion;

4. help teachers become aware of their attitudes
    toward formal and informal manifestations of
    religion and how their attitudes influence their
    teaching and their relationships with students
    (such assistance should include experiences de-
    signed to develop objectivity and empathy in
    teachers);

5. stress why and show how teachers must be noncon-
    fessional and pluralistic in their approach;

6. help teachers discover the complexities and prob-
    lems involved in teaching about religion in a
    pluralistic society;

7. introduce teachers to printed and nonprinted
    materials for classroom use--as well as field
    trips, guest speakers, etc.--and to sound
    criteria for evaluating them;

8. demonstrate how to relate particular curricular
    materials to pedagogical methods appropriate to
    them;

9. provide learning conferences with adherents of
    faiths different from the teachers';

10. provide adequate supervision of the teachers'
    development of lesson plans and courses and ob-
    servation of their practice teaching;

11. stress the importance of using primary sources in
    teaching and only secondary sources that are
    faithful to primary sources; and

12. point out that competency in one area of religion
    does not assure competency in all areas of reli-
    gion studies.

GUIDELINES FOR TEACHER COMPETENCY

Developed By
Professional Advisory Council
Public Education Religion Studies Center
May, 1973

Ideally, teacher competency in religion studies is no different from teacher competency in any other discipline.
However, the legal and political problems created by our
constitutional separation of church and state, the long-
standing Protestant domination of our culture and its
frequent misrepresentation and/or rejection of minority
religious views and the religious pluralism of our present
society require special additions to the usual guidelines
established for evaluating teacher competency. Thus, the
following guidelines consist of one section dealing with
dimensions of teacher competency common to all fields and
a second section presenting aspects of teacher competency
unique to religion studies in American public education.

I.

Competent religion studies teachers, like all teachers,
should be professionally qualified, emotionally mature,
and pedagogically sound.

A. Professional qualification is demonstrated by
certification by the state in which a teacher
practices and by the maintenance of good professional standing.

B. Emotional maturity is demonstrated by the
possession of a secure self-image and set of
values which enable a teacher to be open with
and accepting of students with different views
and life-styles.

C. Pedagogical soundness is demonstrated by
1. use of the same procedures for planning,
developing, and evaluating curricula as are
employed in designing other academic programs;
2. use of pedagogical methods appropriate to the
particular materials for given courses;
3. choice of materials which show awareness of and
sophistication in educational methodologies
appropriate to the age level of students for
which the materials are intended;
4. knowledge of developmental psychology and of
the concepts and teaching methods appropriate
to each stage of maturation; and
5. knowledge of and ability to use a wide variety
of print and non-print materials and media.

II.

Competent religion studies teachers should also be well-
versed in the legal issues surrounding religion studies in
public education, academically qualified in religion as an
academic subject, and non-confessional in approach.

A. Understanding of legal issues is demonstrated by a
    thorough knowledge of the U.S. Supreme Court deci-
    sions as well as state and local laws pertaining
    to religious practices and religion studies in the
    public schools and of the parameters suggested by
    these laws for academic study of religion in the
    public schools.

B. Academic qualification in religion studies is
    demonstrated by
    1. an adequate knowledge of religion in its formal
        and informal, institutional and non-institu-
        tional, communal and personal, inherited and
        experienced manifestations;
    2. a knowledge of the diverse ways in which
        religion is expressed, such as ritual, myth,
        ceremony, festival, symbols, stories, music,
        and art;
    3. awareness of and ability to use several dif-
        ferent methods of studying about religion,
        such as the history of religions, the
        phenomenology of religion, the philosophy of
        religion, the psychology of religion, the
        sociology of religion, etc.; and
    4. a knowledge of both the positive and negative
        functions of religion in human culture and
        history.

C. A non-confessional approach to religion studies is
    demonstrated by
    1. a pluralistic approach;
    2. self-knowledge about one's religious and value
        commitments, about one's attitudes toward
        formal religion, and about one's religious
        biases and cultural limitations so as to be
        free to present fairly and discerningly
        various religious options and to teach about
        religions without proselytizing for one's own
        position;
    3. openness to and empathy for alternative
        religious and non-religious points of view
        among students and a willingness to listen to
        them and accept their feelings and underlying
        beliefs; and
    4. dedication to building a sense of human com-
        munity through cultivating an understanding of
        and respect for all people and an appreciation
        of our common humanity in the midst of our
        diversities.

Given the special requirements needed for competency as a
teacher of religion studies, it is vital for colleges,
universities, and professional schools to provide a comprehensive range of pre- and in-service training and
experiences. Interdisciplinary work is especially needed
to help teachers experience the interrelatedness of
religion studies with other academic disciplines.

STANDARDS FOR APPROVAL OF THE ACADEMIC STUDY
OF RELIGIONS FOR THE CERTIFICATION OF TEACHERS

Officially Adopted by the
State of Michigan
Department of Education
April, 1970

The standards which follow are designed to supplement
existing policies and procedures for teacher education
program review actions.

DEFINITION OF THE AREA

Religion as an academic discipline describes, interprets
and compares sacred writings, creeds, theologies, mythologies and cultic practices or cultures. It is one key to
the understanding of a culture and the value orientation
of individuals. To protect the integrity of the discipline
and assure its maximum benefit in the elementary and
secondary schools, the following standards are proposed for
the training of persons to teach religion in the elementary
and secondary schools.

I.   INSTITUTIONAL ELIGIBILITY

Any institution undertaking to provide a minor in the
academic study of religions for the certification of
teachers for elementary and secondary schools should be
approved by the State Board of Education for the preparation of teachers, accredited by the North Central Association, and approved for the training of teachers in at
least three other certification areas.

Questions:
    --What evidence demonstrates accreditation?
    --What evidence demonstrates that this institution is
      approved for training teachers? (Specify three
      other areas in which the institution now certifies
      teachers.)

II. QUALIFICATIONS OF INSTRUCTIONAL STAFF

Each instructor responsible for the training of teachers
of religions shall have earned academic degrees appropriate
to the level and content of the courses he teaches in the
academic study of religions and should be involved in research activities and appropriate professional societies.

Questions:
    --What evidence demonstrates that instructors in this
      academic area have earned academic degrees?
    --What evidence demonstrates that instructors in this
      academic area have degrees appropriate to the level
      of the courses they are teaching?

--What evidence demonstrates that instructors in this
academic area have degrees in the fields in which
they are teaching?
--What evidence demonstrates that instructors in this
academic area are involved in research (e.g, publications and scholarly papers)?
--What evidence demonstrates that instructors in this
academic area are involved in professional learned
societies?

III. PROGRAM COMPONENTS

An institution preparing teachers of religions should offer
a comprehensive curriculum in the academic study of religions. The instructors of such courses should have some
direct involvement in the field where the teachers will be
working.

Questions:
--What evidence demonstrates that the curriculum
provides exposure to the breadth of cultures represented and extent of courses in both the structure
and the history of religions?
--What evidence demonstrates that the curriculum is
comprehensible, (i.e., what is the rationale)?
--What evidence demonstrates that instructors are
involved on a continuing basis with elementary and
secondary schools offering such programs?
--What evidence demonstrates the availability of
complementary courses in other departments? (e.g.,
anthropology, philosophy, psychology, etc.)
--What evidence demonstrates institutional plans to
incorporate in the professional education component
experiences (including plans for student teaching)
appropriate to the academic study of religions?

IV. RESOURCES FOR INSTRUCTION

An institution preparing a person to teach religions should
have adequate library and staff resources both in the field
of religion and such cognate fields as anthropology,
philosophy, psychology, history and languages.

Questions:
--What evidence demonstrates the adequacy of the
library? (Approximate number of volumes and key
journals in each field.)
--What evidence demonstrates the adequacy of the
related faculty resources?
--What evidence demonstrates the availability of
instructional materials appropriate to teaching
the academic study of religions?

State of Michigan
Department of Education

PROGRAM DEVELOPMENT SUGGESTIONS FOR TEACHING
MINOR IN THE ACADEMIC STUDY OF RELIGIONS

Standards have been developed for State Board Approval of
institutional requests in the Academic Study of Religions
for the certification of teachers. The suggestions below
are intended to supplement these standards to assist institutions in preparing requests for the committee of
scholars' review and State Board action.

1. The program should have a systematic design which
    reflects its intention--the academic study of reli-
    gions. It should not be simply a collection of
    courses.

2. The program should include offerings representative of
    all the great religions of the world. It should not
    reflect a particular religious orientation.

3. The program of study should be distinct and be desig-
    nated in institutional catalogs and bulletins.

4. A program administrator should be designated, respon-
    sible for management, development and evaluation.

5. Staff assigned to the program should be cosmopolitan
    in training and experience, with backgrounds appro-
    priate for the nature of the offerings.

6. At least one-half of the proposed minor should be
    composed of basic or core courses required of all but
    exceptional candidates.

7. Courses should include offerings in Eastern, non-Judeo-
    Christian religions and these should be a part of the
    required core. The program should include an intro-
    ductory course which provides a common orientation for
    students concerning methodology and ontology which is
    relevant to the academic study of religions.

8. Courses for this program drawn from related and sup-
    porting disciplines should be double-titled and double-
    numbered in order to specifically identify their
    attachment to the academic study of religions and as a
    legitimate part of this minor.

9. It is suggested that institutions give serious consid-
    eration to offering a course which focuses on the
    contemporary American religious situation.

10. Teaching and curriculum materials appropriate for use
    in the public and private schools should be provided
    and specific provision made for the development of
    student familiarity with these materials to enable
    them to develop programs and teach this field in
    schools in which they will be employed.

11. Library and instructional holdings should be reviewed
    to insure that these are representative and inclusive
    of the range of religious offerings incorporated in
    the program.

12. The institutional budget should provide adequate and
    visible resources for the development of this program.
    The level of support in the early years of program
    development should reflect an institutional commitment
    to the acquisition of appropriate resource levels.
    These will be staff, library holdings and instruc-
    tional materials.

13. A system for periodic and orderly review on this
    program should be devised by the institution to insure
    that appropriate changes are made where necessary.
    Provision for review should be included in the early
    planning for program development.

CREDENTIAL PROGRAM

CALIFORNIA STATE UNIVERSITY, NORTHRIDGE
Social Science--Religious Studies

1. Religious Studies Major - 36 units

Lower Division - 6 units

Units

RS 150 Man's Religions   3
One 200 level course from the following   3
  RS 200 Religion in America
  RS 205 Contemporary Ethical Issues
  RS 270 Western Religions
  RS 280 Asian Religions

Upper Division - 30 units

One course in religion in America   3
  (from four offered)
One course in ethics   3
  (from five offered)
One course in classical religious texts   3
  (from seven offered)
One course in religious thought in the West   3
  (from nine offered)
One course in religious thought in the East   3
  (from eight offered)

Proseminar: RS 497   3

Elect 12 units, 9 of which must be upper
division, chosen in consultation with an
adviser, in Religious Studies or in closely
related courses from other departments.   12

With approval of an adviser, students may apply a
Topics in Religion course (RS 496 A-Z) to the appropriate category listed above.

2. Social Science Component - 30 units

Six history courses   18
  History 150-151 Western Civilization
  History 270-271 United States History
  Two topical courses in United States History
  (at least one of which must be in the history
  department)

One political Science course   3
  Political Science 155 or 305 American
  Political Institutions

One Geography course   3
   Geography 301 Cultural Geography

One ethnic studies course
   Either Chicano Studies or Pan African   3
   Studies (could be in another department
   with approval)

One elective from other areas of the social   3
sciences

WESTERN MICHIGAN UNIVERSITY
Department of Religion
22 semester hours
Approved by the State Board of Education - January, 1974

Required Courses:

1) Religion 200 - Introduction to Religion (4 semester
   hours)
2) Religion 521 - The Teaching of Religion in the Public
   School (2 semester hours)

Elective Courses:

1) one course in primitive religion, within the category
   of Historical Studies (4 semester hours)
   Religion 300 - Prehistoric and Primitive Religions
   Religion 500 - Historical Studies in Religion (topic
                  varies) 2-4 semester hours
2) one course in the Christian, Jewish, or Islamic reli-
   gions, within the category of Historical Studies (4
   semester hours)
   Religion 305 - The Christian Tradition
   Religion 306 - The Jewish Tradition
   Religion 307 - The Islamic Tradition
   Religion 500 - Historical Studies in Religion (topic
                  varies) 2-4 semester hours
3) one course in Morphological and Phenomenological
   Studies (4 semester hours)
   Religion 310 - The Morphology and Phenomenology of
                  Religion
   Religion 311 - Myth and Ritual
   Religion 312 - Religious Forms in Modern Literature
   Religion 510 - Morphological and Phenomenological
                  Studies in Religion (topic varies) 2-4
                  semester hours
4) one course (4 semester hours) in either
   (A) any religion other than those specified above in
       the category of Historical Studies:
       Religion 301 - Protohistoric Religions: Ancient
                      Near East, Greece, Rome, and Meso-
                      American
       Religion 302 - Religion in the Indian Tradition
       Religion 303 - Religion in the Chinese and Japanese
                      Traditions
       Religion 304 - African Religions
                  or
   (B) Methodological Studies
       Religion 320 - The Philosophy of Religion
       Religion 321 - The History of the Study of Religion
       Religion 520 - Methodological Studies in Religion
                      (topic varies) 2-4 semester hours

HOPE COLLEGE
Department of Religion
23 semester hours
Approved by the State Board of Education - May, 1975

Required Courses:

1) Religion 130 - Phenomenology of Religion (3 semester
                  hours)
2) Religion 110 - Literature of Judaism and Christianity
                  (3 semester hours)
   (possible substitutes: Religion 140 - Religion in
                                          Society
                           Religion 322 - Intertestamentary
                                          History)
3) Religion 242 - Near Eastern Religion (3 semester hours)
4) Religion 341 - Asian Religions I (3 semester hours)
5) Religion 342 - Asian Religions II (3 semester hours)
6) Religion 331 - Philosophy of Religion (3 semester hours)
   (possible substitutes: Religion 451 - Religion and
                                          Psychology
                           Religion 452 - Religion and
                                          Sociology)
7) Religion 321 - Religion in America (3 semester hours)
   (possible substitute: Religion 431 - Contemporary
                                         Religious Thought)
8) Education 328 - Teaching of Religion in Elementary and
                   Secondary Schools (two credit hour
                   course in Department of Education)

CENTRAL MICHIGAN UNIVERSITY
Department of Religion
23 semester hours
Approved by the State Board of Education - November, 1976

Required Courses: (8 semester hours)

Religion 540 - Teaching of the Academic Study of Religion
               in Public Schools (2 semester hours)
Religion 545 - Approaches to the Study of Religion
               3 semester hours)
Religion 130 - Introduction to American Religion
               3 semester hours)

Elective Courses: (15 semester hours)

One from Religion 220 - The Chinese Religious Tradition
         Religion 221 - The Japanese Religious Tradition
         Religion 222 - The Hindu Religious Tradition
         Religion 320 - The Buddhist Tradition

One from Religion 210 - Religions of the West
         Religion 313 - Christianity
         Religion 314 - Islam
         Religion 315 - Judaism

One from Religion 250 - Old Testament and Its Age
         Religion 260 - New Testament and Its Age

One from Religion 304 - Religion and Psychology
         Religion 235 - Religion and Social Issues
         Religion 301 - Myth and Reality
         Religion 334 - Death and Dying: Religious
                        Dimensions

One elective from the courses listed above or:

         Religion 101 - Introduction to Religion
         English 365 - The Bible as Literature

Students must take at least eight hours of 300-500 level
courses.

UNIVERSITY OF DETROIT
Department of Religious Studies
24 semester hours
Approved by the State Board of Education - January, 1978

Required Courses: (fifteen semester hours)

1) Religious Studies 198:   Religion and Man
2) Religious Studies 190:   World Religions I (Eastern
                            Religions
3) Religious Studies 191:   World Religions II (Western
                            Religions
4) Religious Studies 343:   Religion in America
5) Education 457:   Curriculum, Methods, and Materials in
                    the Academic Study of Religions

Elective Courses: (nine semester hours)

Three courses elected from the following areas:

a) Textual Studies
   Religious Studies 100 - New Testament: Introduction
   Religious Studies 101 - Old Testament: Introduction
   Religious Studies 194 - Religious Literature of the East
   Religious Studies 207 - Mark, The First Gospel
   Religious Studies 210 - Jesus and the Church: Gospel of
                           Matthew
   Religious Studies 208 - Jesus, Man for Others: Gospel
                           of Luke
   Religious Studies 311 - Jesus and the Gospels

b) History of Religions
   Religious Studies 265:   Black Religions in America
   Religious Studies 293:   Islamic Religion and Thought
   Religious Studies 294:   Contemporary Religious Move-
                            ments in America
   Religious Studies 393:   Anthropology of Religion
   Religious Studies 491:   Christianity and World Religions
   Religious Studies 493:   History of Religions: Methods
                            and Approaches
   Religious Studies 497:   Buddhism; the 'Little' and 'Big'
                            Rafts
   Cross-Disciplinary Course 42144:   Hinduism
   Religion Studies 412:   Modern Jewish Life and Thought

c) Historical and Cultural Studies in the Western Tradition
   Historical Studies - eight courses listed
   Cultural Studies - ten courses listed

WESTERN MICHIGAN UNIVERSITY
Master of Arts in Teaching of the
Academic Study of Religions

The Master of Arts in Teaching of the Academic Study
of Religions is deliberately designed to be a small and
flexible program, with individual planning for each student.
This will enable the student and advisor to select a curriculum option and particular courses that will effectively
relate the teaching about religions to the student's own
teaching situation. The program is built around an Education core, plus three options in Religion designed to meet
the needs of different types of students.

The Education Core:

Nine hours selected from the following four offerings:

1. TEED 601 Introduction to Research in   3 hours
        Education
2. TEED 602 School Curriculum   3 hours
3. TEED 603 Social and Philosophical   3 hours
        Foundations
4. TEED 604 Psychological Foundations   3 hours

The Religion Options:

Option I (for experienced teachers holding the B.A.
or its equivalent)

1. Religion 621 Introduction to the   2 hours
        Academic Study of Religions
2. Three courses chosen from the following.
        One of these must be Religion 500:

        Religion 500 Historical Studies*
        Religion 510 Morphological and
            Phenomenological Studies*
        Religion 520 Methodological Studies*
        Religion 530 Constructive Studies*   12 hours

3. Religion 622 Seminar-Practicum on the
        Teaching of the Academic Study of
        Religions in the Public Schools   3 hours
4. Religion 710 Independent Research
        (Curriculum Project)   4 hours

Option II (cognate option for experienced teachers)

1. Religion 621 Introduction to the Aca-
        demic Study of Religions   2 hours
2. Three courses chosen from Religion 500,
        510,520,530. One of these must be
        Religion 500   12 hours
3. Religion 622 Seminar-Practicum on the
        Teaching of the Academic Study of
        Religions in the Public Schools   4 hours

4. Suitable cognate at the 600 level
   (preferably in an area in which
   the student has had previous
   training and/or teaching
   experience)   3 hours

Option III (for undergraduate majors, minors, and
teaching minors in religion)

A. (for undergraduate minors)

   1. Three courses chosen from
      Religion 500,510,520,530.
      One of these must be
      Religion 500   12 hours
   2. Religion 622 Seminar-Practicum
      on the Teaching of the Aca-
      demic Study of Religions in
      the Public Schools   3 hours
   3. Religion 710 Independent Research
      (Curriculum Project)   6 hours

B. (for undergraduate majors and teaching minors in
   religion)

   1. Three courses chosen from the
      following: Religion 500,
      Religion 510, Religion 520,
      Religion 530   12 hours
   2. Religion 622 Seminar-Practicum on
      the Teaching of the Academic
      Study of Religions in the Public
      Schools   3 hours
   3. Religion 710 Independent Research
      (Curriculum Project)   6 hours

*All graduate-level courses in Religion are variable-
topics courses, repeatable for credit when the subject
matter is different.

WRIGHT STATE UNIVERSITY
Master of Education for
Secondary Teachers Religion Studies

The Master of Education degree program is open only
to those qualified for at least a provisional teaching
certificate. However, individuals who have degrees in
disciplines other than education and who are not qualified
for a provisional certificate can obtain Ohio certification
in secondary teaching concurrently with the master's degree. Such programs are individualized and must be
approved by the College of Education.

The Program	Course Requirements	Credit Hours
Core 12 hours	ED601 Communication in Education	3
	ED704 Foundations in Education	3
	ED751 Educational Statistics I	3
	REL629 Foundations for Religion Studies	3
Education Requirement 15 hours	ED733 Improvement of Teaching/ Secondary	3
	ED756 Introduction to Educa- tional Research	3
	ED820 Seminar in Secondary Education	3
	ED630 Teaching About Religion in Public Schools	3
	One of the following:	
	ED707 History of Education	3
	ED701 Advanced Educational Psychology	3
	ED702 Social Foundations of Education	3
	ED703 Philosophy of Education	3
	ED708 Comparative Education	3
Religion Component 21 hours	Three courses in non-Western religions	9
	Three-course sequence selected from the following:	9
	Western Religions	
	Religion in American Life	
	Religion and the Social Sciences	
	Philosophy of Religion	
	Religious Literature	
	Individually designed sequence	
	One religion elective	3

Total 48 hours

WRIGHT STATE UNIVERSITY
Education/Religion 430/630
Teaching About Religion in the Public Schools
Quarter Course

Instructors: William E. Collie, Nicholas Piediscalzi

Goals of the Course

This course is an introduction to the historical
background and court decisions pertaining to teaching about
religion in the public schools, to the current ways in
which religion is being taught in the public schools, and
to new experimental approaches to teaching about religion
with special reference to the process of values and moral
education as they relate to religion studies.

The goals of the religion studies program which are
stressed in this course include enabling the enrollee in
the following areas:

Knowledge:

1. To understand the religious dimension of human exis-
    tence and the many and diverse ways it is embodied
    and expressed in historical groups and individual
    lives;
2. To understand the way in which religions function in
    history and culture, with special emphasis on how
    religions influence institutions and in turn are in-
    fluenced by them;
3. To understand the difference between practicing and
    studying about religion;
4. To understand the variety of methods by which religion
    may be studied, e.g. phenomenological, sociological,
    psychological, anthropological, as well as philosophi-
    cal and theological;
5. To understand the appropriate context for public
    education religion studies as defined by U.S. Supreme
    Court decisions;
6. To understand the complexities and problems involved
    in teaching about religion in a pluralistic society;
7. To understand both the importance of and the methods
    of teaching about religion in a nonconfessional and
    pluralistic approach;
8. To understand his/her own attitudes toward formal and
    informal manifestations of religion and how their
    attitudes influence their teaching and their rela-
    tionships with students;
9. To understand the appropriate methods to plan, design
    and implement religion studies programs including how
    to select and utilize appropriate print and non-print
    materials from both primary and secondary sources; and
10. To understand the limited nature of his/her prepara-
    tion and to be able to identify the areas of competency
    in which he/she should be providing instruction.

Skills:

1. Help students accurately understand the religious
   dimension of human existence;
2. Utilize methods of study appropriate to the public
   school classroom;
3. Apply the processes of inquiry to religious concepts;
4. Enable accurate description of religious phenomena;
5. Encourage fair-minded explanations of religious
   practices and beliefs;
6. Enable reasoned analysis of differences and similarities among religions; and
7. Lead to responsible evaluation of religion's function
   in both individual and cultural contexts.

Attitudes and Values:

1. To appreciate:
   a. The place of religion in human history;
   b. The role of religion in private motivations,
      habits, and aspirations;
   c. The varieties of religious expressions, understand-
      ings and effects; and
   d. The necessity for mutual tolerance.
2. To be committed to the conduct of public education
   religion studies in keeping with the pluralistic and
   nonconfessional approaches stressed.
3. To be as objective as possible in dealing with diverse
   manifestations of religion both under study and as
   expressed by students.

Texts

Nicholas Piediscalzi and William Collie, eds. Teaching
About Religion in Public Schools. Niles, Il: Argus
Communications, 1977.

Cushing Strout. The New Heavens and the New Earth:
Political Religion in America. Harper Torchbooks. New
York: Harper and Row, 1975.

Course Requirements

1. For all students:
   a. attend every session.
   b. complete all reading assignments in texts and
      reprints for the given date before coming to class.
   c. complete and submit on time all written assign-
      ments. Study sheets may be hand written; other
      papers should be typed.
2. Graduate students:
   Complete a graduate project to be arranged with the
   instructors on an individual basis. Topics should be
   selected by the third class session.

Evaluation

Study questions on Strout	20%
Community survey on attitudes toward religion studies	30%
Paper on objectivity and autobiographical reflections	10%
Evaluation of religion studies programs/wrapup	30%
Participation	10%

Class Schedule and Assignments

1. -Preassessment and introduction to the course
2. -Religion, the State and the Public School I
    Strout: Forward, intro., 1,2,5,6,7,8 & study questions
3. -Religion, the State and the Public School II
    Strout: 12,13,16,18,20 and study questions
4. -Goals and Purposes of Public Education Religion Studies
    Guidelines for community survey
    Piediscalzi and Collie, Intro. & Part 1
5. -Public School Curriculum and the Instructional Process:
    Implications for p.e.r.s.
    Evaluation of Curriculum Materials: what to look for
    Objectivity paper due
6. -Religion Studies in Social Studies: Elementary and
    Secondary
    Piediscalzi and Collie, Part 3
7. -Religion Studies in the Humanities and the Fine Arts
    Piediscalzi and Collie, Part 2, Followup field trip
8. -Examining Exemplary Instructional Programs
    Piediscalzi and Collie, Part 4
9. -Values and Moral Education and Religion Studies and
    Community Concerns
    Piediscalzi and Collie, Part 5, Community survey due
10. -Final class on exam day. Wrapup. Attendance
    required.
    Evaluation of religion studies programs due.
    Graduate assignment due.

WRIGHT STATE UNIVERSITY
Religion 429/629
Foundations for Religion Studies
Quarter Course

Instructors: William Collie, Nicholas Piediscalzi

Purpose of the Course

The purpose of the course is to examine the different
ways in which religion may be studied academically, and,
in the process, to introduce the student to the complex
problems and issues which arise when one attempts such
study.

Course Requirements

For all students:

1. Attend every class session.
2. Participate actively in class discussions.
3. Complete and hand in on time a work sheet on each
    reading assignment.
4. Submit "take home" final examination.

For graduate students (additional):

Complete an independent research project mutually
agreed upon with the instructors at the third class
meeting.

Determination of Final Grade:

Work Sheets   40%
Class Participation   10%
Final Examination   50%

Texts:

DeVries, The Study of Religion: A Historical Approach.
Bettis (ed.), Phenomenology of Religion.
Shinn, Two Sacred Worlds.
Selected articles on library reserve.

Class Schedule and Reading Assignments:

(* = on library reserve)
1. Introduction to the Course
2. a. "From Classical Antiquity to the European Enlight-
        enment"
        deVries, Introduction and Chapters 1,2,3,4,5
3. "The Nineteenth and Twentieth Centuries"
    deVries, Chapter 10,11,12,13,15 and 16
    Bettis, pp. 111-168
4. "Psychological Explanation"
    deVries, Chapter 17
    *S. Freud, "The Phenomenon of Religion"
    *P. Ricoeur, "Reaction to Freud"
    *R. Bechtle, S.C., "C.J. Jung and Religion"
    *V. Frankl, "Man's Search for Meaning"

*W. James, "Meaning and Experience"
*N. Piediscalzi, "Erik H. Erikson's Psychology of
   Religion"
5. "Anthropological and Sociological Approaches"
    deVries, Chapter 18
    Bettis, pp. 179-198
    *Geertz, "Religion as a Cultural System," and
    "Ethos, Worldview and an Analysis of Sacred Symbols"
6. "Phenomenology and History of Religions"
    Bettis, pp. 1-4; 31-52; 53-84; and 199-218
7. Two Sacred Worlds (I)
    Shinn, pp. 11-120
8. Two Sacred Worlds (II)
    Shinn, pp. 121-186
9. "Theology of Culture"
    Bettis, pp. 169-178
    *Tillich, "Selections"
10. "Summary, Synthesis and Conclusions"
    "Take home" examination due.

WRIGHT STATE UNIVERSITY
The Bible and Literature: A Workshop
for Secondary English Teachers

Instructor: Peter Bracher

Goals of the Workshop:

The three-week workshop offers an intensive study of
selections from the Old and New Testaments chosen for
their inherent literary interest and for their special
interest as literary sources. The course of study should
familiarize participants with materials that will provide
them with a general biblical background to literary study
and will also enable them to deal directly with biblical
texts as literature. The workshop will also introduce
participants to the use of biblical materials in poetry,
fiction, and drama as sources of allusion, symbol, mythic
pattern, plot, and character. The emphasis will be on the
literature of the 19th and 20th centuries that secondary
school teachers are most likely to deal with in the classroom. In addition, some attention will be given to biblical backgrounds, to the methods and materials of teaching
the literature of the Bible, and to audio-visual resources.
For those interested, there will be opportunity to develop
curricular materials.

Textbooks:

Participants should provide their own copies of the
Bible in any of the standard English translations. A
collection of stories, poems, short plays and other related
reading materials will be distributed to workshop participants. The following texts should be purchased:

MacLeish, J.B. (Houghton-Mifflin)
Hemingway, The Old Man and the Sea

Supplementary Texts:

Abbot, W. M., and others, eds., The Bible Reader: An
Interfaith Interpretation (Bruce Publishing Co.)
Chase, Mary Ellen, The Bible and the Common Reader,
rev. ed. (Macmillan)
Ackerman, James S., Teaching the Old Testament in
English Classes (Indiana University Press)
Gros Louis, Kenneth, and others, eds., Literary Inter-
pretations of Biblical Narratives (Abingdon)
Ryken, Leland, The Literature of the Bible (Zondervan)

Writing:

The written work in this course is intended to provide
a variety of experiences similar to those that teachers
might require of high school students in a course on the
Bible.

266   Resources

A.
   1. Pre-test (1st meeting)
   2. Brief objective or short-answer quizzes on assigned
       biblical readings:
       a) 4th meeting: Genesis 1-11, and Abraham, Isaac,
          and Jacob
       b) 8th meeting: Joseph, Exodus, Samson, Saul, and
          David
       c) 11th meeting: the New Testament selections
   3. Quiz on terms selected from the following list
       (11th meeting):

       canon, apocrypha, decalogue, pentateuch, parable,
       gospel, anthropomorphism, apocalyptic (apocalypse),
       scribe, Douay, Authorized Version, King James
       Version, Revised Standard Version, Torah, 1611,
       the Vulgate, Documentary Theory, Masoretic,
       Tyndale, Converdale, Synoptic, Higher Criticism,
       "The Law, the Prophets, the Writings," typology,
       Septuagint

B.
   1. Map work
       a) the migration of Abraham
       b) the route of the Exodus and the Conquest of
          Canaan
       c) principal towns, rivers, and mountains of the
          Holy Land, especially those appearing in impor-
          tant biblical stories

   2. A set of study questions on the Joseph material
       (due 5th meeting)

   3. A psalm (to be written in class, 8th meeting)

   4. A parable (due 11th meeting)
       a) write an original parable, or
       b) recast one of Jesus's parables in different
          terms and/or different language; see, for
          example, the C.F. Burke material (handout)

   5. Write a brief "literary" analysis of some passage
       from the Saul-David material (due 7th meeting)

   6. Choose a literary work from the anthology and write
       a brief paper explaining its relationship to the
       biblical material it draws upon. Explain what use
       is made of the biblical material, how it is treated,
       and what is added to the "meaning" of the literary
       work as a result.

C. Graduate Students Only: Choose 1 and 2 or 3.

   1. Prepare a set of notes tracing the development of
       one of the following themes in your reading from
       the Bible: the concept of God, covenant, justice,
       evil.

2. Read and prepare a brief report (2-3 pages) on one
   of the following: Esther, Daniel, Proverbs,
   Ecclesiastes, Song of Songs, Tobit, Susanna, Judith,
   commenting on its literary and/or thematic values
   and its relationship to other biblical materials.

3. Develop a curricular project. Most typically this
   will be a unit or course outline, but it might also
   be to develop some teaching material or a resource
   list or resource material. It could be a more
   typical academic research project or it could be a
   media project. Do what you want and what will be
   most helpful to you but discuss your project with
   the workshop director during the first two or
   three days of the workshop. You may develop your
   unit and course outline in terms of local resources
   and format, but you should be sure to include a
   statement of objectives and then show how these are
   worked out in course content and activities. Also
   make provision for evaluation and resources.

INDIANA UNIVERSITY
Institute on Teaching the Bible
in Literature Courses

Faculty and Staff

James S. Ackerman, Dept. of Religious Studies, Indiana
    University (Director)
Thayer S. Warshaw, formerly Dept. of English, Newton North
    High School, Newton Mass., (Associate Director)
Hillel Barzel, Depts. of Hebrew and Comparative Literature,
    Bar Ilan University, Tel Aviv, Israel
Nancy Fuchs-Kreimer, Dept. of Religion, Temple University
David Greene, Dept. of Religion, Wabash College
Kenneth R. R. Gros Louis, Dept. of English, Indiana
    University
Henry J. Hoeks, Dept. of Religion, Calvin College
Bernard Scott, Dept. of Scripture, St. Meinrad School of
    Theology

All participants are required to attend three introductory sessions. Then the Institute will switch over into
separate ten-day tracks. Although there are a few exceptions caused by scheduling difficulties, each track will
generally meet at a specific time each day. And although
some of these tracks will have guest lecturers speaking in
them, each track will be presided over by one Institute
faculty member.

8:30: Bible in the Classroom; with Thayer Warshaw.
There will be lectures, discussions, and individual
conferences--as indicated by participant interests and
needs. Participants attending this segment and completing
a curricular unit or project will receive two hours of
credit. The only advanced preparation for this segment is
to read Alan Paton's Cry, the Beloved Country.

9:30: Bible as Literature; with Ken Gros Louis.
Reading assignments will be from the Bible, with several
mimeographed secondary readings--to be handed out at the
Institute. For one hour of credit participants may write
a short paper (6-10 pages) analyzing a biblical passage or
take a brief test on the last day of class.

10:45: Bible in Literature; with Hillel Barzel.
Reading assignments will be from The Bible as/in Literature by Ackerman and Warshaw, with several mimeographed
readings, to be handed out at the Institute. For one hour
of credit participants may write a short paper (6-10 pages)
analyzing a piece of modern literature which uses a biblical story, or take a brief test on the last day of class.

1:00: Historical-Cultural Background of the Biblical
Period; with Jim Ackerman. Reading assignments will be
from the Bible, Teaching the Old Testament in English
Class by Ackerman, et. al. and An Introduction to New
Testament Literature by Juel. For one hour of credit par-
ticipants can take a brief test on the last day of class.

2:15: The Bible in Art and Music; with David Greene. Will not be given for credit. These lectures will be offered to provide enrichment for teachers desiring to use audio-visual media in their classes.

NOTE: the maximum number of hours of credit given is four, either in Religious Studies (R515) or English (L580). Any of the tracks not taken for credit may be audited.

A Teacher Education Institute
On The Religious Dimensions
of World Cultures
Summer 1976, 1977
Public Education Religion Studies Center
Wright State University

Funded by the National Endowment for the Humanities

Institute Overview:

The Institute will provide elementary and secondary
teachers who deal with world cultures a five-week 1976
summer training session in academic religion studies and
in preparation of resource units coordinated with their
existing textbooks and curriculum. The summer '76 session
will provide teachers with academic study of various
approaches to religion; Eastern, Western and African
religions; and curriculum development of resource units
for world culture/world history studies in elementary and
secondary schools. Teachers will field test their resource
units during the '76-77 school year with consultation and
supervision from the Public Education Religion Studies
Center staff. The second five-week 1977 summer session for
teachers will include additional academic preparation and
professional assistance to enable them to evaluate, adapt,
and refine the resource units based on the previous year's
experience. The resource units then will be edited by the
PERSC staff for publication for more general usage by
other teachers.

The Institute is set for June 14-July 15, 1976 and the
comparable period in 1977. Six hours of graduate credit
will be given for each summer session.

Objectives - First Summer:

The Institute is planned to provide participants with
appropriate information regarding:

- the legal and pedagogical issues surrounding the
  academic study of religion,

- academic preparation in the study of world
  religions, and

- resource materials for world religion studies

in order to enable the participants to plan, implement,
evaluate, and revise curriculum resource units appropriate
for their instructional settings which incorporate the
religious dimension in the study of world cultures.

Since the Institute participants reflect a diversity
of backgrounds--elementary and secondary level; public and
parochial schools; varied discipline orientations--social
studies, English, humanities; inner city schools to rural

schools; one year's teaching experience to many years'
experience--the resulting outcomes are expected to reflect
that diversity. Some participants will be planning for
courses of study specifically identified as "world religions"; others will be integrating the religious dimension
into world cultural studies that may be labeled "social
studies" with a heavy geographic orientation or into an
"English" or "language arts" curriculum emphasizing world
literature.

Regardless of the curricular labels teachers work
with and under, the purpose of the Institute is to broaden
both the participants' vision and competency to incorporate
the religious dimension in the study of world cultures. It
is the commitment and conviction of the Institute staff
that culture cannot be comprehended adequately unless one
also understands religion as an integral part of culture.

The first summer session will emphasize study of the
apporpriate ways in which religion can be studied academically in a school setting. Much of the content of the
formal instructional sessions will provide background information on the major world religions.

Objectives - Second Summer:

1) Refine instructional units to not merely describe
religion but to actually show religion as an integral part
of the culture under study, both shaping and shaped by the
cultural context in which it functions.

2) Develop a unit of study to fit the level of conceptual sophistication of the students to be taught.

3) Plan appropriate methods of instruction to
actively involve students in considering the role of
religion in culture rather than just learning information,
details, and facts about the religions.

4) Incorporate resources for use with students which
are appropriate to the teaching situation including both
teacher developed and commercially available resources,
print, audio-visual, etc.

5) Submit your resource unit in final form typed and
ready to be shared with other teachers.

Readings:

Nicholas Piediscalzi and William Collie, Teaching About
    Religion in Public Schools.
PERSC Introductory Packet
        Guidelines
        Symposium Papers
        World Religions Packet
        Bible Packet
John Noss, Man's Religions
Chaim Potok, The Chosen
Marmaduke Pickthal, The Meaning of the Glorious Koran
Frederick Streng, "Four Ways of Being Religious"
Clifford Geertz, Islam Observed

272

THE UNIVERSITY OF DETROIT
Workshop on Teaching About Religions in the Schools
Religions Studies 504 -- Three Graduate Credits
June 27 - July 16, 1977 1:00 - 4:00 p.m.
Professor Paul J. Will

Objectives:

1) To clarify the basic concepts and terms for the world's major religious traditions
2) To discuss the problem of objectivity in teaching about religions
3) To gain an understanding of the legal basis for religion studies in the public schools
4) To discuss a variety of methods and approaches to the study of religion
5) To survey and evaluate the various available media resources for instruction about the major religions

Textbooks:

Public Education Religion Studies Center - Religion Studies in the Curriculum: Retrospect and Prospect, 1963-1983 (PERSC softcover)
Huston Smith - The Religions of Man (Harper paperback)
Various Handouts

Written Requirements:

1) One/two page reaction essay to question: "What does 'objectivity' mean?"
2) Three/four page critique of a teaching unit
3) Ten/fifteen page research project. The purpose of this assignment is to give students a chance to examine material in their area of special interest in more depth. This project may take several forms but should center on the field of religion studies and education. Students are especially encouraged to consider developing a curriculum unit but may also elect other projects such as a research paper, media presentation, or course outline.

Tentative Course Outline

Monday   Introduction
June 27   Course goals
            Student introductions
            Film: "The Supreme Court Speaks: Learning About Religion in the Public Schools"

Tuesday   Lecture: Evolution of Religion Studies in
June 28   Public Education
            Discussion: Legal Basis for Public Education Religion Studies

Wednesday
June 29
	Lecture: Religion and Public Education:
	     Prospects, Programs, and Problems
	Discussion: Religious Education and Religion
	     Studies: The Difference

Thursday June 30	Lecture: What is Religion? Discussion: Objectivity and Subjectivity in the Classroom NOTE: Reaction Essay Due
Friday July 1	Lecture: Basic Concepts of Hinduism Discussion: Criteria for Evaluating Curricular Materials
Monday July 4	Holiday
Tuesday July 5	Lecture: Basic Concepts of Buddhism Film: "Learning About Religion in World Culture Courses"

Wednesday
July 6
	Lecture: Karma and Samsara in Hinduism and
	     Buddhism
	Demonstration: Teaching Strategies and
	     Resources for Religion Studies

Thursday July 7	Lecture: Basic Concepts in Chinese Religion Discussion: Review of Teaching Units and Their Problems NOTE: Critique of Teaching Unit Due
Friday July 8	Lecture: Basic Concepts of Japanese Religion Discussion: Media Materials in Religion Studies (Optional Field Trip to Detroit Institute of Art)
Monday July 11	Slide and Filmstrip Without a Camera Workshop
Tuesday July 12	Lecture: Foundations of Christianity Discussion: Textbook Bias
Wednesday July 13	Lecture: Islamic Principles Discussion: Student Project Possibilities Use of Primary Source Materials

Thursday	Lecture and Discussion: Aspects of Judaism
	     Rabbi Richard Hertz
	NOTE: Class will be held at Temple Beth El,
	     Birmingham, Michigan

Friday July 15	Summary and Evaluation Research Papers Due

CENTRAL MICHIGAN UNIVERSITY
Second Regional Day-Seminar on Teaching
About Religion in the Public Schools
Wednesday, April 25, 1979

8:30- 9:00 Registration ($7.00 fee)
            Coffee/Tea/Donuts

9:00- 9:15 Opening Session -- Curricular Display Table

	English	Social Studies
9:15- 9:55	"Interpreting the Bible: A Reading and Writing Approach" Robert Root, English, CMU	"Meditative and Mystical Traditions of Asia" Kendall Folkert Religion, CMU
9:55-10:10	DISCUSSION	DISCUSSION
10:10-10:50	"Religious Biography in American Studies" Jeri Lou Wagstaff Ypsilanti Senior High School	"Aspects of Judaism" Fredric Brandfon Religion, CMU
10:50-11:05	DISCUSSION	DISCUSSION
11:05-11:45	"Jesus' Parables: Different Levels of Meaning" William Reader Religion, CMU	"Cults and New Religious Movements" Roger Hatch, Religion, CMU Jane Hurst, Religion, CMU
11:45-12:00	DISCUSSION	DISCUSSION

12:00- 1:15 Luncheon - University Center

1:30- 3:30 WORKSHOPS: Teaching strategies and concepts
            for classroom use related to the
            respective themes of the mini-
            sections (i.e., Bible and Litera-
            ture, American Religion, and World
            Religion). Results will be repro-
            duced and distributed to partici-
            pants.

3:30- 4:00 Summary Session

OREGON STATE UNIVERSITY
Corvallis, Oregon
"Awareness Conference"
March 2, 1974
Memorial Union

The Conference will:

•supply historical background and court decisions pertaining to teaching about religion in the public schools;

•offer new experiment approaches to teaching about religion;

•explain current ways in which religion is being taught in our schools;

•suggest services, resources, and materials available to those interested in adding religion studies to their curriculum.

Program

8:30 Registration -- Coffee

9:00 Opening of Conference

9:15 General Session I:
"The Supreme Court Speaks" (Film)
"Trends and Issues in Public School Religious Studies in Oregon"

10:30 Break -- Coffee

10:45 General Session I, continued:
"Trends and Developments in Oregon"

12:00 Lunch -- Preview
Preview of Seminars

1:15 General Session II
"Review of National Material and Services"

2:00 Seminars:
1. The Bible as Literature, New Testament
2. The Bible as Literature, Old Testament
3. The Teaching of World Religions in Public Schools
4. Attitudes and Concepts in the Social Sciences

3:15 Break -- Coffee

3:30 Wrap-up Session
"Trends and Issues in Public School Studies"

4:00 Adjournment

RELIGION AND THE PUBLIC SCHOOLS OF IOWA
Project of the Iowa Educator's Task Force on Teaching
About Religion in the Public Schools
Funded by The Iowa Board for
Public Programs in the Humanities

Specimen Conference Meeting

Time Frame: 3½ hours   (Afternoon: 1:00 p.m.- 4:30 p.m.)
                         (Evening: 7:00 p.m.-10:30 p.m.)

Part I: "Religion and Culture"

5 min. - A.   Introduction & Orientation (Humanist-Coordi-
               nator)
20 min. - B.   Presentation: "The Impact of Religion on
               American Culture" (Historian)
10 min. - C.   Break & Informal Discussion of Circulated
               Questions

Part II: "Church/State Separation & Religion in the
               Schools"

20 min. - A.   Presentation: "The Principle of Church/
               State Separation and Its Impact on Dealing
               with Religion in the Schools" (Theologian)
15 min. - B.   Question & Answer Period (Humanist-Coordina-
               tor, Historian, and Theologian participating)
10 min. - C.   Break & Informal Discussion of Circulated
               Questions

Part III: "Religion and the Public Schools: The Legal
               Climate"

30 min. - A.   Film Presentation: "Abington vs. Schempp"
               ("Great Legal Cases Series: Encyclopedia
               Britannica Films")
5 min. - B.   Recap of Film's Main Points (Humanist-
               Coordinator)
20 min. - C.   Presentation: "The Aftermath of Abington
               vs. Schempp" (Lawyer)
5 min. - D.   Break & Informal Discussion of Circulated
               Questions

Part IV: "Should Religion be Taught in Iowa's Schools?"

20 min. - A.   Presentation: "What's Happening in the
               U.S.? Current Efforts to Teach about
               Religion (Educator)
40 min. - B.   Group Discussions: Five Groups (Leaders:
               Historian, Theologian, Education Specialist,
               Law Professor, Humanist-Coordinator)
               (10 min. - movement; 30 min. - discussion)
30 min. - C.   Conclusion: Panel Discussion & Wrap-Up
               "Should It Be Done? Why or Why Not"
               (Issues: Can religion be taught "objectively"?
               Are there qualified instructors? Are there
               appropriate materials available?)

UNITY AND DIVERSITY
A Conference On Teaching About
Religion in Public Schools
Monday - February 3, 1975

Paul's Place Inn
St. Paul, Minnesota

8:30 - Registration Check-In Begins

9:00 - Welcome and Introductions

9:15 - Panel on Development of Courses or Curriculum
Units on Religion

"Example of What's Happening in Minnesota"
Roland DeLapp, Principal, Washburn High;
Lee Smith and Wes Bodin, St. Louis Park High
School

	Section A	Section B	Section C	Section D
10:00- 11:00	Religious Holidays, Seasons and Other Issues	World Cul- ture World Religion Studies	Religion Units in Literature	Value Clar- ification
11:00- 12:00	Community Support and Guide- lines	World Reli- gion Studies	The Bible As Litera- ture	Religion, Ethics and Values
12:00- 1:00	Luncheon at Noon - 12:00 p.m. to 1:00 p.m.			
1:00- 2:00	Teacher Education and In- Service	Social Studies	Science and Reli- gion Studies	Religion and Humani- ties
2:00- 3:00	Religion Unit and Curriculum	Junior High World Cultures	American Culture and Bicenten- nial Bible as Source	Resources at Social Studies Center

Training Workshop on Teaching About
Religions in Minnesota Public Schools
February 2 - February 3, 1978   10:00 a.m. - 2:00 p.m.
Spring Hill Conference Center near Wayzata, Minnesota

Co-Sponsored By:

1) Minnesota Committee on Religion & Public Education of
   the Minnesota Council of Churches,
2) Nolte Center for Continuing Education of the University
   of Minnesota, and
3) Social Studies Unit of the State Department of Education.

Funded by the Bremer Foundation, the Spring Hill Foundation
and the Minnesota State Department of Education.

Instruction Team:

   Dr. Charles Bruning, Professor of Curriculum & Instruc-
   tion - College of Education, U of M.
   Dr. Lee Smith & Mr. Wes Bodin, Teachers in Social
     Studies at St. Louis Park High School (Minnesota) and
   Co-Directors of the World Religions Curriculum
   Development Center
   Mr. Roger Wangen, Social Studies Consultant, Minnesota
   State Department of Education
   Gerald C. Fahrenholz, Director-Coordinator of Educa-
   tional Ministries, Twin Cities Metropolitan Church
   Commission

Participants:

   Ten teams of five members each from ten different
Minnesota cities. Each team consists of a public school
administrator, teacher, clergy, school board member and a
parent. Cities participating included: Duluth, Rochester,
Owatonna, Faribault, Minneapolis, St. Paul, Bemidji-LaPorte,
Robbinsdale, St. Cloud, and Winona. Participants recruited
through members of the Minnesota Committee in their own
locale.

Purpose:

   An attempt to provide a continuing education experience for local community teams that would: 1) clarify
issues surrounding the teaching about religions in the
local public schools, and 2) develop skills for follow-up
discussion and action in each participating community.

Long-Range Goals:

   1) Programs which will enable students to better understand the religious diversity of mankind and develop
attitudes of respect and action patterns that will improve
human relationships.

2) Participating communities will develop and adopt their own guidelines for teaching about religions in their schools and identify their curricular and training needs for such a program.

Immediate Objectives:

1) To initiate informed discussion among community leadership teams on the proposed state guidelines.

2) Use the proposed state guidelines plus community action materials to train local discussion/action leaders. These leaders will initiate discussion and action on guidelines as they apply to their local community.

I. Part I - A Simulation Learning Experience

A learning experience showing the different issues as reflected by different constituencies in a community --to raise awareness of the issues and problems in developing a program for religions in the school curriculum.

II. Part II - Action Training

Groups discuss and formulate plans for developing discussion and action in their own communities (based on a community action training model developed by Charles Bruning).

Each of the ten teams assemble in their own group and remain as separate teams for the remainder of the training workshop. This gives the teams an opportunity to work at their own community problems and determine plans and strategy for carrying out their plans back home. Each team sets its own goal and develops plans to move toward that goal in their community.

A. Identify the Problem - This consists of developing a list, prioritizing and choosing one.

B. Write the Problem Statement - This is to set a goal to be achieved by the end of six weeks.

C. Choose the most promising solutions and sequence the action steps to achieve them.

D. Determine the means of implementing action strategies - Each set of action strategies is listed per accomplishment in a) six weeks, b) three months, c) six months, and d) nine months.

E. Share plans and action strategies with one other community team. For this segment, two teams are assigned to meet together for an hour and exchange information with one another.

F. Final segment brings all the teams together for an overall evaluation process.

BIBLIOGRAPHY

Books

Boles, Donald E. The Bible, Religion, and the Public
    Schools. Ames, Iowa: Iowa State University Press,
    1965.

Boles, Donald E. The Two Swords: Commentaries and Cases
    in Religion. Ames, Iowa: Iowa State University
    Press, 1967.

Bracher, Peter et al., eds. Public Education Religion
    Studies: Questions and Answers. Dayton, Ohio:
    Public Education Religion Studies Center, 1974.

Duker, Sam. The Public Schools and Religion: The Legal
    Context. New York: Harper and Row, 1966.

Engel, David E., ed. Religion in Public Education. New
    York: Paulist Press, 1974.

Fellman, David, ed. The Supreme Court and Education. New
    York: Columbia University Press, 1975.

Holm, Jean L. Teaching Religion in School. New York: Ox-
    ford University Press, 1975.

"Papers and Selected Bibliography from Texas Consultation
    on Religion and Public Education," Journal of Church
    and State, volume 14, number 3 (Autumn, 1972).

Kauper, Paul G. Religion and the Constitution. Baton
    Rouge, Louisiana: Louisiana State University Press,
    1964.

Michaelsen, Robert. Piety in the Public School. New York:
    Macmillan, 1970.

Piediscalzi, Nicholas and William E. Collie, eds. Teaching
    About Religion in Public Schools. Niles, Illinois:
    Argus Communications, 1977.

Sizer, Theodore R., ed. Religion and Public Education.
    Boston: Houghton Mifflin, 1967.

Warshaw, Thayer S., Religion, Education, and the Supreme
    Court. Nashville, Tennessee: Abingdon, 1979.

Films

Keystone for Education. A 28 minute, color print is available through the Education Communication Association, 960
National Press Building, Washington, D.C. 20004. An accompanying study guide includes the complete text of the
film and supplemental material. An award-winning documen-
tary film designed to answer the many questions on religion
and the public schools. It includes an analysis of the
court decisions by leading experts and an explanation of a
variety of curricular activities by classroom teachers.

Learning About Religion. This series of four color films
was developed by the Religion-Social Studies Curriculum
Project, Florida State University, Tallahassee, Florida
32306. The first film, "The Supreme Court Speaks: Learning About Religion in the Public Schools," (27 minutes) is
a general introduction dealing with the overall possibilities for the study of religion in public schools, including
legal questions. The other three films (each 33 minutes)
are similar in format to each other and each emphasizes a
different subject. The first deals with the study of
religion in American culture or history courses ("Learning
About Religion in American History Courses"); the second
with the study of religion in world cultures or world
history courses ("Learning About Religion in World Culture
Courses"); and the third with the study of religion in
social issues courses, such as civics, problems of democracy, etc. ("Learning About Religion in Social Issues
Courses"). The effective use of these films would involve
showing the first film and only one of the last three, as
they are repetitious.

Religion in Public Schools. A 29 minute, black-and-white
film produced by the National Broadcasting Company is
available through the Broadcasting and Film Commission,
475 Riverside Drive, New York, New York 10029. The film
features Dr. Philip Phenix, professor of philosophy and
education at Teachers College, Columbia University, who is
interviewed by Henry J. McCorkle. The discussion begins
with the implications of the 1963 Supreme Court decision
on Bible reading in the public schools and moves on to
examples of religious issues in literature, history, and
even mathematics.

The Schempp Case: Bible Reading in Public Schools. This
34 minute, color film was produced by Encyclopedia Britan-
nica Educational Corporation, 425 North Michigan Avenue,
Chicago, Illinois 60611. It documents the issues of the
Schempp decision in dramatic fashion and includes a re-
creation of the emotionally charged issues as presented to
the court as well as an analysis of the guidelines established by the court.

Teaching: A Question of Method. A 6 minute, color film
in the series "Citizenship: Whose Responsibility?" is
released by International Film Bureau, 332 South Michigan
Avenue, Chicago, Illinois 60604. This film is concerned
with the question of the degree to which a high school
teacher has the right to deliberately attempt to alter or
change beliefs which are common to contemporary American
culture. Among such beliefs are those in the sanctity of
capitalism, democracy, the home, and the Judaic-Christian
body of ethical and religious teachings.